$6.25

GLOBALIZATION AND ITS VICTIMS
As Seen by the Victims

GLOBALIZATION AND ITS VICTIMS
As Seen by the Victims

Edited by
Michael Amaladoss, S.J.

Vidyajyoti Education & Welfare Society/
ISPCK
1999

Jointly published by the Revd. Ashish Amos of the Indian Society for Promoting Christian Knowledge, Post Box 1585, Kashmere Gate, Delhi–110006 for the Vidyajyoti Education & Welfare Society, Delhi–110054.

© Michael Amaladoss, S.J., 1999

ISBN: 81-7214-480-6

Laser typeset by ISPCK, Post Box 1585, 1654, Madarsa Road, Kashmere Gate, Delhi–110006, Phone: 2966323

Printed at Cambridge Press, Delhi-110006

CONTENTS

Introduction   vii

Part 1: Globalization: Its Social Consequences

1. Globalisation, Liberalisation and the Victims of Colonialism
   Walter Fernandes, S.J.   2

2. Globalisation and Money: An European Perspective
   Johannes Hoffmann   26

3. Globalisation: Implications for Africa
   Peter Henriot, S.J.   65

4. Is the Answer in the South: A Latin American View
   Xabier Gorostiaga, S.J.   77

Part 2: Globalization: Its Cultural Bases

5. Globalization and Its Cultural Underpinnings
   Léon Diouf   104

6. Beyond the Fatal Impact Theory
   Frans Wijsen   122

7. Globalization and Counter-Culture: Liberation movements in Asia
   Michael Amaladoss, S.J.   132

8. Globalization and Culture: A View from Oceania
   Mikaele N. Paunga, S.M.   137

Part 3: The Global and the Local: Theological Perspectives

9. Theology in the Global and the Local
   Diego Irarrazaval   160

10. Globalization and 'Postmodern' Culture Politics
    Georges De Schrijver, S.J.   171

11. The Global and the Local: An African View
    Laurenti Magesa   187

Part 4: Emerging Alternatives to Globalisation

12. Emerging Alternatives to Globalization and Transformative Action
    Horst Sing   194

13. Alternatives to Globalisation: Philippine-Asia-Pacific Experience
    Mary John Mananzan   206

Conclusion: Towards Global Community
Michael Amaladoss, S.J.   217

Appendices:
Reports of Group Discussions   233
Final Statement   243
Authors   247

Introduction

Globalization can be looked at from many points of view. Its basis is in *economic* globalization that seeks to bring the whole world under one market system with free movement of capital and of products. But in practice this means the dominance of the MNCs, supported by the IMF, WB and WTO. The relationship is one of domination-dependence between the rich and poor countries. It is a form of economic colonialism. It leads to the further impoverishment of the poor countries who are obliged to follow policies set by the richer nations under the guise of structural adjustment programmes. It may permit the emergence of a few rich people also in poor countries, but who are in league with the rich everywhere. The proportion of poor people in rich countries also increases.

Economic globalization is supported by *political* globalization. We are living in a uni-polar world, supported by military might. In spite of the talk about the free market the richer countries use their political power to support and promote their own economic machines.

Cultural globalization seeks to spread the 'gospel' of modern culture as a necessary underpinning of economic and political globalization. A materialistic outlook on life and reality, a spirit of individualism and competition, an attitude of consumerism, an approach of autonomy in the name of science from ethical and religious control, profit-oriented commercial activity are some of the characteristics of this culture. There is also an ideal of unity as uniformity and intolerance of pluralism. Life is mechanized. This culture is ardently propagated by the media, controlled by business interests, through advertisement, propaganda and selective information, which becomes mis-information. People are expendable. There is no sense of the common good.

This thrust towards globalization has its consequences in the *social and psychological* sphere. The gap between the few rich and the mass of the poor keeps increasing. The majority are excluded from any role in society. The other may not even be recognized as fully human and certainly not as equal, whatever be the democratic facade. The victims interiorize the cultural system through the media and feel powerless to confront an impersonal system. People take refuge and seek security in fundamentalist or alienating religion.

Religious institutions also may exhibit globalizing tendencies trying to promote unity or universalism either through administrative centralization or through certain types of mission.

We can already see the emergence of *subaltern movements of protest* against globalization. They can take many forms: ecological, feminist movements; the rise of indigenous peoples; the defence of local cultural identity; the search to build up people's power to exert control over the economic and political systems. The media itself can be used for rapid communication and networking in support of the protest movements so as to give them a global character.

We can therefore see already *alternatives* to globalization: Social, participative and democratic control of economic and political processes; the humanization of science and technology; promotion of appropriate technologies; a desire for the common good and a preferential option for the poor; respect for the different local identities in a perspective of a positive appreciation for pluralism; an active quest for equality; an emphasis on the quality of life.

The 500th year after *Vasco da Gama* landed in India seemed to offer a good occasion to explore the implications of globalization, especially as they are seen from the perspectives of its victims and to do so in India. So the Institute of Missiology of Missio, Aachen, Germany and Vidyajyoti College of Theology of Delhi, India collaborated in organizing an International Consultation on *Globalization from the Perspective of the Victims of History,* in Delhi, January, 18–22, 1998. About 35 Scholars from the five Continents took

INTRODUCTION   ix

part in the Consultation. We regret to have missed the participation of a couple of persons from Africa and Latin America owing to problems in crossing frontiers. This is perhaps an indication that the world is not, after all, as global as it is made to appear. After analysing the phenomenon of globalization and its social consequences, its cultural underpinnings of were examined. This lead to a reflection on the theology of the global and the local. A search for emerging alternatives and transformative action concluded the exploration. This last stage suffered from the absence of invitees who could not make it to the Consultation. The lead papers in each section were given by people from different continents: Asia, Africa, Latin America and Europe respectively. In each case others from different continents responded to this paper. Then the participants met in groups to discuss and to pursue the themes further.

The present volume brings together all the papers that were presented and discussed at the Consultation, as well as the report of the group discussion and the final statement. As it was felt at the end that the theological reflection was not sufficient, given the fact that it was primarily a Consultation of theologians, I have added a brief theological conclusion.

Analysing the social consequences of globalization, *Walter Fernandes* sees it as a continuation of colonialism characterized by phenomena like the debt trap, the internationalization of capital and trade, but not of labour, the exploitation of nature by a few, the increasing ranks of the poor, homogenization of a consumer culture and the apparent absence of alternatives and a sense of powerlessness. *Johannes Hoffmann* sees the world-wide subsidization of monetary wealth as the structural cause of job elimination, private and public debt, white-collar and organized crime, and environmental destruction. He also proposes a number of measures to control the savage impact of naked money power through political action: taxing of exchange transactions, reform of the compound interest system, the ethical mobilization of economic subjects, and the prevention of money-laundering from which every one seems to benefit. From an African perspective, *Peter Henriot* shows how the structural adjustment programmes imposed by international financial institutions on poor African countries further increases the gap between the rich and the poor both within and between the countries, leading to the destruction of both nature and culture. Possible remedies are the globalization of solidarity leading to the building of relationships and communities locally and globally and a sense of all peoples being the "family of God". *Xabier Gorostiaga* sees a real solution emerging from the south. What is needed is the control by people of economic systems. This is possible only through political systems that are democratic, efficient, participatory and transparent, both at national and at international levels. These in turn will emerge from a culture of resistance.

Léon Diouf detects two sorts of cultures in conflict in the process of globalization in Africa. On the one hand is the culture of western hegemony characterized by the fruits of the Enlightenment: the promotion of reason, the domination of nature, belief in progress and efficiency, trust in science and technology, rationality in planning, individualism and competition. On the other hand are the African cultures marked by their experience of slavery, and political and economic colonialism: the complexes of forgetfulness, self-justification, inferiority and borrowed personal and national identity. However Africa's trust in transcendence, life and community offer creative and constructive antidotes. *Frans Wijsen* argues that subaltern and marginal groups, both in Europe and Asia, have always resisted homogenizing conformity and affirmed their identity and independence in various ways. *Michael Amaladoss* points out that, in Asia, while instrumental values may have changed under the impact of globalization, categorical values have withstood the attack. Besides, Asian religions have promoted and are promoting counter-cultural movements which affirm a spiritual humanism that is critical of egoism in all its forms, speaking of duties rather than rights and affirming life, community and active non-violence. Oceania, according to *Mikaele Paunga,* has been economically and culturally plundered by colonial powers. Its natural resources have been contaminated by the nuclear powers. Foreign exploiters have been joined and helped by the local elite. There are however signs of a new awareness among the people which could lead to social control of the economy.

Diego Irarrazaval finds hopeful signs in a new kind of theological reflection that rises from local and marginalized groups of

INTRODUCTION

people that stresses the local and the historical leading to an affirmation of pluralism and a demand for dialogue. Small groups of people, living symbols of a counter-culture, linking themselves in a network are harbingers of hope. *Georges De Schrijver* looks at globalization in the context of postmodern culture and suggests that the totalizing market is indeed postmodern in so far as it escapes the controls of the modern nation-state and becomes daring, inventive and purely consumer-oriented, making ample use of postmodern media. Such totalization is being opposed by subaltern groups who stress the local as the sacramental mediation of the Absolute and who build community by linking up with other similar sacramental units. Reflecting from an African point of view *Laurenti Magesa* emphasizes the aspect of power. In an unequal society, globalization means in practice the domination of the powerful. The victims are then called to get organized and gain participative control of the systems that govern their lives and humanize and socialize them. Respecting the pluralism of cultures and peoples is one way of countering globalizing tendencies.

Underlining the self-reliance of the poor as an emerging alternative to globalization, *Horst Sing* suggests that the poor need, not only to be conscientized, but to be empowered. While the Church remains an important counter-cultural force, even it cannot pretend to have a universally valid remedy. But it can provide a prophetic voice to the poor. Speaking from her personal experience in the Philippines, *Mary John Mananzan* points to four areas in which the women's movements have been active is seeking for alternatives for globalization: organizing grassroots women's groups for protests and alternative projects, promoting consumer protection, supporting small, sustainable bio-diverse farms and making the school an agent of social transformation. Their collective strength will give a new voice to women.

In the concluding chapter, *Michael Amaladoss* suggests that God's own plan for the world suggests the construction of a global community. There can therefore be a right kind of globalization that respects pluralism and identity but promotes convergence and communion, making proper use of the facilities of science, technology and the media.

One of the problems in editing the proceedings of an international Consultation has to do with differences in language styles and spellings. Only one of the contributors in the present volume is a native speaker of the English language and that too of its American variety. I have decided to respect the differences of linguistic style and also of the spellings. The word *globalization* itself can be spelt with an "s" or an "z". Trying to homogenize the spelling is also an element of globalization. So I have decided to respect a healthy pluralism in the matter.

As I present the fruits of the Consultation to a wider public I think gratefully of the many who have helped to make the Consultation a success. Among these, the Missio Institute of Missiology, Aachen, deserves pride of place. This is the third in a series of International Consultations on Third World Theology that the Institute of Missiology has been sponsoring and it has offered full financial support to the Consultation and to the present publication, besides collaborating in the organization of the Consultation itself. The Staff and the Students of Vidyajyoti were helpful in many ways besides collaborating with planning the Consultation. . The Indian Social Institute and its Hostel offered us their facilities for holding the Consultation. They were good and efficient hosts. Finally I thank all the participants for a very participatory, stimulating and lively Consultation.

November 1, 1998.   Michael Amaladoss, S.J.
Feast of the All the Saints.

PART 1 :
Globalization:
Its Social Consequences

Globalisation, Liberalisation and the Victims of Colonialism

Walter Fernandes, S.J.

During the closing months of 1997, two international conferences were held around issues arising from the present form of globalisation: the Third Meeting of Parties on Climate Change, at Kyoto in Japan, and the follow up of the World Trade Organisation (WTO, formerly GATT), at Geneva. The issues they raise are referred to as "arising from its present form" because globalisation may not be bad in itself, if by it one means going beyond one's selfishness and limited horizons to the world around. But its present form is viewed as neocolonialism that results in the impoverishment of former colonies in general and of the poor in them in particular. As such it is an ethical issue, and a challenge to those who believe that Jesus came to "give the good news to the poor" (Lk 4.18). It impoverishes the communities whom the God of History created in His own image (Gen. 1.27) and on whose side He has shown Himself. These people are denied access to the fruits of His creation over which He gave command to all of them (Gen. 2.15).

The discussion at Kyoto and Geneva was precisely about using this creation. At Kyoto it was about climate change causing emissions. Many rich countries particularly USA, that account for most emissions, refuse to reduce them for fear of affecting the life-style of their citizens. They demand that poor countries too reduce them, in other words, that they sacrifice many of their developmental schemes. They refuse to see the difference between the survival emissions of the poor, and what they themselves cause through overconsumption. They refuse to recognise that poverty in the global South is caused by overconsumption in the North and by the middle and upper classes in the poor nations. At Geneva the question was around foreign investment in the financial sector, which most poor countries would like to protect. It was a follow up of the GATT Agreement on Investments that demands free access to capital from other countries.

That gives the following distinguishing features of globalisation:

1. Basic to it is the foreign debt trap.
2. Then follows the internationalisation of capital and trade, but not of labour.
3. Monopolisation of the natural resources to the profit of a few, and the consequent denial of the rights of the poor over their livelihood and subsistence. It often results in their displacement, further impoverishment, pollution and ecological destabilisation.
4. Technological transformation resulting in the reduction in employment and livelihood opportunities, particularly to the poor.
5. Withdrawal or drastic reduction of subsidies required by the poor.
6. Homogenisation of culture and information and the consequent desensitisation of the middle class that adopts the consumerist lifestyle.
7. Apparent absence of alternatives and the consequent powerlessness.

The Debt Trap

Basic to the single economy is the balance of payments crisis and the foreign debt trap. It is a consequence of the pattern of development chosen by many newly independent countries, of the present unjust international economy and decades of unequal trade relations. This imbalance is the most visible in Sub-Saharan Africa, much of which depends on a single commodity whose international price keeps falling while that of the finished goods they import from the rich countries keeps rising (Kurien 1996: 4).

To restrict ourselves to foreign debt, in 1995, the countries of the South together owed more than $2 trillion to the rich countries.

35 poorest countries owed $226 billion. Among them the 28 countries of Sub-Saharan Africa, minus South Africa, owed a total of $199 billion which is 20% more than their total annual income. In 1994 they could repay only 10% of the total due that year. Between 1990 and 1993, Mozambique paid only 10% of what it owed (Mahony 1997). More importantly, in the 1980s the Balance of Payment crisis forced them to shift to commercial crops in order to earn foreign exchange. As a result, their staple food production declined and starvation followed (Dreze and Sen 1989). The Sahel famine of the 1980s which we shall discuss later, is an example of a group of countries becoming bread basket cases as a result of the debt trap that ensued from this unequal trade pattern.

The Single Economy and A Consumerist Society

The seven rich countries known as G-7, take most economic decisions for the rest of the world. Instead of dealing with this imbalance, they want to keep these countries only as suppliers of cheap raw materials. In the event of a Balance of Payment crisis, the G-7 impose the single economy through the World Bank and IMF. Basic to it is the Structural Adjustment Programme with conditionalities such as reducing financial deficit to 5% of GDP, privatisation of the services and elimination of subsidies.

These decisions are presented as free trade or free market. In reality it is freedom of unequals geared to the profit of a few. To be considered fair, liberalisation should include free trade, free flow of capital and of labour (Kurien 1996: 21-22). In practice, the 30 OECD countries in general and G-7 in particular, limit freedom to movement of capital, not of labour. They demand free access of their capital to the South but put ever more restrictions on visas for their citizens. Thus it is a one way imposition by the powerful.

An easy mode of ensuring foreign investment by exploiting a BOP crisis, is swapping debt for equity. It has been practised in countries as far apart as Argentina, Mexico, Ghana and Nigeria. The recent food riots in some African countries and in Indonesia are linked to the price rise and impoverishment resulting from the Structural Adjustment Programme. That the poor do not count in this search for profit but pay the price of such policies, is seen from

PART 1 : GLOBALIZATION: ITS SOCIAL CONSEQUENCES

the fact that between 1984 and 1988 the net outflow of capital from the Structural Adjustment Programme affected countries of Latin America and Africa alone was of the order of $143 billion (Reddy 1995: 215).

Thus the free market the rich countries demand, is based on structural inequalities. They, and the middle and upper classes in the poor countries, have appropriated for themselves, the creation that Genesis 2.15 symbolises. It has resulted in the impoverishment of the majority at the global as well as the national levels. With enormous economic power concentrated in their hands, those few having access to capital can destabilise a whole country or economy, as the recent events in South-East Asia and Mexico testify.

A sign of this impoverishment is the growing disparities in the global income and resource use. According to estimates, in the late 1960s, 32.5% of the world's population accounted for 87.5% of its income (Johnson 1974: 58). In 1978 the global income was US $8.5 trillion and the world population 4.4 billion, thus giving a per capita average of a little over US$ 2,000. But roughly $7 trillion of it, or 82%, was generated in the North which contained around 25 of the population. The 75% living in the South shared the remaining $1.5 trillion (Demeny 1981: 298). A decade later, 784 million of the world population of 5,101 millions or 15.4%, had an income of $13,394 billions or 78.2% of the total of $17,135 billions (Chossudowsky 1991: 25-28). According to estimates, today 80% of the world's income is enjoyed by 15% of its population. The ratio of low to high income economies, grew from 1:28 in 1970, to 1:50 in 1990 (Oommen 1997: 23).

Income is one of many signs of differential access to the resources. For example, 17% of the world's population living in the rich countries uses 70% of the global energy, 75% of its metals, 85% of its wood and 60% of its food (Desrochers 1997: 141). This disparity is visible also in world trade. In the total world exports of US$ 2,730 billions in 1992, the share of the South was $920 billions or 33.7%, much of it from the Asian Tigers (Roy 1996: 179).

Given this unequal partnership, any talk of a free market makes little sense. Overconsumption by a few and the impoverishment of many is integral to the present economic order. That in itself is not new in the sense that it is basic to a colonial economy. The difference today is that such an economy is imposed on the whole world as the only possible alternative.

Growth in foreign investment is integral to this economy. Even as poverty grew, foreign investment increased from $77 billion in 1983 to 200 billion in 1992 and 320 billion in 1995 (Kurien 1997: 137). Such investment leads to temporary economic growth counted in terms of GNP (gross national product). Most such investment is on high profit making luxury items, meant for the minority that can afford them. Their price increases, so does the income of this minority. But the basic needs of the people are neglected (Reddy 1995: 210-211).

One more of its features is that in countries like India that had developed an autonomous economy, most capital inflow is portfolio investment i.e. to buy up local companies rather than in new units even for the limited production of luxury items. In India, 70 to 75% of capital inflow during the last six years is portfolio investment (Kurien 1997: 138). In financial terms such inflow improves BOP liquidity and facilitates repayment of debt, but does not provide the stability and security that the country requires. It is speculative capital that is subjected to the world market. It puts pressure on the local currency. At times it has resulted in the revival of a sagging stock exchange and at other times in its weakening. But since this genre of capital does not have a long term stake in the local economy, it moves around the world where the highest profit is possible. So it is neither productive nor stable (Ghosh 1997: 6-7). We shall later study also its role in the loss of employment.

Given its profit orientation, the single economy is geared to the consumerist society, based on creating new needs and providing money to a few consumers to buy them. It is easier in countries like India with a large population than in smaller ones. But even some of the latter, for example the Philippines, follow it. Basic to it is concentration of wealth in a few hands. In India, for example, according to estimates the middle class had grown from around 10% at independence to about 30% in the 1980s, when the process of liberalisation began. This proportion is expected to decline since

PART 1 : GLOBALIZATION: ITS SOCIAL CONSEQUENCES

poverty has grown in recent years (Desrochers 1997a: 201-202). But the middle class will have more money than in the past to spend on luxury items.

Overconsumption and Ecological Degradation

Such overexploitation of the world's resources has often been legitimised in the name of religion, particularly Christianity. Based on Gen. 2.15, the focus of colonialism and of Judaeo-Christian history has been more on human mastery over nature than on equitable sharing.

> It is western Christianity that has taught us to see ourselves as the centre of things with the right, even the duty, to conquer, subdue and have dominion over nature. Early scientific thought reinforced this view of ourselves, by seeing the earth as the centre of the universe, with the planets, the stars and the sun all circling round it (Rajotte and Breuilly 1986: 6).

This approach has resulted in the monopolisation of the natural and other resources on behalf of the middle class to whom they are only a raw material. Environmental degradation is an integral part of this unjust national and international economic order. While such monopolisation is coterminus with colonialism, a major contribution of globalisation is recent agreements that legitimise it in the name of a free i.e. market economy. Through the agreements, those who overconsume the resources, ensure that the poor preserve the environment on their behalf. This effort is symbolised by the Convention on Bio-diversity signed during the 1992 Rio de Janeiro United Nations Conference on Environment and Development, and by the GATT Agreement whose negotiations were completed at Geneva in December 1993 and was signed at Marakash, Morocco, on April 15, 1994.

Convention on Bio-diversity Nos 3 and 4 speak of the sovereign rights of States. Art. 10 (c) 2.4 acknowledges the contribution of farmers and other rural, indigenous and tribal communities to the preservation of biodiversity, but does not recognise their right over it (Shukla 1994: 589). Thus despite the efforts of the North to legalise their stand that biodiversity belonged to the whole world, the countries of the South succeeded in asserting their sovereign right over the natural resources. So Convention on Bio-diversity safeguards the interests of the South that accounts for more than 90% of the world's biodiversity. But the governments that fought for this sovereignty, failed to recognise the rights of the communities that have preserved it for centuries. They are not entitled to compensation for the loss of biodiversity they have preserved or for the genes the corporate sector pirates from them.

Though signed only two years later, the GATT Agreement does not recognise even the sovereign right, much less that of the local communities. Its Agreement on Trade Related Intellectual Property Rights (TRIPS) allows mutated genes to be patented, though not living organisms in their natural form. Besides, based on its claim that traditional knowledge is in the public domain, it denies the communities that have developed it, all rights over it. Only what it calls inventions can be patented.

In reality, a large number of patents particularly of pharmaceutical products, are based on knowledge pirated from the rural communities. They have developed many uses for the products but have not patented them. Biotechnology is monopolised by the multinationals of the North who have been smuggling genes from the South, using them for research and trying to take control of the biodiversity in these countries (Mooney 1979: 5-6).

Often what are called new products are minor modifications of what exists in the South. In other cases patents are got for user practices already prevalent in the South. For example, more than a dozen patents have been taken in USA and Japan since 1985, on different products of neem (*Azadrachta Indica*) alone, though it has been in use in India for centuries as medicine, pesticide etc. But research on these resources has remained non-commercial. No patent has been taken, since most of it was done by institutions that believed in Rabindranath Tagore's dictum that knowledge is free. Estimates of patents based on traditional herbal knowledge range from 40 to 60% of all the pharmaceutical patents in use today (Shiva and Holla Bhar 1994: 8).

Consequently, the communities that have developed these knowledge systems through centuries, do not have a right over them once

PART 1 : GLOBALIZATION: ITS SOCIAL CONSEQUENCES

multinational companies that monopolise biotechnology patent them on claims of being new inventions. Thus the economic forces that had till now tried to take control of the natural resources, are going beyond it to monopolise the traditional knowledge systems by delegitimising the communities that have developed them. This is an attack on their very identity, as such goes beyond impoverishment, to dehumanisation.

The second important demand is control over land. For example, the draft rehabilitation policy of the Ministry of Rural Development, Government of India, begins by stating that the new economic policy will result in greater investment and more land will be required. It thus implies that there will have to be more displacement of people for development projects. Hence the need to have a national rehabilitation policy (MRD 1994: 1.1). It adds that most natural and mineral resources are found in the tribal areas (ibid: 4.1). Hence much displacement will be in these regions. In other words, displacement for development, particularly of the marginalised communities, is taken for granted, to facilitate investment. Some sops are offered in the name of rehabilitation. But the right of the poor to inhabit any part of India's territory and to a life with dignity, is not recognised.

To understand its consequences, one should remember that in India at least 30 million persons have been displaced by development projects since 1951. More than 40% of them are tribals who form only 7.58% of the country's population. Another 40% are from other rural poor communities. Fewer than a quarter of them have been resettled even partially (Fernandes 1994: 22-32). The draft policy geared to the needs of liberalisation, ignores this situation. The context of globalisation demands new efforts to make land acquisition easier in order to attract foreign capital. Thus many more persons, mostly poor, will be displaced to give land to the investor. What is said about India is equally true about other countries, for example the Amerindians of Amazonia, those to be displaced by the Bio-Bio river projects in Chile (Downing 1997), Moun‍ Apo in the Philippines and others elsewhere.

Thus the few who control the natural resources, render the already weak further powerless and ensure an ecological crisis. One such case is the Sahel famine of the 1980s. These countries depended on the single commodity of groundnuts that were exported mostly to France to be processed into cooking oil. As the price of this commodity declined, more and more land till then under staple food was shifted to it and fenced off. Forests were destroyed to grow staple food. With it the link between the pastoral and farming communities broke down. Cattle died first, followed by human beings (Agarwal 1985: 52). This process may be intensified by the GATT Agreement on Agriculture that stipulates, among others, that 3% of food be imported and other measures aimed at changeover of agriculture in the South from staple food to commercial crops (Singh Gill 1996: 52-54).

Despite such consequences on human beings, most persons in the rich countries and the middle and upper classes in the poor nations, concentrate on saving the natural environment, and ignore the communities that are the victims of this degradation. Many do it in the name of religion, by calling it the creation of God that has to be rejuvenated. This effort often takes the form of saving nature from the communities that have managed it sustainably for centuries. As examples we may mention the World Bank Forestry and Ecodevelopment projects. The former is meant, in practice, to turn natural forests into plantations for the forest produce based industries and the latter to preserve biodiversity to the benefit of outsiders (Cheria 1996).

Globalisation and Employment Reduction

Another feature of globalisation is reduction in employment despite rise in production. "Employment adjustment" is an IMF conditionality, integral to the Structural Adjustment Programme, imposed on the poor countries as a precondition for loans from the international agencies. The technological progress of the last two decades, gives to the industrial decision maker, access to the most profitable option. Mechanisation being an integral part of Structural Adjustment Programme, the industrialist often opts for it.

A reason why, as mentioned above, the middle class is shrinking, is loss of jobs, mainly to mechanisation. In India, for example, in 1985, the year in which the process of liberalisation became

PART 1 : GLOBALIZATION: ITS SOCIAL CONSEQUENCES 11

visible, the formal sector employed around 30 millions in a total workforce of 300 millions. 23 millions of them were in the public sector and 7 millions in the private sector. By 1987, the number in the private sector had declined marginally. In 1991, when liberalisation was formalised, the number in the private sector had come down to 6 millions (Patnaik and Panda 1992: 210). During the last six years, annual GNP growth has been of the order of 6 to 8%, but employment generation has been negative. Today the workforce in the formal sector is around 28 millions. With every job lost in the formal sector, several are lost in the informal sector. ILO estimates that 8 million jobs have been lost in India since 1991 (VAK Team 1996: 167).

Studies and field experience show its impact. For example, by official count, all the subsidiaries of Coal India together gave a job each to 11,901 (36.34%) of the 32,751 families (1,64,000 persons) they displaced in 1981-1985. In the 1980s, the company began to mechanise its mines, and started transferring employees to other mines instead of giving jobs to new DPs. The first 5 of the 25 mines under construction in the Upper Karanpura Valley of Jharkhand (Bihar) are expected to displace 1,00,000 persons, over 60% of them Dalits and tribals. But Coal India gave a job each to only 638 (10.18%) of the 6,265 families (32,000 persons) they displaced till 1992 (BJA&NBJK 1993: 36).

There are indications that also reduction in the subsidies of agricultural inputs and the price rise have resulted in negative employment generation and poverty in the rural areas (Sen 1997: 92-96). Fertilisers had functioned as a land substitute. Farmers with two acres of land were able to make their farms viable through the use of fertilisers. With subsidies being reduced or dispensed with, the price of fertilisers rose by 30% in a year. The small farmer could not afford it. This change seems to have pushed many of them below the poverty line.

To this should be added portfolio investment that focuses on acquiring control over locally owned companies. The monopoly that results from it makes smaller units non-competitive. A basic norm of liberalisation is that the economy of a poor country should be globally competitive. Its impact on local competitiveness and the viability of small units is not taken into consideration. Preliminary data indicate that a large number of small enterprises have closed down, with loss of jobs as a consequence (INSAF 1997).

That impoverishment is a consequence has become obvious from many studies. Even by official statistics, in India the Below the Poverty Line proportion increased from 37% in 1989-90 to 48% in 1992-93 (VAK 1996: 167). One does not have to repeat that most Below the Poverty Line population is Dalit and tribal.

Structural Adjustment and Impoverishment

Another IMF conditionality is reduction or elimination of subsidies that are essential for the survival of many poor families. For example, the GATT Agreement on Agriculture stipulates that no food subsidies be allowed except to the population. That many millions of families remain above the poverty line through these subsidies is ignored. They may end up below the poverty line, in the absence of viable alternatives. "Therefore it is imperative to provide safety nets to cushion the poor against rising prices" (David 1997: 231).

Besides, food for the public distribution system has to be bought in the open market, not through government procurement. This arrangement can hold in a year of plenty. In a lean year food would have to be imported at market prices and that can cause a BOP crisis. This measure will also increase the burden on the tax payers because of which there may be pressure from the middle class to reduce subsidies further. Thus Public Distribution System may be affected because its clientele is powerless and cannot defend its interests (Ray 1993). A result of Structural Adjustment Programme is that the price of rice and wheat rose by 20 to 35% during 1992 and continues to rise. But the quantity made available under Public Distribution System declined by 50% (CWDS 1995).

Intrinsic to globalisation is industrialisation of agriculture. For example, the GATT Agreement on Agriculture stipulates that 3% of a year's consumption be imported even when a country is self-reliant. Meant to support the farmers of Europe and the Americas who have industrialised their agriculture and have an excess to export, it will go against most farmers in the South who depend on subsistence agriculture (Rao 1994: 727). They may be further impoverished because more than 70% of the farmers in the South are small and medium peasants who do not produce an excess (VAK Team 1997: 170). Thus globalisation raises the basic question of food security particularly in the context of the malnutrition related death of children.

Also other subsidies have to be reduced or given up completely. India, for example, has cut down on fertiliser subsidies. As a result, the price of fertiliser rose by 30% in a year. The small farmer owning less one hectare of land often used fertilisers as a land substitute to double production. Because of the sudden rise in fertiliser prices, many small farmers had to stop using fertilisers. There are indications that many of them have gone below the poverty line and have probably sold their land. Instead, subsidies continue on water and power which are in practice accessible only to relatively big farmers.

The Structural Adjustment Programme demands that fiscal deficit be reduced to 5% of GDP. In India it is done by cutting down on what is known as planned sector i.e. development schemes, subsidies and welfare measures like health, not by reducing wasteful expenditure that is called unplanned expenditure. Such reduction is often linked to repayment of foreign debt and to the conditionalities attached to its adjustment. For example, the 10% interest on foreign debt that Mozambique paid on its foreign debt between 1990 and 1993 and the 20% it paid in 1994, represented more than what it needed for its health services, environment protection, education and other forms of social welfare. All these fields suffered. Today 60% of its estimated population of 16 millions does not have safe drinking water. One million children are out of school (Mahony 1997). But IMF suggests it as the only solution.

The scenario can be expected to worsen because of the role IMF and the World Bank are playing in the international economy. An impression has been gaining ground in recent years that these financial institutions are becoming all important and that technical organisations like FAO, ILO, UNICEF and UNESCO are being marginalised. Till now agriculture was dealt with by FAO, labour by ILO, patents by various conventions, environment by UNEP etc. Some Northern countries like USA had alleged that the Soviet bloc was using the Third World to control them, and had stopped their annual contribution to them.

Through trade linked agreements on all of them, WTO has in practice integrated their functions with trade which the North dominates. WTO will also have the World Bank and IMF as its affiliates. The technical organisations only had moral authority. The financial institutions can use the force of money to impose their will, as has been done effectively in case of a Balance of Payment crisis, for example in Mexico and South-East Asia. Centralisation under the single umbrella of WTO, gives the North greater say in the economic agenda of the South.

The Middle Class, the Media and Alternatives

Besides, during the last four decades, several alternatives were developed to the neo-colonial economy. They gave some hope to the poor countries. Most of them like State control, Pan-Arabism and Ujama have failed either because of their internal weakness or more often because of the powerful forces arraigned against them. Some countries, particularly in East and South-East Asia, had succeeded in combining productivity with social justice. But in recent months one has witnessed the collapse of these Asian Tigers. Thus in the absence of alternatives, today there is a sense of powerlessness in the South, particularly their poor. Globalisation is not an alternative to the systems that have failed. But the apparent absence of alternatives increases their sense of powerlessness.

However, in most cases, the middle class in these countries supports globalisation as the only alternative. In other words, no colonialism, internal or external, is possible without local collaboration (de Boschere 1967: 43). Thus the elite of the poor countries supports foreign economic control as the only alternative, since it caters to their needs. The North, in its turn, ensures the acceptance of the value system accompanying it, by controlling the means of communications (Rajagopal 1994: 1660). Thus while it is true that the single economy is imposed on the poor nations by the OECD countries in general and G-7 in particular, through the IMF and the World Bank, a strong demand for it comes from the domestic elites themselves. They see a definite advantage for themselves in a globalisation which effectively improves their living standards even as it leaves the mass of the population without any obvious benefit, and, in some cases, may even worsen their material conditions (Ghosh 1997: 3).

With the middle and upper classes accepting consumerism, the talk of poverty alleviation all but disappears even as an ideology. Under pressure from them, the political leadership moves away from the altruistic tradition of freedom movements that had enabled them to express their concern for the marginalised at times through relief measures and at others by creating a social infrastructure (Kothari 1991: 554-555). This class is now desensitised to poverty around it.

The media thus play the role of imposing the value of consumerism on the middle class that has the financial resources to buy the new products. Through its technological sophistication the media also make it possible for this class to watch problems around it from the comfort of the drawing room without feeling responsible for them. Desensitisation is an offshoot.

Globalisation and Religious Fundamentalism

One can also ask whether it is a coincidence that consumerism and fundamentalism grow together. In other words, do the media also divert attention from the problems of the poor, through a fundamentalist message? This can have the consequence of further desensitising the middle class. An example is the "Christian-Muslim" or "Civilised-Uncivilised" country division that USA and Europe presented as basic to the Gulf War that resulted in Iraq being bombed back to the stone age. In other words, colonial injustice has often been defended in the name of religion, particularly Christianity. It results in another cultural backlash from the colonised elite, that felt its identity threatened, and rediscovers it in a fundamentalist revival.

That brings one to the link between the market economy, the consumer society and fundamentalist revival. It is not purely by accident that the middle class, the most fervent supporter of consumerism, is also the strongest foundation of fundamentalism. This class, the main beneficiary of the single economy, has been brought up in the western value system of productivity as the symbol of progress. Consequently, in much of Asia of the 1980s, the two phenomena of the middle class strengthening its hold on society and the growth of fundamentalism went hand in hand.

To limit ourselves to India, the economic crisis that weakened the country and resulted in the new policy of 1991 is related directly to concentration on producing and importing more and better quality goods for the middle class during the 1980s. As a result, foreign debt rose from $7.9 billion in 1975, to $20.6 billion in 1980 and $70.1 billion in 1991 (Desai 1993: 8-10). During the same decade, under middle class pressure the political leadership, moving away from the post-independence altruistic tradition, abandoned all talk of poverty alleviation. The earlier efforts in the direction of social justice, were weakened. Even the limited reforms made till then were abandoned when in fact the country needed more radical reforms (Narayan 1986: 96-106). The resistance of these classes to concessions being extended to the marginalised groups, is symbolised by many anti-low caste riots in different parts of India during the 1980s (Engineer 1986: 15-16).

That is where religion becomes a convenient tool. While demanding a western type of lifestyle, this class also needs an alternative to the loss of the social dimension in their life. It goes in search of indigenous identity that can help them to enjoy the benefits of a western type of consumerist society without qualms of conscience. The middle class finds such an identity in a fundamentalist approach to life, as reaction to what in their perception is a colonial past which the minority religious groups supported.

In their thinking the same minorities are trying to deprive them of the benefits of national development, which they perceive as belonging by right to their community. That is the main basis of the growth of fundamentalism in former colonies. To the Muslim World it is the end of the Crusades and of the "Christian Empire" that had defeated them. To the Hindu upper classes, it is reacquisition of power and an identity that they perceive to have lost at first to the Muslims and then to the Christians (Hasan 1989: 128-129).

The attitude of the middle class is the major reason why in these countries, fundamentalism has grown side by side with consumerism. Both the middle class aspirations of a consumerist society and religious fundamentalism are turned by the media into a national identity. This role of the media is crucial for integrating the middle class in the global system. It creates in the country, a single "platform that could be 'shared' in some sense right across the country" (Rajagopal 1994: 1660). This is followed by other forms of control of the media such as advertisements and TV commercials sponsored by big business and meant to exploit the middle class market that has lost the post-independence perspective of social justice (Gueriviere 1991: 160-162).

In relation to the third world, cultural imperialism can be defined as the systematic penetration and domination of the cultural life of the popular classes by the ruling class of the west in order to reorder the values, behaviour, institutions and identity... to conform with the interests of the imperial classes. In past centuries the church, educational system and public authorities played a major role in inculcating native peoples with ideas of submission and loyalty in the name of divine or absolutist principles..... In the contemporary world, Hollywood, CNN and Disneyland are more influential than the Vatican, the Bible or the public relations rhetoric... (Petras 1994: 2070).

Thus the media become instrumental in internal and external colonialism coinciding with fundamentalist revival. In their search for profit, the global industrial forces find an ally in the middle class that has lost the sense of distributive justice and is finding a new identity in the combination of a consumerist culture with religious fundamentalism. The economic forces thus succeed in legitimising their domination and ensuring the continuation of their culture.

Marginalisation and Women

While the poor suffer, women among them are the worst victims. According to one estimate, of the 1.4 billion absolute poor in the world, 70% are women (Desrochers 1997: 141). To understand the impact on women, one should firstly remember that despite other changes, their traditional role remains more or less unchanged. But for exceptions, they continue to be viewed by others and by themselves, as secondary producers in the family. Secondly, because of the need to do unpaid work and the need to do even paid work at home, most women in poor countries remain in the informal sector. Thirdly, they continue to be viewed as being primarily responsible for household provisioning. The three together can become extremely exploitative and their status can deteriorate, if the socio-economic foundation of these functions is weakened

That is what globalisation intensifies. To begin with employment, because of the perception of the woman being the secondary income earner, in case of loss of jobs through mechanisation, men are preferred for the few jobs available. So she tends to remain unemployed and turned into a housewife alone, with no economic independence (Fernandes and Raj 1992: 142). In other cases, an enterprise owning many units, transfers the man with a temporary or lower category job, to another unit, with better or permanent employment. The woman who often works in the same unit on a temporary or even permanent basis, is forced to resign her job "voluntarily" in order to accompany her husband to the new place (Sen 1992: 392-394). Besides, a feature of globalisation is centralisation of decision making and localisation of production. Loss of jobs through mechanisation is accompanied by much production being shifted to the "sweat shops" or to the home-based "putting out system". This work is done mostly by women and children, in exploitative conditions (Kurien 1996: 36-38).

To her role of provision supplier is linked the disappearance of or reduction in subsidies, particularly the Public Distribution System. Due to gender differential within the household in access to essential items like food and health care, the price rise that ensues has disastrous effects on poor women in particular. A recent study (CWDS 1995) shows that women perceive price rise, access to food and violence as their three main problems. Malnutrition is a major problem women face. It has been substantiated by the experience of the tribal women of Tamil Nadu. Till recently they saved a rupee a day to add lintels to the little rice they got. Today the shopkeeper laughs at them if they ask for lintels worth a rupee. So the family is deprived of even this little protein and the woman suffers more than the rest (Thekkekara 1993: 70-71).

The situation looks grim if one is to believe recent reports that following privatisation the Public Distribution System is being systematically dismantled in large parts of rural India. Studies show that provisions are not available in fair price shops and the number of shops has decreased (CWDS 1995). In the hilly regions, such shortage in addition to the decline in local production of food grains due to steady environmental degradation caused by indiscriminate felling of forests, has more serious effects on women than on men. Studies show that hill women consume less food than they should, eat what is left over after feeding their children and husbands, are malnourished and susceptible to diseases (SHERPA 1990; Rawat 1993).

Studies (e.g. Vashishta 1990: 138) also show that with employment reduction, persons with access to some literacy and numeracy take over jobs till then held by poorer and less literate sections. Men take to areas traditionally reserved to women. For example, hawking has traditionally been the occupation of low status and poor persons, mostly women. With other jobs disappearing, men from a slightly higher caste and better off class than them take to these occupations.

To this can be added ecological degradation that affects poor women the most. The tribal family, for example, gets more than 50% of its food from the forests in the form of non-timber forest produce Non-Timber Forest Produce like edible fruits and flowers. With deforestation, the distance between the village and the forest has increased, for example in Orissa, from 1.5 km in the mid-1960s to 7 km in the mid-1980s. So the housewife has to walk the extra distance to collect NTFP. But she collects less than in the past since older women and children cannot accompany her (Fernandes and Menon 1987: 72). The World Bank Forestry and Ecodevelopment projects should be situated in this context. With its focus on commercial timber, plantation forestry deprives the woman of the Non-Timber Forest Produce she requires to play her role as provision supplier. In the name of ecodevelopment, the people are denied access to the Non-Timber Forest Produce with more negative consequence for women than the rest of the family.

Conclusion

The basic feature of globalisation is the marginalisation of the majority for the profit of a few. It is thus a challenge to the Christian conscience because 6 of the G-7 countries claim to be Christian. At times they defend their decisions in the name of Christianity, for example in the Gulf war. That it was a colonial war meant to take control of petroleum was never mentioned. Nor was it stated that the countries that condemned Iraq's occupation of Kuwait had colonised the South for two centuries. One does not defend the occupation of another country by anyone in the South. One only states that it was a clear sign that after the end of the Cold War, the major conflicts in the unipolar world are North-South. In the absence of alternatives, the countries of the South are forced to join the North. In fact, addressing the US Congress at the end of the Gulf War, President George Bush announced that it was assured that now, with the end of the Cold War, the UN was in a position of playing its rightful role and imposing a new international order the world over (Koshy 1997: 5).

That is the challenge of people committed to the Gospel of Him who came to give the good news to the poor. One cannot assume that in the past the South had all the alternatives it needed. Many of them had accepted a colonial system and had developed an economy of internal inequalities that reproduced the international iniquitous order. So the solution does not lie in defending national independence alone. One has also to search for alternatives to the present form of internal and external colonialism which is today called globalisation.

If one believes in Jesus who chose to work in Galilee, the backwaters of Palestine, inhabited by people considered inferior (Soares-Prabhu 1981: 12), then one has to take sides with the victims of colonialism. Today this sinful society condemns the majority to a sub-human existence. Making all things new involves acknowledging our share in the processes in this state of sinfulness. It also demands that the sinful state be remedied and the Lord's Jubilee be proclaimed prophetically. It may mean a more meaningful search for alternatives, in cooperation with all people of good will.

In this search one has to go beyond condemning sin. Prophetical proclamation is only accidentally condemnation. It is easy to give oneself peace of conscience by condemning globalisation as evil. One has to go beyond it by first and foremost, announcing a positive message. With such a proclamation in view, one has to identify the type of globalisation that is acceptable, the factors that have resulted in its present form and viable alternatives to it. For example, one is justified in asking whether division among the countries of the South is basic to the failure of trade and economic blocs in regions like South Asia, Central America and much of Africa. If that is the case, then those searching for alternatives have to join the forces attempting to find solutions to existing conflicts and build new trade blocs. The reconciliation that Christ preached would not then be only absence of conflict but empowerment of the powerless.

References

Agarwal, Anil. 1985. "Ecological Destruction and the Emerging Pattern of Poverty and People's Protest in Rural India," social Action 35 (n. 1, Jan.-March), pp. 54-80.

BJA&NBJK. 1993. Social Impact: Piparwar and the North Karanpura Coal Fields. Hunterganj and Chauparan: Bharat Jan Andolan and Nav Bharat Jagruti Kendra.

Cheria, Anita. 1996. The World Bank in Nagarahole: A Story of Human Rights Violations, Lies and Deceit. Bangalore: With the Author.

Chossudovsky, Michel. 1991. "Global Poverty and the New World Economic Order," Economic and Political Weekly, 26 (n.44, November 2), pp. 2527-2537.

CWDS. 1995. Shifting Sands: A Report on the Workshop on Gender Implications of Structural Adjustment Perspectives From India and Canada. New Delhi: Centre for Women's Development Studies.

David, James. 1997. "The Public Distribution System," Integral Liberation, 1 (n. 4, December), pp. 224-229.

De Boschere, Guy. 1967. Autopsy de la Colonisation. Paris: Aubin Michel.

Demeny, Paul. 1981. "The North-South Income Gap: A Demographic Perspective," Population and Development Review, 7 (n.2, June), pp. 297-310.

Desrochers, John. 1997. ""Complementary Insights on Colonialism," Integral Liberation 1 (n. 3, September), pp. 141-145.

Desrochers, John. 1997a. "Guidelines for the Anti-Poverty Struggle," Integral Liberation 1 (n. 4, December), pp. 17-223.

Desai, Meghnad. 1993. Capitalism, Socialism and the Indian Economy: Annual Export-Import Bank Commencement Lecture. Bombay: Exim Bank.

Downing, Theo E. 1997. "Wolfensohn: Indian Killer," Unpublished Paper Circulated by Documentation Centre, Indian Social Institute.

Dreze, Jean and Amartya Sen. 1989. Hunger and Public Action. Oxford: Clarendon Press.

Engineer, Asghar Ali. 1986. "Communalism: Its Facts and Roots," Mainstream 24 (n. 43, June 28), pp. 15-19.

Fernandes, Walter. 1994. Development-Induced Displacement in the Tribal Areas of Eastern India. New Delhi: Indian Social Institute, (mimeo)

Fernandes, Walter and Geeta Menon. 1987. Tribal Women and Forest Economy: Deforestation, Exploitation and Status Change. (New Delhi: Indian Social Institute).

Fernandes, Walter and S. Anthony Raj. 1992. Development, Displacement and Rehabilitation in the Tribal Areas of Orissa. New Delhi: Indian Social Institute. Fernandes, Walter and Indrani Choudhury. 1997. "Liberalisation, the Environment and Impact on Women," Women's Link, 3 (n. 4, Oct.Dec.), pp. 23-31.

Ghosh, Jayati. 1997. "Gender and Macro-Economic Policy in India Since 1991," Women's Link, 3 (n. 4, Oct.-Dec.), pp. 3-11.

Gueriviere, Paul. 1991. "The Information Industry: Political Economy of Media," Social Action, 41 (n. 2, Apr.-June), pp. 156-175.

Hasan, Mushirul. 1989. "Indian Muslims: Insecurity, Economic Aspirations and Identity," Social Action, 39 (n. 2, April-June), pp. 142-151.

INSAF. 1996. The United Front Government and the People. Social Action in the Post-Election Period: Policy Document of INSAF. Indian National Social Action Forum.

Johnson, Stanley. 1974. Population Problem. London: Newton Johnson.

Koshy, Ninan. 1997. "World Order - A Critical Review," in Ajit Muricken (ed). Globalisation and SAP: Trend & Impact. Mumbai: Vikas Adhyayan Kendra, pp. 5-20.

Kothari, Rajni. 1991. "State and Statelessness in Our Time," Economic and Political Weekly, 26 (n. 11&12, Annual Number), pp. 553-558.

Kurien, C.T. 1996. Global Capitalism and the Indian Economy. New Delhi: Orient Longman. Kurien, C.T. 1997. "Globalisation: What Is It About?" Integral Liberation, 1 (n. 3, September), pp. 133-140.

Mooney, P.R. 1979. Seeds of the Earth: A Private or Public Resource? Ottawa: International Coalition for Development Action.

MRD. 1994. National Policy for Rehabilitation of Persons Displaced As A Consequence of Acquisition of Land. New Delhi: Ministry of Rural Development, Government of India. (Second draft)

Narayan, K. Laxmi. 1986. "Growth of Metropolitan Cities and Their Migrants -- A Historical and Demographic Profile," in M.S.A. Rao (ed). Studies in Migration. New Delhi: Manohar, pp. 85-159.

Oommen, M.A. 1997. "Transnational Capital, GATT/WTO and the Crisis of National Soverregnty: The Case of India," in Ajit Muricken (ed). op. cit. pp. 21-44.

Patnaik, Gopabandhu and Damodar Panda. 1992. "The New Economic Policy and the Poor," Social Action, 42 (n.2, Apr-June), pp. 201-212.

Petras, James. 1994. "Cultural Imperialism in Late 20th Century," Economic and Political Weekly, 29 (n. 32, August 6), pp. 2070-2073.

Rajotte, Freda and Elizabeth Breuilly. 1986. "What is theCrisis?" in Elizabeth Breuilly and Martin Palmer eds). Christianity and Ecology. London: Cassell Publishers Ltd, pp. 1-18. Amiya. 1994. "The Drama called GATT," Economic and Political Weekly, 29 (n. 3, March 26), pp. 721-723.

Rawat, A.S. 1993. Deforestation in the Lesser Himalayan Kumaun and Its Impact on the Peasant Women and on the Van Rajis. New Delhi: Nehru Memorial Museum and Library, Centre for Contemporary Studies.

Ray, Parshuram. 1993. "Dunkel Forces us to Import Food," The Patriot, Dec. 20, p. 4.

Reddy, D. Narasimha. 1995. "Political Economy of Crisis and the Strategy of Structural Adjustment Programme in India," in M. A. Oommen et al. Political Crisis in India: Studies in Political Economy. New Delhi: Khama Publishers, pp. 196-219.

Sen, Abhijit. 1997. "Structural Adjustment and Rural Poverty:

Variables that Really Matter," in G. K.Chadha and Alakh N. Sharma (eds). Growth, Employment and Poverty: Change and Continuity in Rural India. New Delhi: Vikas Publishing House, pp. 110-122.

Sen, Ilina. 1992. "Mechanisation and the Working Class Women," Social Action 42 (n. 4, Oct.-Dec.), pp. 391-400.

SHERPA 1990. Environmental Status Report, 1990. District Chamoli. Vol.I. Lucknow: Society for Himalayan Environmental Rehabilitation and People's Action.

Shiva, Vandana and Radha Holla-Bhar. 1994. "Intellectual Piracy and the Neem Free," The Ecologist Asia, 2 (n. 2, Mar.-Apr), pp. 7-14.

PART I : GLOBALIZATION: ITS SOCIAL CONSEQUENCES

Shukla, S.P. 1994. "Resisting the World Trade Organisation: Agenda for Marakesh," Economic and Political Weekly, 29 (n.11, March 12), pp. 589-592.

Singh Gill, Sucha. 1996. "GATT Agreements and Sustainable Development of Agriculture in India," in K. Gopal Iyer (ed). Sustainable Development: Ecological and Socio-cultural Dimensions. New Delhi: Vikas Publishing House, pp. 49-57.

Soares-Prabhu, George. 1981. "The Kingdom of God: Jesus' Vision of a New Society," in D.S. Amalorpavadass (ed). The Indian Church in a Struggle for a New Society. Bazngalore: National Biblical, Catechetical and Liturgical Centre, p. 8.

Thekkekara, Mari. 1993. "Tribal Women: The Trauma of Transition," Social Action 43 (n. 1, Jan.-March), pp.23-31.

VAK Team. 1997. "The New Economic Path - Trends and Impact," in Ajit Muricken (ed). op. cit. pp. 151-180.

Vashishta, Prem, S. "Urban Informal Sector: A Profice of Marginalised Irregulars," Social Action, 40 (n. 2, April-June), pp. 126-145.

Globalisation and Money: An European Perspective

Johannes Hoffmann

Preliminary remarks:

The point of departure of the following statement or position paper is constituted by the effects of the globalization of monetary structures. This is not to overlook the fact that globalization does of course comprise a number of globally interconnected areas. To begin with, there is the world-wide interconnection of all economic activities, which brings about the joint operation and interpenetration of "capital flows, labor markets, information, raw materials, management and organization—all of which takes place to a planetary extent in a uniformly internationalized, concurrent, and totally interdependent manner".[1]

There is further the phenomenon of ecological, political, cultural, societal and psychological globalization, together with its interworking with the economic sphere.

This process has been emerging and developing for the last four decades. In the 1960s global competition started with labor, and the production of textiles, etc. was shifted to an increasing extent to the so-called low-wage countries. This development was followed in the 1970s with the shift—due to more favorable conditions such as environmental parameters—of production capital, machinery, and the manufacture of chemicals and automobiles. In the 1980s the new communication technologies entered the arena of

---

[1] Manuel Castells, "European Cities, the Informational Society, and the Global Economy", in: *Tijdschrift voor Economische en Sociale Geografie* 84 (1993): 249; quoted in: Jürgen Friedrichs, "Globalisierung - Begriff und grundlegende annahmen", in: *Aus Politik und Zeitgeschichte*, supplement to the weekly newspaper *Das Parlament* B 33-34/97, 8 August 1997, pp. 3-11; here: p. 3.

global competition, as is evidenced by telecommunications and recreational electronics. And most recently the 1990s have been characterized by the global competition of financial services and the media, to name two examples, which has been made possible by the new conditions governing information exchange.[2]

Globalization should also be gauged from hegemonic perspectives: From the Age of Discovery — that is, the era of European exploration—up into the 19th century, global development had been under the sway of Europe's rise to power and subsequent hegemony. In the 20th century the United States assumed the role of shaping the world's course. And according to the prognoses of the World Bank, "in twenty to thirty years China will probably be the largest economic system world-wide, simply because of its great population size".[3] In that case, in the 21st century the decisive impulses and influences affecting economic, social, ecological and cultural development are most likely going to come from Eastern Asia. All this needs to be kept in mind in the course of my discussion of globalization from an European perspective.

My perception of the perspectives of other cultures has no doubt been broadened and sensitised as a result of the work begun in 1985 by the project of Intercultural Theology in the Department of Roman Catholic theology at the University in Frankfurt. Thus the road to intercultural communication in a global context has been taken by us as well. I would like to characterize the aim of Intercultural Theology with the words of its initiator, Hermann Pius Siller: "The task of a theology operating within an intercultural framework is to work out in its own theology the differences between theologies, in dialog with theologians of regional churches in other cultural contexts. The aim of a theology working on an intercultural basis is to grasp the perspectives of autochthonous members of a given culture and bring them to bear in one's own theology. Put otherwise: if theology is going to be done interculturally, then its task is to grasp in cogent outlines the integrating horizons of meaning in both its own culture and in the respective foreign culture and to understand

---

[2] Cf. John M. Stopford and Susan Strange, *Rival States, Rival Firms: Competition for World Market Shares* (Cambridge 1991), p. 36

[3] Yeo George You-Boon, "*Ostasien wird die Weltordnung in ihren Grundfesten erschüttern*", in: Frankfurter Allgemeine Zeitung, 21.11.1997, no. 271, p. 10.

their relationship to the Christian faith".[4] The path that we have taken in the course of our dialog with representatives of other cultures—concerning the issue of human rights, for example—has led us to take our starting point from the factors that disturb intercultural communication. In the course of so doing we have learned that listening is the first condition of intercultural communication.[5] We have then learned that by listening we perceive the disturbances that we ourselves have constituted for other lands and cultures since the beginning of the modern era. We must be prepared to be made aware of how much havoc we Europeans have inflicted upon the value systems of other cultures, of what anomies we Europeans have brought about in functioning systems of norms and values in other cultures just simply with the large amount of exports of mass products.[6]

Our dialog partners have also made it clear to us that the destructive potential[7] unleashed by the processes of rationalization, industrialization and modernization—and under whose culturally

---

[4] Hermann Pius Siller, "Überlegungen zur Methode von 'Theologie Interkulturell'", in: Maria Hungerkamp and Matthias Lutz, eds., *Grenzen überschreitende Ethik*, Festschrift for Prof. Dr. Johannes Hoffmann on his 60th birthday (Frankfurt 1997), pp. 99-114; here: p. 111.

[5] Attaching political strings to development aid without taking this into consideration is doomed to failure from the start. Cf. Franz Nuscheler, "Menschenrechtsschutz durch Konditionierung der Entwicklungshilfe?", in: Brock, *Menschenrechte und Entwicklung*, op. cit., pp. 65 - 72; here: pp. 67f.; as is described by Hermann Sautter, director of the Ibero-America Institute for Economic Research at Göttingen University, the following is characteristic of the lack of intellectual competence in joint development work at a national and international level: "It is no exaggeration to say that the existence and the content of the social pact was long unknown to the donor organizations of the bilateral and multilateral EZ; it was not until 1995, in connection with the 'social world summit', that there was some change in this respect. It is symptomatic of this ignorance that until recently it was still possible for an employee of the World Bank, when asked about the social pact, to remark that he had never heard of it". Hermann Sautter, "Soziale Menschenrechte und Entwicklungszusammenarbeit: Von der Konvergenz der Ziele zur Komplementarität der Mittel", in: Brock, *op. cit.*, pp. 181 - 193; here: p. 185.

[6] According to Peter Atteslander, "anomie means actual or subjectively perceived hopelessness, hence a societal condition of obstructed or impossible self-development". Idem, *"Kulturelle Eigenentwicklung als Kampf gegen Anomie", in:* idem., ed., *Kulturelle Eigenentwicklung* (Frankfurt 1993), pp.13-32; here: p. 13.

[7] Tzvetan Todorov, *Die Eroberung Amerikas: Das Problem des Anderen* (Frankfurt 1985); Enrique Dussel, *Von der Erfindung Amerikas zur Entdeckung des Anderen: Ein Projekt der Transmoderne* (Düsseldorf 1993).

erosive and humanly denigrating impact they themselves have suffered and continue to suffer[8]—does not stop at our own gates. The violence of this process is manifested by the consumerist and egoistic avarice of the golden calf called the market[9]—a type of avarice to which we have all fallen prey and which dictates our relationship to ourselves, our fellow human beings, as well as to our social and natural environment. In the process of reflection on, and assimilation of, the experiences in our intercultural dialogs and meetings it has become evident to me that we in the West must take seriously the task of analyzing and deconstructing our universal claims. I would therefore like to make an attempt along these lines and put forward some reflections on the deconstruction of the universal claim to validity implied by our economic system and monetary structures.

1. The obstruction of intercultural communication resulting from the globalization of the capitalistic economic system

The thesis that constitutes my point of departure is as follows: The systematic privileging and subsidizing of monetary wealth leads to ecological destruction and job elimination all over the world.[10] The increased productivity resulting from technological progress reduces the number of workers that are required. At the same time the continuing process of rationalization brings about a higher rate of exploitation of natural resources such as soil, air, water, and raw materials.

---

[8] Jon Sobrino writes in his book: *Sterben muß, wer an Götzen rührt: Das Zeugnis der ermordeten Jesuiten in San Salvador. Fakten und Überlegungen* (Fribourg 1990), p. 55: "I understand that it is difficult for those living in the First World to grasp the extent of the tragedy. For for those who enjoy life and freedom it is of course difficult to understand what poverty and repression mean in countries of the Third World; hence they have a tendency to ignore this reality, to act uninvolved and remain silent. But perhaps they are also silent because of an unconscious sense of guilt: One cannot continue to live in abundance, to possess practically everything and always want to have more, while many millions of people die of hunger every day. It is the totality of thses kinds of actions and omissions that kill both the poor and those who defend them. Thus the question of who the murderers are is one that is directed at all of us".

[9] Hugo Assmann and Franz J. Hinkelammert, Götze Markt (Düsseldorf 1992); Hinkelammert, *Die ideologischen Waffen des Todes: Zur Metaphysik des Kapitalismus* (Freiburg and Münster 1985).

[10] Cf. Gerhard Scherhorn, *Arbeitsplatzvernichtung und Umweltzerstorunghabendiegleichen Ursachen,* draft paper, version dated 2 May 1997, Stuttgart, pp. 1-6.

2. The consequences of monetary structures for one's own ecological and social structures

2.1 From An Ecological Perspective

Monetary value thrusts itself between man and nature. The money of the economy induces progressive growth and makes it mandatory to utilize nature from the vantage point of calculability, and in the interest of the instrumental rationality of money—to destroy nature bit by bit. The primary orientation to money, to interest and compound interest means exponential growth. This induction of exponential growth leads to ecological disaster. "For"—as H. Creutz has rightly demonstrated—"in a limited space there cannot be unlimited growth. For every healthy and natural form of growth there is an optimum upper limit. In their development all parts of an organism must orient themselves to the whole. All developments that ignore the laws of nature are condemned to break down."[11] A comparison of growth curves makes this clear.

FIGURE 1

The figure above shows various courses of growth: a natural course of growth (decreasing, tending to stabilization); b: lineal course of growth (constant growth rates in the same time periods); c: exponential course of growth (increasing with doubled rates of growth in the same time periods).

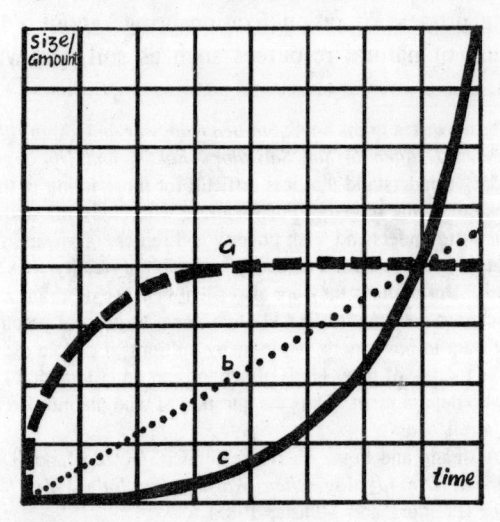

---

[11] Helmut Creutz, *Das Geldsyndrom: Wege zu einer krisenfreien Marktwirtschaft*, (Munich, 1993), p. 300.

2.2 From a Societal And Social Perspective

More and more people are becoming aware of this situation and more and more are asking themselves how this development could be turned in a positive direction. This requires learning to think and act along other lines than previously. Here it is helpful to consider the growth of the economy in relationship to the growth of wealth and to reflect on the steps taken by the economy in the Federal Republic of Germany from 1950 to 1990 in order to bring itself into line with this growth in wealth. The following chart elucidates these events

FIGURE 2

The curves above represent growth and monetary wealth. The overproportional increase of monetary wealth necessitate every higher indebtedness and ever-repeated surges of growth.

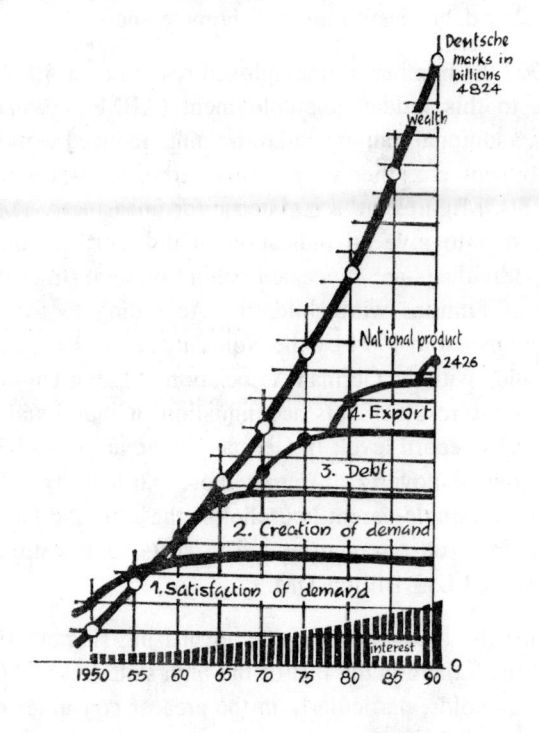

On the one hand the surges of growth become recognizable. After the immediate demand had been met in the first phase of postwar development and the saturation point had been reached, a new demand had to be created, new needs had to be generated at another level in order to be able to meet the demand of wealth for interest. When this was no longer sufficient, the "Law for the Promotion of the Growth and Stability of the Economy" came into being in 1967. The purpose of this law was to attain, through the incurrence of debt on the part of private households, a further increase in consumption, which in turn was supposed to stimulate economic growth yet again and generate further yields for wealth. Today a large number of families and single individuals are faced with the wreckage brought about by development. Many people incurred debts up to the limit of their financial abilities in the hope of averting a negative economic development for themselves. In this they were disappointed: unforeseen events such as illness, reduced working hours or even temporary job loss plunged them into overextended debt, destitution and homelessness.

In 1997 the number of unemployed rose to over 4,5 million. If one adds to this hidden unemployment (ABM or work-creating measures, additional training and re-training, reduced working hours, early retirement, etc.) then we probably arrive at a figure of over 6,5 million. Such figures are a real cause for uneasiness. Yet they do not even start to give an indication of the fact that the fates of concrete individuals are concealed behind these abstract millions— the fates of families with children. According to the report on poverty published in 1994 by the Non-Partisan Welfare Association in cooperation with the German Association of Labor Unions (DGB), we have—as a result of this accumulation of individual plights— reached a new record level: In Germany there are now 7.25 million people living in poverty. Among those particularly affected are large families, single-parent households, the sick, the handicapped, and those from other countries. The costs of unemployment in 1995 grew to 142,5 Billion DM.

Against the background of the advertising slogan "Buy today, pay tomorrow" there is the fact of the high state of indebtedness of private households, particularly in the area of consumer credit. By now the interest balance in nine-tenths of all private households is negative. This is added to by the burden that results from the growing national debt. In the last few years the net additional Federal debt has been roughly 66 billion DM. That means that by now every third DM of every male and female in Germany goes for interest payments, including every third DM spent, say, by a welfare recipient for bread.

The other side of the coin reveals further facts: There are top earners who earn 1,500 DM per working day. There are several thousand individuals who are millionaires fifty times over; they earn 15,000 DM on interest per working day. And, according to the economics magazine "Forbes", there are 400 millionaires in the Federal Republic of Germany who each own 500 million DM, and therefore each earn 150,000 DM per working day. That has led to the situation that, as a result of interest transfers, in 1990 eight tenths of the poorer households became 116 billion DM poorer, and mainly the top tenth of the richer households were made even richer—which strengthens the trend not only that the rich are becoming fewer but also that they are becoming older, and that the number of poor is not only increasing but also that there are more and more young people among them.

The interest burdens imposed by great fortunes have an effect on the labor market as well. A comparison of the development of the capital-market interest rate with the number of business failures (in 1997 about 33000) and the number of unemployed shows that an increasing interest rate is accompanied by an increase not only in the number of business failures but also in the number of unemployed. Here it should be noted that after a decrease in the interest rate the level of employment prior to the interest hike is never regained; the number of unemployed levels off at a higher level for the reason that the boost in the interest rate ushers in a new round of rationalization, which of course rationalizes away jobs as well.

Development of unemployment and the capital market interest rate in the Federal Republic of Germany 1950-1986 including the development of insolvencies (bankruptcies) since 1970

34   GLOBALIZATION AND ITS VICTIMS

FIGURE 3

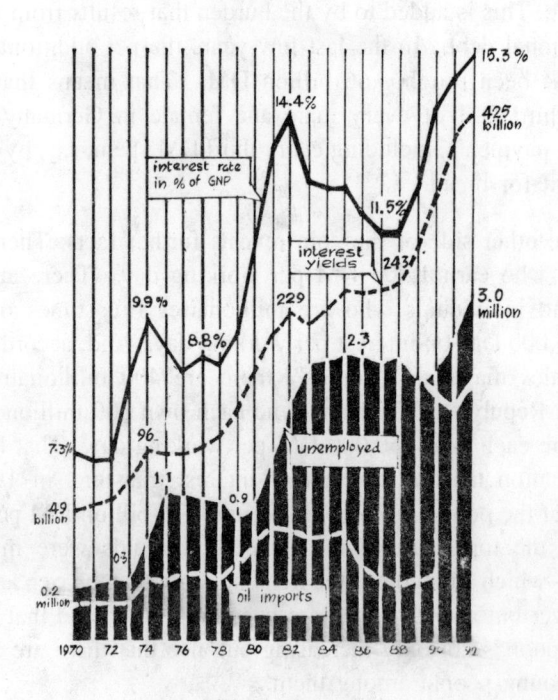

FIGURE 4

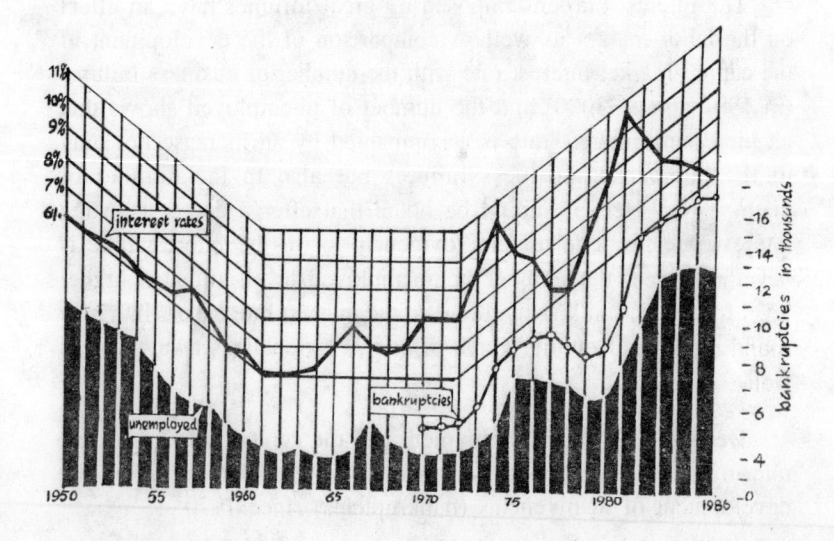

This results, among other things, in the following: inequitable distribution of income from wealth, and inequity due to redistribution of income from interest charges. In other words: The number of loser households rises constantly.

Not only is the fact of these inequities being increasingly registered by the public, but also—in the face of unemployment, indebtedness, homelessness and spreading poverty—their injustice.

Money is a good that is guaranteed by the state. It would be to no person's advantage if this good were not guaranteed in its value and as a means of exchange by the economic performance of the working population on the one hand and by the state on the other. But it is also just and reasonable, on the model of the social market economy, that everyone should receive a portion sufficient for an existence worthy of a human being. There is no good reason why some few people with a large amount of wealth at their disposal should enjoy a privileged use of the social medium money. In point of fact, however, due to the maladjustment in the monetary system brought about by economic change, the use to be had from money is enjoyed at the present time almost exclusively by the owners of wealth freely disposable beyond the necessities of existence. No attempt is being made to remedy the situation by bringing about a just equalization either by means of appropriate taxation or by an adjustment of the ground rules. The social obligation of ownership required by our Constitution is not insisted upon, despite the fact that the State guarantees the monetary system, thereby establishing the basis for the possibility for gaining profits from wealth.

I think that these relationships suffice to show where and what adjustments need to be made in the social market economy. In this context and in view of this state of affairs we should start thinking about drawing consequences and undertake the necessary adjustments to the monetary system in order to conform it to the social market economy. The crisis in which we presently find ourselves could release the requisite creativity. And even if this involves sacrifice, particularly for the owners of more considerable amounts of wealth, we should still attempt to bring about the necessary adjustments if we have an interest in maintaining a social market economy and a democratic political order. To reiterate my thesis:

The security that our State gives to all shall also be enjoyed by all. For the safeguarding of a life lived in dignity the social market economy is a good of high value. Of this we must take good care and make the necessary adjustments where they need to made, as we have been entrusted to do by the fathers of the social market economy, Alfred Müller-Armack and Ludwig Erhard.

If we look at the situation rightly, then the present situation between the rich and the poor in our society is like the situation described in the prisoner dilemma: If we want to extricate ourselves from our dilemma both groups, rich and poor, will have to work together. That means that no one can have an eye simply to his own advantage. Everyone has to give proper consideration to the interests of the other. If everyone in the two groups proceeds in this manner then the results for both sides will be the best that can be obtained: The one group lets the other group have a share in its wealth, in the form, say, of foregoing interest. In return they can live in peace and security and safeguard their possessions. For the other group jobs can be either saved or created anew, enabling them to provide for their own existence, make their way in dignity, live in contentment and thereby add their guarantee to the security of all. Such a modus vivendi falls short of the Christian injunction to love one's neighbor; it functions simply according to the rule *"Do ut des"*, that is, "I give, that you give". But by means of this maxim it is possible to attain a high degree of justice and domestic security.

This proposal is not utopian, on the contrary: it is well in accord with the real facts of the matter. In order to elucidate this I would like to briefly outline a few illustrations.

To start with, it is certainly to be welcomed whenever entrepreneurs can breathe more easily at every drop in the interest rate. The servicing of debt with uncertain margins of interest creates more problems for enterprises than the relatively high but calculable incidental labor costs. Furthermore, the burden of the most wage-intensive companies and workshops could be lightened if incidental labor costs were not deducted from the wage sum but rather from the net product. That could also have the effect that, on the one hand, fewer jobs would be rationalized away. On the other hand, in the interest of the competitiveness of the company the phantasy of the managers would be directed more to the development of intelligent products and procedures. The way things look so far is that German managers prefer to avail themselves of newer and newer versions of the rationalization concept whenever pressure is put on them by the majorities on their respective supervisory boards, who are bankers and think primarily in terms of yield. But that is very shortsighted and counterproductive. The superiority of the other strategy is proven by companies in other countries. Substantial causes for the endangerment of Germany as an economic site lie buried right here, namely in the widespread lack of phantasy among our management. The perpetual moaning on the part of managers and industrial associations about the relatively high incidental labor costs sounds like an alibi for the lack of creativity and inability to deal with the situation on the part of those doing the moaning.

What lies behind the misguided planning in management is quite likely the fact that banks—and along with them money—have largely usurped the function of problem definition in society and in the economy. Here something will have to change. It is possible that our present crisis and the social pressure created by it will have the effect of focusing on the perspective of the victims, the unemployed and the poor, for the problem definition of politics and economics.

As is also shown, at the end of the 70s and the beginning of the 80s exports were vigorously promoted in order to create further economic growth to satisfy the demands of wealth. This development ushered in the increasing debt of Third World countries from which many countries suffer. Free trade intensifies this still further.

3. The consequences of monetary structures for the world economy and for other countries and cultures

3.1 The Dangers Of Free Trade

The orientation of all values to money had a definitely positive side in the 19th century. What was least needed by a world economy oriented to profit and no longer to subsistence was war. It is therefore no wonder that in the English century high finance attempted by all possible means to secure the system of the balance of power.

For this reason it seemed from the European point of view that peace had come about as a result of free trade.[12] The last quarter of the 19th century was of course also a time of colonial expansion; the Berlin Conference of 1884/85, which took place in the wake of this, deserves special mention. At this conference Africa was divided up on the drawing board among the most important colonial powers, with no regard for the rights that Africans had inherited from their ancestors, and with no regard for the boundaries between tribes and peoples that had established themselves in Africa over the centuries and that had made it possible for all to live a good life in peaceful coexistence. But in Europe, too, the orientation of life to the value of money left behind deep destructive traces. Here, as well, social and societal structures were revolutionized in the course of money-oriented profit seeking in connection with the idea of a self-regulating market. And thus the peace created by the balance of power in Europe turned out to be a peace that had been obtained at the price of enormous domestic conflict within the European nations. From this Karl Polanyi concludes "that the origins of the catastrophe lay in the utopian efforts of economic liberalism to establish a self-regulating market"[13]. He continues in this vein: "The mechanism that was set in motion by profit seeking was comparable in its effectivity with the wildest outbreaks of religious enthusiasm in history. Within a generation the entire human world was subjected to its compact influence. As is generally known, in the first half of the 19th century profit seeking reached its zenith in England in the wake of the industrial revolution. About 50 years later it reached the European continent and America. Finally it came to the point that in England, on the European continent and even in America similar eventualities forced the questions of the day in a direction whose main characteristics were essentially the same in all Western countries. Hence we must look for the origins of the catastrophe in the rise and fall of the free market."[14]

The tremendous social and ecological wounds resulting from the transvaluation of values and their orientation to money and

---

[12]Cf. Karl Polanyi, The Great Transformation: Politische und okonomische Usprunge von Gesellschaften und Wirtschaftssystemen, German edition (Vienna, 1977), pp. 34ff. (hereafter cited as Transformation).

[13] Ibid., p. 49.

[14] Ibid., p. 50.

profit in the course of the industrial revolution have not healed to this day. But we are becoming more and more aware of them. Money, and profit-seeking oriented to the increase of money, makes everything subservient to it: man and nature. Nature becomes just as much a subsystem of the economy, a mere means of production, as does man, who is no longer of any interest except as manpower. Whoever cannot be utilized as manpower becomes redundant in the market economy. Thus entire continents, if they are no longer required or no longer seen to be of interest for profit seeking or for increasing money, can be declared redundant—Africa, for example. Although we still talk about over-population, from the perspective of the profit maximization of the market economy it is rather a question of population redundancy. This transvaluation of values requires "a change of the motivation of the members of society. The motive of making a living must be replaced by the motive of making a profit. All transactions are transformed into money transactions. ... The dislocations caused by such mechanisms must necessarily tear apart interpersonal relationships and threaten with destruction the natural living space of human beings."[15] Whoever calls to mind the highly differentiated and closely intertwined complex of rituals that obtains between people's economic activity and their social relationships will be able to understand the import of this. Here also belongs the regulation of relationships involving barter and markets, which has existed in all societies for the regulation of the division of labor.[16] In societies prior to the introduction of the

---

[15] *Ibid.*, pp. 63f.

[16] Polanyi points out that there has always been some kind of economy and markets in societies, but that before our time there had never been a form of economy "that was steered, even in principle, by the market. Despite the stubborn dissemination of academic incantations in the 19th century, yield and profit had never before played an important role in the exchange of goods in human economic activity. Although the institution of the market had been fairly widespread since the late Stone Age, it had played merely a secondary role in economic activity.

We have good reason to insist with all emphasis on this observation . No less of a thinker than Adam Smith maintained that the division of labor in society is based on the existence of markets, or as he put it, on the inclination of people to barter, to trade and to exchange one thing for another. This formulation was later to lead to the concept of homo economicus. Looking back it can be stated that no misunderstanding of the past has demonstated itself to have been so prophetic of the future: Whereas this tendency had in no known society up to the time of Adam Smith manifested itself to any larger degree, and had played in economic life at best

market economy, the social constellations and relationships were such that the subsistence requirements of all persons were ensured by the obligation of reciprocity and by an "attitude of give and take"—as has been recommended by the Plenary Meeting of the Catholic Bishops' Conference of Nigeria[17]. "Thus the principle of reciprocity in the wider sense serve(d) to ensure production as well as the maintenance of the family."[18] In many places and times the distribution of production was also regulated with the help of the principle of gathering and redistributing. The decisive point of this kind of economic activity is that reciprocity and redistribution are ensured by social relationships and social behavior. Reciprocity grounded in social relationships generates a type of solidarity that ensures a just distribution of goods as well as appropriate participation at both the intra-social and inter-social level. From this it can clearly be seen that social relationships formed the basis of the economic system. Production was therefore geared to consumption and redistribution in accord with social requirements.

---

a. subordinate role, a hundred years later an industrial system held sway over the greater part of the earth that carried the practical and theoretical implication with it that mankind was virtually defined by this one particular tendency - in all its economic activities, and possibly even in its political, intellectual, and spiritual activities as well. In the second half of the 19th century Herbert Spencer, who had only a superficial knowledge of economics, was able to equate the principle of the division of labor with barter and trade, and fifty years later Ludwig von Mises and Walter Lippmann were able to repeat the same misapprehension. But by this time arguments were no longer needed. An untold number of authors who concerned themselves with political economics, social history, political science and general sociology followed in Smith's tracks and took over as axiomatic for their respective sciences his paradigm of savages engaging in barter. It may be added that Smith's contentions concerning the economic psychology of early man were just as false as were Rousseau's views on the political psychology of natural man. Division of labor, a phenomenon as old as society itself, develops out of the natural difference between the sexes, out of geographical circumstances and out of individual abilities, and man's alleged inclination to barter, to trade and to exchange is doubtful in the extreme. Whereas history and ethnology have cognizance of various economic forms, most of them exhibiting the institution of the market, they have no knowledge of any economy prior to ours that comes even anywhere close to having been so dominated and regulated by markets.", in: Karl Polanyi, *Transformation*, p. 65f.

[17] "Plenary Meeting of the Catholic Bishops' Conference of Nigeria Held at Eunugu on September 12-16, 1994", Communique, no. 3.

[18] Polanyi, *Transformation*, p. 71.

In contrast, production in a market economy is oriented to profit; society, social relationships and the natural environment are turned into "adjuncts" of the market, as analyzed by Polanyi.

The market form, on the other hand, which is connected with its own specific objective, namely exchange, barter, is capable of giving rise to a specific mechanism: the market. This is ultimately the reason why the domination of the economic system by the market is of such immense significance for the total structure of society: it means nothing less than the treatment of society as an adjunct to the market. The economy is no longer imbedded in social relationships; social relationships are rather embedded in the economic system. The decisive significance of the economic factor for the existence of society excludes every other result. As soon as the economic system is organized in separate institutions based on specific objectives and bestowing a particular status, society must itself also be structured in such a way that the system can function in harmony with its own laws. This is the real meaning of the well-known dictum that a market economy can only function in a market society.

The step that transforms individual markets into a market economy, and regulated markets into a self-regulating market, is of decisive importance. Apart from whether this fact is praised as the apex of civilization or bemoaned as a cancerous growth, in the 19th century it was naively believed that such a development was the natural outcome of the expansion of markets. There was no awareness of the fact that the transformation of markets into a self-regulating system of enormous potency was not the result of a natural, indwelling tendency of markets to expand indiscriminately, but was much rather the consequence of the thoroughly artificial stimuli applied to the body of society in order to cope with a situation that for its own part had been created by the no less artificial phenomenon of the machine. The limited and non-expansive character of the market form as such was not recognized; and nevertheless it is just this fact that emerges convincingly from modern research.[19]

---

[19] *Ibid.*, p. 81.

From all of this the dangers of our market economy and of free trade become clear. If free trade is organized in a world-wide market economy on economic principles alone—that is to say, on the basis of financial interests, profit and competition—then "the maximization of profits and production" is striven for "without taking into consideration the hidden social and ecological costs"[20]. Man and nature are just simply "adjuncts" of financial market interests. But for both man and nature that can lead only to disaster. Free trade is being demanded world-wide because the international division of labor offers cost advantages. That is no doubt beyond dispute.

If no international trade takes place then the production of every country is limited only by its capital and its resources. If there is free trade, countries are able to specialize because of comparative cost advantages. In the last analysis the entire capital of a country could theoretically be invested in the production of a single product. In this respect the absolute cost differences between countries plays no role—but only on the silent assumption that capital is not able to move across national borders. If capital is also able to move then it can pursue the absolute instead of the relative cost advantage.[21]

Since money is the most moveable factor in the world economic system, and is furthermore at the top of the value list, its logic alone is followed. In other words: The fundamental aims of economic policies, namely "effective allocation, equitable distribution and sustainable utilization of resources"[22], do not need to be taken into consideration at all as long as the bottom line shows that profit has been made. Beyond that, from the perspective of profit maximization it is a matter of indifference if, as a result of competition with lowered barriers, man and nature world over suffer grave injury, and social systems break apart. "Capital will flow out of one country and into another, and in the process perhaps wash away

---

[20] Herman E. Daly, "The dangers of free trade: As a rule economic researchers ignore the hidden costs imposed by deregulated world trade on the environment and society in general", in: *Specturm der Wissenschaft* (January, 1994), pp. 40-46; here:p.40.
[21] *Ibid.*, p. 42.
[22] *Ibid.*, p. 42f.

jobs and prosperity along with it. This international division of labor will indeed bring about a total increase in world production; but that is by no means to say that all countries involved get something out of it."[23]

Thus it is clear why the transvaluation of values discussed at the beginning, which has come about in the course of the absolutizing of money and profit in the market economy, must once again be transformed. "Economic rationality must once again be systematically brought back in line with ethical criteria respecting the good life and fair coexistence among people"[24], as is postulated by Peter Ulrich. What is necessary, therefore, is just the opposite of economic globalization—the opposite course as recommended by John Maynard Keynes: "Hence I sympathize with those who do not wish to maximize the economic entanglements between nations but rather to keep them as slight as possible. Ideas, knowledge, art, hospitality, travel—such things are international in their essence. Goods, however, should be made at home whenever it is reasonable and practicable to do so; and, above all, finances should remain predominantly national."[25] If this were taken to heart by those responsible in corporate business and industry, as well as by those owning large fortunes, then the current talk about economic sites, which is oriented solely to profit maximization, would be given a different content. At a time in which twenty times more money dances around the world each day than is required by the world economy—at such a time it has become absurd to give priority to the maximization of profit and the further accumulation of stockpiles of money. This will lead to a crisis of world society ending in the collapse of economic and monetary structures. It is now already apparent that the demands of these vast heaps of money can no longer be satisfied with real production and that they are therefore seeking an escape by dealing with fictitious products, that is, in a virtualizing of reality—which was unmistakably revealed to everyone by the stock-market crash in the fall of 1987.[26]

---

[23] *Ibid.*, p. 43.
[24] Peter Ulrich, *Transformation der ökonomischen Vernunft: Fortschrittsperspektiven der modernen Industriegesellschaft*, 3rd. ed. (Bern/Vienna/Stuttgart, 1993), p. 5.
[25] Quoted in *ibid.*, p. 40.
[26] *Cf.* Matthias Albert, "Internationale Beziehungen in cyberspace? Virtualisierungsprozesse im Weltwirtschaftssystem" (International relationships in

Quite apparently we have not succeeded—even within the concept of a social and ecological market economy—in mediating between competition and solidarity, that is, between the market economy on the one hand and the social and ecological systems on the other. We have to begin to understand that, according to the creator of the concept of the social market economy, the principle of competition is acceptable only on the condition that the state, as the embodiment of social solidarity, provides sufficient social security for all persons. What is further required is "a socially acceptable formation of international political ground rules"[27], and the organization of the economy as a subsystem of nature, requiring from the economy a maximum limit to its utilization of material and energy, as well as the attainment of a stationary condition.[28] We should start with haste to move in this direction.

3.2 Conclusion and alternative possibilities

The greatest obstacle to a lasting improvement of the situation of human beings and of the social environment in the world is constituted by the monetary parameters and structures that have been formed by the neoliberal economic system. They have neither dropped down from heaven nor are they unalterable. They are the result of social processes in the societies of rich industrial nations and can and must be changed if their condition is experienced by people as destructive and if the natural, social and cultural foundations of life appear to be endangered by them. There is a growing awareness of the fact that the present-day form of economic growth no longer serves the economic well-being of human beings and the preservation of their natural environment; on the contrary, it has attained the status of an end in itself and no longer serves any purpose other than the further accumulation of monetary assets.

---

cyberspace? Virtualization processes in the world economnic system), paper read at the symposium "Construction and Reality" of the ethics group within the interdisciplinary work group "Technological Research" of the Johann Wolfgang Goethe University, Frankfurt, 23-25 June 1994.

[27] Lothar Czayka, "Mehr Wettbewerb ist kein Allheilmittel: Und ausreichende soziale Sicherung ist keine Wohltätigkeitsveranstaltung" (More competition is no universal remedy: And sufficient social security is no charitable undertaking), in: *Frankfurter Rundschau*, no. 219, 20 October 1994, p. 16.

[28] *Cf.* Daly, *loc. cit.* (note 30), pp. 44f.

Rightly calculated, it even tends to reduce general economic wellbeing rather than to improve it.[29]

Gerhard Scherhorn interprets the capital-oriented growth strategy as follows: The first component is the cost reduction of natural resources: "The exploitation of natural resources costs relatively less than the exploitation of manpower, because no one has to bear the (full) costs for the regeneration or replacement of natural resources. For manpower, on the other hand, wages and social-security contributions are paid. It is comparatively less cost-intensive to utilize capital goods. Therefore it is required by the logic of business administration to replace the more expensive means of production with the less costly ones.

Hence one cause of job elimination and environmental destruction lies in the cost reduction of natural resources. This is one part of the growth strategy by means of which the state has promoted the formation of capital since the beginnings of industrialization. Hence the real cause lies in just this strategy. It was conceived at a time in which capital was the bottleneck factor. Therefore the course was set for an expansion of capital. (This was also the case, *mutatis mutandis*, with respect to "socialist" economies).

The regulations governing property rights confer control over business enterprises on investors (= those who place equity and/or debt capital, including bank loans, at the disposal of a business enterprise), thus putting them in a position to determine the direction and pace of technological progress. The makeup of capital markets makes it possible for them, among other things, to discipline companies that neglect the goal of expansion, that is, by lowering stock quotations. This possibility for exerting influence has been significantly reinforced both by the concentration of monetary assets (in the hands of large-scale enterprises and investment companies) and by globalization (that is, the international mobility of capital).[30]

---

[29] Gerhard Scherhorn *et al., Wohlstandskosten und verantwortliches Handeln,* Report on the findings of an experimental study of the research branch "Mensch und globale Umweltveränderungen" of the German Research Foundation. Arbeitspapier 68 (Stuttgart: Hohenheim University, Lehrstuhl für Konsumtheorie und Verbraucherpolitik, 1997).

[30] Gerhard Scherhon, Arbeitsplatzvernichtung, *loc. cit.*, p. 2.

Thus "unchecked capital expansion" brings about "a kind of economic growth that devaluates itself. It is the objective of the capital-oriented growth strategy to increase economic well-being, the number of employed, as well as tax revenues. This it succeeds in doing only as long as the initial parameters remain more or less unchanged: that is, capital is the scarcest production factor, the substance of the totality of natural goods or resources—the natural environment—is intact, the working population benefit from the increases in affluence. Today these conditions no longer obtain. Capital is abundantly available (its high price is a function of power, not scarcity—see below). Despite the fact that the national product continues to increase, people in general, as well as the social environment, derive less and less benefit from it: as a result of four side-effects of growth, material well-being is becoming increasingly divested of its value:

The natural environment is not being preserved and enhanced, but gradually destroyed, as has been set forth above. The destruction of nature detracts from the value of the growth of the national product as a result of the progressive increase in defensive expenditures, in noncompensated damage to the environment and to health, and in the irremediable exploitation of nonrenewable resources.

The claims of capital exert downward pressure on income from wages. Investors (= all those who place equity and/or loan capital, including bank loans, at the disposal of business enterprises) require returns (interest, dividends), over and above production increases. They can only obtain that much if there is a reduction of the share of the production result received by other stakeholders (= employees, suppliers, the state, customers). Technological progress has seen to it that they can push their claims through; labor costs, in particular, have been reduced. This devaluates growth: A part of the national product is set aside for unemployment compensation, people willing to work go idle, their material existence and occupational identity become endangered, and their faith in the market economy is undermined.

The discretionary power of capital compels the state to waste its resources. It leads to a situation in which multinational corporations are no longer under the necessity of paying any heed to political considerations; they are in a position to play off various production sites (cities, regions, nations) against each other. Potential locations compete with one another for the relocation and settlement of companies by offering privileges (costs, taxes, regulations) and direct subsidies—all of which distracts from the task of putting the powers of production to the best possible use. This does not lead to the creation of jobs; innovations and jobs are more likely to be generated by medium-size and small enterprises. The only certain effect is that the national economy wastes its resources on uninnovative companies—which devalues the growth of the national product.

The demands made by capital reinforce the unequal distribution of income and assets. The greater the monetary wealth, the more its growth is fed by interest rather than by savings. The interest yield brings about an exponential growth rate of monetary capital, which is accompanied by a corresponding increase in the sums that have to be raised for interest payments. This type of growth benefits only a small fraction of the population, for monetary assets are extremely unequally distributed, and this inequality is becoming more acute. The price of the increase in monetary fortunes is paid for by the working population, who receive a correspondingly smaller share of the returns on production, as well as by consumers, to whom the interest burden is passed on in the form of higher prices. The increasing inequality of distribution also adds to the devaluation of the growth in prosperity.

In the final analysis, capital bears no responsibility for production. It is exempted from all responsibility apart from a single task: its own expansion. The growth strategy which banks on the illimitability of capital leads in the short run to an increase in returns, in favorable cases to an increase in growth rates as well; for a short period it can also raise the employment rate; but it can achieve a lasting reduction of unemployment only under certain conditions (reconstruction, remedial development), which in industrialized countries are no longer given.

The growth strategy can postpone the decline of growth rates and returns (at preset values by means of globalization) but it cannot delay it indefinitely. The world is finite, and the desire for goods finds its limit precisely in the devaluation of economic well-being. For this is becoming ever more clearly identified as a progressive development in the costs of prosperity. Desires for goods are insatiable only as long as the costs for additional goods seem justifiable.

The totality of monetary wealth represents potential demands on the national product despite the fact that growth predicated on interest results from redistribution. That should lead to a greater responsibility on the part of the recipients of interest to buy more goods with their money and/or to reinvest it in production. But there is no provision that prompts them to assume such a responsibility, and the inclination to assume this responsibility of their own accord is steadily diminishing.

Since it is already the case that high returns are more likely to be achieved by cost recovery and company takeovers rather than by the production of goods, to an increasing extent investors are turning to purely financial schemes, even to speculative ones. This tendency is given further impetus by the exponential growth of monetary wealth and by the excessive increase in state debt creation. To an ever greater degree it is leading to a situation in which capital neglects responsibility for production and is concerned solely with its own growth. Conclusion: it can be demonstrated that in the infancy of industrial development it was necessary to promote the formation of capital. In a time of advanced economic development, however, it turns out to be disadvantageous if no limits are put on the formation and utilization of capital.[31]

The necessary adjustments can be forced through by cultural pressure—pressure that emanates from the grassroots level, from the disadvantaged. This group constitutes the innovative and creative power providing the catalyst, as it were, for change. Creativity in any society is generated on the periphery. In the interest of the preservation of the system as a whole this creativity must be taken advantage of by the ruling classes in the society and translated into practice. If that does not happen then the end of the system is preordained. We have to ask the following question: At

---

[31] *Ibid.*, pp. 2-4.

what points can leverage be brought to bear on monetary structures to effect change? I see four basic ways:

3.2.1 The first way: The Tobin tax

The first way would go into effect entirely within the framework of existing power structures. I am referring here to the Tobin tax. It was suggested by the economist James Tobin "in order for governments to be able to regain their autonomy with respect to decisions concerning the national economy".[32] James Tobin, who received the Nobel prize for economics in 1981, made the proposal of taxing exchange transactions worldwide. Here are some figures to illuminate the context: "According to data of the Bank for International Settlement, foreign exchange dealings in 1995 reached an extent of 1300 billion dollars per day (over against $18 billion at the beginning of the 1970s). By way of comparison, the annual turnover of goods and services worldwide amounts to a value of 4300 billion dollars. Furthermore, in 80 percent of exchange dealings the transactions back and forth take place within a maximum of seven days, and in most cases even on the same day. In London, the world's most important foreign exchange center, four-fifths of all transactions are no longer directly connected with trade movements or investments."[33] They constitute speculations that have no positive effect whatsoever on investments in the economy. On the contrary: they endanger the market and the autonomy of the economy up to and including entire national economies and serve the sole purpose of enriching speculators without imposing any social responsibility on them.

Taxation would have a twofold effect: On the one hand, the principle of the social responsibility of monetary wealth and the ensuing profits would be brought to bear. On the other hand, taxation of foreign exchange dealings would facilitate the cash flow in the economy, as well as the financing of the implementation of ecological and social innovations. In addition, short-term investing would be reduced and a development in the direction of long-term

---

[32] Ibrahim Warde, "Die Tobin-Steuer - ein wenig Sand im Getriebe, in: *Le Monde Diplomatique*, 12. Feb. 1997, p.1.
[33] *Ibid.*

investing would be encouraged, since short-term investments would be most strongly affected by the Tobin tax. Considerable sums would be generated in any case. "At a tax rate of 0.25 percent annual revenues would amount to circa 290 billion dollars".[34] In spite of this, the Tobin tax is not applied, notwithstanding the fact that the financial ministers and heads of state of the Group-of-Seven states are aware of it, and notwithstanding the fact that a team of experts has established the extremely positive effect it would have on the economy worldwide.[35] This is all the more astounding inasmuch as state debt could be reduced by means of the funds gained from the Tobin tax. Instead, Waigel, Rexrodt and Kohl tolerate the situation that the continuing favored treatment of, and tax exemptions for, speculative capital forces the Federal Republic of Germany, and other states as well, to increase state debt and reduce social-security benefits.

3.2.2. The second way: Reform of the compound-interest system

The second way would be a way of changing the monetary structures. It implies a fundamental change in the ground rules of the monetary system, i.e. a change in the interest system. In other words: "The formation of (speculative) liquidity reserves must be made more difficult by burdening them with expenses ..., that affect everyone with, say, 4% of his average cash reserves to the extent that incoming monetary sums are not forthwith rechanneled into consumption, investment, or payment into a savings account. This circulation safeguard, i.e. prevention of blockages in economic circulation, no longer relies on the inadmissible reward of interest as its driving force, ..., but rather the consistently effective punishment of the withdrawal of liquid funds from economic circulation ...".[36] Thought of in terms of ethical criteria, this is justifiable by virtue of the fact that money becomes publicly acknowledged as money, as constituting a social institution, i.e. socially guaranteed in its value, as has been set forth above. To this extent money can

---

[34] *Ibid.*

[35] Mahbub ul-Haq, Inge Kaul, and Isabelle Grunberg, eds., *The Tobin-Tax: Coping with Financial Volatility* (Oxford: Oxford University Press, 1996).

[36] Ernst Winkler, "Vor einer Mutation unseres Wirtschaftssystems", *in: Sozialökonomische Arbeitstexte* 3, 2nd edition (Lütjenburg 1994), p. 16.

take on the functions both of a means of exchange and also of a means of value conservation. And it acquires a universal value for everyone in possession of money due to the fact that it can be exchanged for any product at any time. For owners of money incur no storage costs for the conservation of money, nor does money become spoiled if it is hoarded—in contrast to the potatoes of a farmer, who must dispose of them as quickly as possible if he wants to avoid the risk of losses from old or rotting potatoes. Compared with a farmer's potatoes, money has the characteristics of a joker, with the result that money is highly desirable and can be made available on a time basis, can be lent, to those who have none, in exchange for interest and interest on interest. This is different in the case of the farmer. If he lends just one sack of potatoes he is satisfied if at the end of any set period of time he gets back just this sack and no more. Pierre Joseph Proudhon (1809-1865), a contemporary of Karl Marx (1818-1883), recognized this problem and viewed value-added, in contrast to Marx, as a result of money circulation. Following Proudhon, Dieter Suhr formulates the matter as follows: "Exchange transactions and credit transactions in which interest plays a role are phenomena of the circulation sphere."[37] That means that the real capitalist is not the entrepreneur or the "industrial capitalist", but rather the money capitalist, who makes interest and compound interest thanks to the joker advantage of money as a universal means of exchange and communication without making so much as a single contribution to an increase in value.[38]

---

[37] Dieter Suhr, *Befreiung der Marktwirtschaft vom Kapitalismus: Monetäre Studien zur sozialen, ökonomischen und ökologischen Vernunft* (Berlin 1986), p. 14

[38] *Ibid.*, p. 19: "The money capitalists ought to be truly thankful to good old Marx until the Last Judgment for a certificate of good character so good that it frees them from the suspicion of value-added. For the interest that an entrepreneur as borrower has to pay deprives him of a portion of the profit that he has earned through his entrepreneurial efforts: he has to perform 'surplus work" in addition to what he can earn on his own in order to satisfy the interest claims of the monetary capitalists - to the extent, that is, that he does not succeed in passing on to the workers the pressure he is under. If value-added does not originate in the production sphere, however, but rather in the circulation sphere, or more precisely, in the money and capital market, then the indirect cause of the profits from (increasable) tangible assets is also money interest, and with these decisive reflections Proudhon was right - all along the line - after all: the investor is faced with the agonizing choice of whether he ought to put his money in interest-bearing monetary claims (bonds, for example), or in a company, in real estate, or in stocks (real assets). If for the sake

That should make it clear to us where the pressure point in our system lies, namely in the interest system and the monetary structures built upon it. They are at the root of the compulsory growth to which the economy is subjected. Hence they are also at the root of the private, public, and international debt under whose consequences human beings, nature, and cultures suffer. If the circulation of money can be safeguarded by other means than by interest and compound interest and if the withholding of money on the part of the owners of money can be prevented by other incentives, then we should accomplish that by political means and mobilize all the cultural forces necessary for this end. Against this background we consider it to be lacking in foresight and ethically problematic that the Church, which had maintained the prohibition of interest up into the 20th century, dropped this prohibition in the reformulation of ecclesiastical law in 1983. Not the least pertinent factor has no doubt to do with the fact at least the rich churches profit as economic players from the unjust monetary structures. Hence they also have a share in the responsibility for the harmful consequences to human beings and nature, are entangled in structural sin and involved in the continued working and hardening of sinful structures. It is to be hoped that the bishops of rich dioceses and their chief financial administrators, as well as their governing boards and investment consultants, face up to this problem and take steps to ensure that their financial activities do not stand in contradiction to the proclamation that is their calling.

---

of simplicity one abstracts from theoretical, portfolio-related nuances of the problem (risk calculation and so forth), then the following holds true: The investor shifts his liquidity to where he anticipates higher yields. His money is available for the increasing of real assets only under the condition that he can expect that their returns will be higher than those of the prospective interest yields from bonds. Therefore real assets never see the light of day unless they hold the promise of a return at least equal to interest rates. This has been known to the pundits of economic science at least since Keynes: The marginal utility of monetary capital sets the standard for the marginal utility of tangilbe assets; the interest rate limits the growth rate of real capital. In other words: monetary interest is the obstacle to a national economy on the path to real prosperity: The formation of tangible assets - be they in the form of production facilities or in the form of valuables that could serve as the basis of capital investment - is slowed down and obstructed if and to the extent they are not profitable, that is, if they cannot beat the competition from monetary interest. That is how different the world looks depending on whether it is looked at through the spectacles of Marx or Proudhon".

PART 1 : GLOBALIZATION: ITS SOCIAL CONSEQUENCES 53

At the present time the only thing lacking for a change in the monetary structures is the requisite social awareness. Those holding positions of responsibility in the churches should lend their full support to the mobilization of all possible forces for a change in the monetary structures. Even if there is not yet sufficiently widespread awareness of this path, which I have designated as the radical path, this could be created quickly with increasing social, ecological and cultural pressure. Besides, there are many who are of the opinion that the worldwide interlocking of our system is an obstacle that condemns a single-handed attempt of the Federal Republic to failure, despite the fact that there have been thoroughly successful attempts at local levels.

3.2.3 The third way: The ethical mobilization of economic subjects
I call this the "gentle way". It proceeds on the assumption of the capacity for ethical motivation on the part of those involved—and banks on this assumption. However, this avenue requires a change in awareness and a capacity for mobilization on the part of consumers just as much as on the part of entrepreneurs, investors, the owners of monetary wealth, and banks. All of these contingents should cease to tolerate the fact that money is the god at the center of every concern in our society. We should no longer allow the god "Mammon" to dictate to us the nature of the problems that we have to solve. We have to contest the definition of the problem given by the god Mammon. In other words: We should no longer be prepared to accept the fact that entrepreneurs and bankers come along and say: "Before we can talk about morality there has to be cash in the till, a profit has to be made". The absolutizing of this formula is economically shortsighted and leads to a dead end.

We have always acted in accordance with this formula, not least in the financial departments of the Church. Hence we require a new way of looking at things in order to grasp the real facts of the situation and see where priorities have to be set. It cannot in earnest be the task of 90 percent of the population to break their backs and make sacrifices for no other purpose than to satisfy money's exponential needs for growth. Human beings do not exist for the sake of money; on the contrary, money exists to serve human beings in their concern for and attempt to realize a life in dignity for all. What follows from this is that the victims of our present monetary ground rules—the unemployed, entrepreneurs ruined by servicing their debts, the poor all over the world, and the ravished environment—must be given priority in the definition of the problem. The primary question is precisely not: "What is good for big money?", but rather: "What is good for human beings and for the entirety of creation?"

We should no longer vote for politicians who do not adopt this definition of the problem, and who are involved in financial scandals on top of that. In this manner we can bring about a change in perspective in the definition of the problem in politics as well. In the economic sector, too, a change in perspective can be effected by many working in concert. Furthermore, not only in politics, but also in the economic sphere and among the owners of disposable monetary funds there are men and women and institutions who would acquiesce to such a change in perspective, who would be open to it if the necessary parameters were put in place.

But how could this work? The first prerequisite is a widespread interest in the preservation of the social market economy. I think that this exists. But is there really no alternative to this that would be better? In our democratic system and the cultural value system connected with it we have developed a form of social relationships and conditions of coexistence in which a balance is to be attained between the economy and the state—in the interest of both a humanly dignified form of society and the preservation of the natural foundations of life. It is on this basis that conditions in the state and the economy are structured and it is in terms of this basis that they must be justified. In other words: The state may not simply be put at the service of economic and monetary structures. The question must continually be put to the state as to the extent to which it has done justice, in the face of pressure from the owners of monetary wealth and from capital, to its fundamental task, which is to set up the ground rules in such a way that humanly dignified life is possible and the natural and cultural foundations of life are safeguarded. That is no easy political task. For on the one hand we have nation states, which therefore have their limits with respect to the implementation of their norms and values, and on the other hand we have monetary fortunes with global mobility which can be shifted to wherever the highest yields are to be had.[39] That means: "The understanding of the development of the nation state cannot be a question of the examination of internal and external determinants, but rather of the attempt to grasp what it means that the nation state is an element of global capital relationships. For the present that means that the development of any given state can be understood only within the context of the global development of capitalistic societal conditions, of which it is a component".[40] It is therefore of importance to draw attention to the fact that money as globally mobile capital has become an end in itself and can everywhere pursue its interest in making profits without having to respect the interests of human beings, nature, the nation state, cultures, etc. Whoever takes note of this will come to the conclusion that "the crises of the conditions of production are manifested in the increasing liquidity of capital".[41] In order to prevent "money as the most impudent and arrogant form of capital"[42] from becoming an end in itself we must work towards the goal that money fulfils its function of being at the service of production and of making decent human coexistence possible. The creation of free trade zones and the expansion of markets all the way up to and including globalization—the World Trade Organization, for example—must demonstrate that they do not primarily serve the interests of money but rather of human beings and that they are capable of guaranteeing social human development.[43] I think that this can indeed be made a reality if use is made of the possibilities inherent in a democracy and if supervisory bodies are created to control the business policies of banks to the end that by means of money-flows the conditions of production are ordered in such a way that a lasting development of the world society is made possible—one in which environmental, social, and cultural compatibility function as criteria with foremost priority. On this point I am also in agreement with the thesis put

---

[39] John Holloway, "Reform des Staates: Globales Kapital und nationaler Staat", in: *PROKLA* 23, no. 90 (Münster 1993), pp. 12 - 33; here: p. 21
[40] *Ibid.*, p. 24.
[41] *Ibid.*, p. 28.
[42] *Ibid.*, p. 30.
[43] Enrique Dussel, "Bye Bye Weltmarkt? Freihandel oder Regionalisierung des Weltmarktes: Das Freihandelsabkommen zwischen Kanada, Mexiko und den USA", in: *PROKLA*, loc. cit. note 39, pp. 129-156

forward by Joachim Hirsch "that capitalism can be lastingly changed if a way can be found to bring the processes of production, investment, and the market under public, democratic control. One conceivable option is a corporation model that, while allowing capital investment and profit, does so in a form that is politically controlled and regulated in a "socially compatible" manner. This is less a question of formal property arrangements and more one of social and political power structures.[44] In Germany there is growing interest in transforming the model of the social and ecological market economy along such lines. If this transformation succeeds then the interest in adopting and/or adapting this model could increase in other countries and contribute to a humane formation of the social environment. Here in Germany there is sufficient cultural pressure that could be channeled in the direction of bringing about the needful adjustments for the sake of preserving the social market economy. In the final analysis the interest in preserving the social market economy implies the demand for changes in the ground rules; if monetary structures can no longer be adequately controlled on the basis of economic assessment criteria alone, then these must be supplemented by an ethical evaluation in such a way that money-flows can be channeled into ethically, ecologically, and socially important areas. Money-flows must be steered in such a way that they serve the new definition of the problem.[45]

There are owners of great monetary wealth who have come to the realization that the further accumulation of money leads to a dead end. They are therefore reducing their monetary stockpiles and are funneling considerable portions of their fortunes into the public community, at both the national and international levels, by means of foundations and other forms of endowment.

3.2.4 The fourth way: The prevention of money laundering

A fourth possibility for making a substantial contribution to the realization of human rights is the prevention of money laundering,

---

[44] Joachim Hirsch, *Kapitalismus ohne Alternative? Materialistische Gesellschaftstheorie und Möglichkeiten einer sozialistischen Politik heute* (Hamburg 1990), p. 181

[45] Peter Roche, Johannes Hoffmann, and Walter Homolka, eds., *Ethische Geldanlagen: Kapital auf neuen Wegen* (Frankfurt 1992).

a practice in which our economic system, the banks, etc. are involved, from which they draw profit, but which can also become a danger for them. To some this thesis may possibly seem far-fetched. A few illustrations should make it more plausible. In the 1984 report on the findings of the President's Commission on Organized Crime, money laundering is defined as a process in which the existence, the illegal source, or the illegal utilization of income is concealed in order to subsequently create the impression that this income has been acquired in a legally permissible manner.[46] According to Thomas Achim Werner, money laundering is "the reintroduction of illegally acquired assets into legal financial circulation. The purpose is the concealment of the origin and the removal of the assets from the possibility of being accessed by criminal prosecution authorities. At the same time it is intended to prevent the possible criminal prosecution of those persons who have perpetrated the antecedent criminal actions."[47] These are the key concepts in need of some illustrative examples.

To start with, there are the antecedent criminal actions through which the illegal profits are made. Foremost among these is the illegal trafficking in drugs, which has an annual turnover worldwide of between 500—800 billion U.S. dollars. "This drug trade constitutes the largest cash business in the world."[48] Another form of antecedent action is the slave trade, in which, for example "women from poorer countries are 'smuggled' under false pretenses into the industrial countries, where they are forced into prostitution"[49] ... as well as "the smuggling of children for adoption purposes, illegal trafficking in human organs, which to some extent is connected with the original crime of organ removal from kidnapped or murdered victims"[50], and as further examples, the arms trade, environmental crime, extortion of protection money, etc.

---

[46] Mark Pieth, ed., *Bekämpfung der Geldwäscherei: Modellfall Schweiz* (Basel, 1992) - quoted in: Thomas Achim Werner, *Wachstumsbranche Geldwäsche: Die Ökonomisierung der Organisierten Kriminalität* (Berlin 1996), p. 13.
[47] Werner, *op. cit.*, p. 14.
[48] *Ibid.*, p. 20.
[49] *Ibid.*, p. 22.
[50] *Ibid.*, p. 22.

In addition to the antecedent criminal actions already named, mention must also be made of the degrading, exploitative dealings of drug dealers with coca farmers in Bolivia and in other countries of the Third World.

Wherein lie the causes? For the U.S.A. and other Western industrial countries to put the blame on the coca-producing countries and demand the containment of drug production is hypocritical—for three reasons: Firstly, drug consumers are primarily to be found in the rich countries. Worldwide there are allegedly 12 million consumers of cocaine and 8 million heroin addicts. To name but one example: measured in terms of the number of inhabitants, on a European-wide scale Switzerland has the highest rates of drug-induced deaths, according to the number of those convicted and suspected under the narcotics statutes.[51] Secondly, the cause of the growing drug production is to be seen in the exploitation of countries of the Third World by the industrial nations, as well as in the debt creation and debt overload induced by the rich countries in the Third World. And thirdly, one of the chief causes of the flourishing trade in illegal drugs is the circumstance that money laundering is successfully engaged in, that illegally acquired money can be funneled into legal money circulation without any great difficulty, with the collaboration of numerous reputable money institutions and banks. Thomas Achim Werner has provided the following list of participants in money laundering:

"1. Members of organized crime who themselves have perpetrated the antecedent crimes and thus acquired the profits and who then further conspire and carry out the money laundering with operations of their own. These include the physical act of smuggling cash across national borders, using in part same means and methods by which the drugs are also smuggled.

2. Persons who knowingly and willingly collaborate with criminal groups but who are otherwise active in the legal sphere and who therefore appear trustworthy and unsuspicious to banks and other institutions. Examples are messengers, couriers, corrupt bank employees, certified public accountants, public,

---

[51] *Ibid., p. 130.*

notaries and legal representatives of the Organized Crimes, as well as financial experts acting as specialized money launderers who operate as well-paid functionaries of the OC.
3. Persons who in the exercise of their normally legitimate service functions are misused for the purposes of money laundering— often without their knowledge. These include bank employees, money couriers, lawyers, trustees, numerous financial consultants, investment companies, real estate agents, etc.

Criminal behavior is manifested by the first two groups; the involvement of the third group is largely unwitting, at the most resulting from negligence."[52]

To summarize: For money laundering practices to operate successfully the involvement of the banking system is mandatory. "Due to their central position in the money and credit system, in the administration of assets, and in the international clearing system, banks function as the centers of money laundering. No other institution can transform and transfer more quickly and more effectively the mass of funds in need of being legalized."[53] A particularly prominent role in money laundering is played by tax paradises and offshore banks. Here optimal conditions for money laundering obtain, for example: the virtual absence of taxes, hardly any bookkeeping responsibilities, no or only minimal bank supervision, refusal of international legal assistance, strict bank secrecy, deregulated foreign exchange dealings, etc. In addition to Luxembourg, Liechtenstein, Monte Carlo, Switzerland, Austria, and others "one of the most important offshore sites is the Cayman Islands, a small island group in the Caribbean with 14,000 inhabitants. Several thousand offshore companies are located here, with 500 registered banks alone"[54]—among which all of the major German banks are to be found, including the Central Bank. In 1987 the IMF set the bank

---

[52] *Ibid.*, p. 30.
[53] *Ibid.*, p. 31.
[54] *Ibid.*, p. 35; Werner quotes here the 1988 yearbook of the Chamber of Commerce of Cayman Island: "Deutsche Bank, BfG [Bank für Gemeinwirtschaft], Bayerische Hypotheken und Wechselbank, Bayerische Vereinsbank, Berliner Handels- and Frankfurter Bank, Deutsche Bundesbank - represented by the Deutsche Girozentrale Overseas Ltd".

reserves of the seven most important offshore financial sites at a total of 973.1 billion U.S. dollars, "which corresponds to more than one fifth of the bank reserves worldwide".[55] According to recent estimates, in Germany 50 to 89 billion German marks are laundered annually. What makes this puzzling is the fact that numerous banks acquiesce to money laundering for reasons of short-term profits, notwithstanding the fact that they thereby provide the Organized Crime with the opportunity for amassing unbelievably high capital reserves in the legal sector, from which dangers can then arise for the banks themselves, as well as for entire national economies: "These laundered funds can be integrated profitably, securely, and legally—or they can be employed in the form of speculative capital as a strategic instrument for gaining economic and political leverage".[56] To this must be added the dangers for society, for democracy, and for the legal system, inasmuch as inhibitions with respect to bribery, cooperation with the Organized Crime, and white-collar crime become further weakened. The Organized Crime and the concomitant worldwide disregard for human rights cannot be successfully countered by putting an end to drug cultivation alone. On the contrary, in addition to the elimination of money laundering as the decisive point of attack in the struggle against the OC there is a whole arsenal of measures which will have to be financed by the rich countries. For their so-called developmental policies and dealings—which since the 1960s have been primarily aimed at subordinating the economies of the countries of the Third World to the interests of their own economies—are responsible for the destruction of naturally evolved subsistence economies in these countries, as well as for the debt creation and debt overload of many countries in the so-called Third World.

Werner also emphasizes this connection: "In order to contain the cultivation of drugs, and thereby the supply, far-reaching measures are necessary, for the cultivation is inseparably linked with the economic situation of the countries in the so-called Third World, whose total indebtedness by the end of the 1980s amounted to over 1,300 billion U.S. dollars. As a result of the decline in world market prices for raw materials and agricultural products, the cultivation of

---

[55] *IMF International Financial Statistics (1988),* quoted in Werner, *op. cit., p. 35*
[56] *Ibid., pp. 77f.*

PART 1 : GLOBALIZATION: ITS SOCIAL CONSEQUENCES 61

coca and poppy plants is in many cases the last source of income for farmers. As long as they can attain far greater profits with the cultivation of coca and poppy plants than with other agricultural products, they can only be induced to refrain from drug cultivation with specifically targeted forms of aid. Some examples are more equitable prices for raw materials, as well as fair trading practices, by which not only multinational corporations make profits, but also the farmers. ... The attempt to contain drug cultivation by means of pressure exerted on the cultivating countries by the industrialized countries is very likely doomed to failure as long as such things as economic conditions, the threat of unemployment, and social problems fail to receive sufficient attention. An effective solution requires measures that manifest solidarity and are of use to the countries involved in cultivation."[57]

Put bluntly: For reasons of the causal involvement described above, the industrialized nations bear the primary responsibility for the present desolate condition of the countries of the so-called Third World—for their indebtedness, for the poverty and hunger in these countries, and for the expansion of the Organized Crime.

Hence the industrialized countries have the obligation to support the following measures with all means at their disposal:

1. Elimination of money laundering through the creation of an effective monetary framework and laws capable of implementation.
2. Immediate and total debt remission for all countries of the so-called Third World.
3. Assistance in the creation of a viable type of subsistence economy in these countries.
4. Deconstruction of the attachment of provisos to development aid

With respect to the deconstruction of the universal claim to validity of the capitalist economic system we have dealt primarily with the deconstruction of the monetary structures connected with it. Of course this is not the only area that needs to be put to debate. In practice, the attachment of conditions, or political strings, to

---

[57] *Ibid., p. 105.*

development aid is a further universal claim that is transported in connection with the monetary sector.

At issue here is the fact that in connection with both bilateral and multilateral cooperation the granting of financial aid or credit is coupled with the requirement of introducing democracy as a form of government and life along Western lines. One frequent assumption made in this connection is that thereby the implementation of human rights is most effectively facilitated. This kind of thinking or conception has its roots in the European development of human rights. From this context emerges the faith in the politics of human rights, which is held to have assumed a universally valid form in liberal democracy. Continuing this line of thought has far-reaching consequences. Ernst-Wolfgang Böckenförde points these out when he writes: "If democracy and human rights are connected so closely with each other that democracy becomes a mandatory prerequisite for human rights, then that means that the realization of democracy must be just as universal as the realization of human rights. Only then does the human being—as human being—come into his right".[58] But that cannot be the case. For in terms of its political structure democracy is too fraught with preconditions and is too highly culture-specific; as a form of political order it does not exist for its own sake. "Political systems are geared to particular goals and ends, in the first instance the safeguarding of the security, rights, and freedom of the people who live under them. In contrast to the individual person political systems are not an "end in themselves", but instrumentalities for other ends. They are entities of action and effect created by people who live under particular socio-cultural and political conditions and have a particular mentality.[59] Although global generalizations should be avoided, it would seem to follow from the self-understanding of democracy in our society that the right of citizenship would be granted as a matter of course to every person living in Germany who is integrated in its socio-economic context and who wants to become a German citizen. What happens in Germany instead of

---

[58] Ernst-Wolgang Böckenförde, "Das Unwahrscheinliche wollen: Demokratie, notwendige Forderung der Menschenrechte?" in: *Frankfurter Allgemeine Zeitung*, no. 102, 2 May 1996.

[59] *Ibid.*

this is the denial of full political participation on the grounds of cultural disparity. To this is added the hypocrisy of offering aliens the alternative of "either placing themselves as a foreign culture at the disposal of cultural exoticism and renouncing political claims (examples: voting right, dual citizenship) or adding themselves to the waves that are already flooding the boat. The question of having or not having a passport becomes a question of cultural difference; issues of rights turn into to issues of culture. ... The message sent to aliens in Germany by events reported in rapid succession by the press was clear: "Stay different and show your folkloristic identity or die!"[60] This illustrates once again the significance and the necessity not only of deconstructing the universal claim made for the Western political form of democracy, but also of measuring actual practice against one's own claim, and of facing the fact that other models of democracy exist in other countries.

Thus it also becomes clear that to tie political strings to development aid by making it contingent upon the introduction or successful implementation of democracy is to furnish a specific political system with a universal claim to validity. Doing this can have devastating consequences for the naturally evolved norms and value structures of a country, as well as impairing the realization of human rights. "The effect in practice is a weakening of the claim to validity of human rights. If democracy is accorded the same unconditional status as human rights themselves, whereas at the same time the preconditions for the life and workability of democracy are lacking, as is frequently the case in the political world of today, then this has repercussions on the unconditionality of human rights".[61] And in point of fact this kind of absolutizing of a specific political form would exhibit a lack of respect for the social and political forms of other cultures, as well as completely underestimate their importance for the realization of human rights. Here, for example, the well-known high esteem in which the individual is held in Central Africa should be borne in mind. There the individual is held in high regard "as a unique and irreplaceable being" that "has nonsubsti-

---

[60] Diedrich Diederichsen, "Wie aus Bewegungen Kulturen und aus Kulturen Communities werden", in: Fuchs *et al., op. cit.*, pp. 126-139; here: p. 130.
[61] *Ibid.*

tutable tasks in the community".[62] But it is not alone for the understanding of individual rights that the perspectives of other cultures such as the African are to be respected: The difference of the African model of democracy from that of the West must be recognized, for example. At the 50th International Congress of Moral Theologians and Social Ethicists in 1997 in Münster, Bénézet Bujo made it clear that in the Black-African universe there is a model of democracy in which the right to have rights and human dignity are both guaranteed. In this model tradition and discourse are an experiential reality in a context of strong reciprocal feedback between the traditional institutions of chief, council of elders, and the people. A chief can be removed by the council of elders, and the council of elders can be removed by the people. In a palaver a majority opinion is not brought about, as it is for example in the Western model of democracy; instead, the discourse is carried on until unanimity has been achieved. The palaver as locus politicus illustrates the sapiential and highly democratic character of the African model of democracy.

In this regard it is understandable that Bénézet Bujo is of the opinion that "In Africa the Western understanding of democracy can only fail". And therefore he rightly asks "Why do the Western powers have to intervene there and save their political system at all costs? Would it not be more humane and make more sense to help the people in Africa to go their own way and find their own political system, which in view of their cultural background should be neither democracy nor dictatorship?"[63]

Similar questions and reservations concerning a universalizing of the Western understanding of democracy have been expressed by other cultures in other continents. The West would be well advised to convince itself, by way of a deconstruction of its own universal claim to validity, of the culture-specific roots of its model of democracy. Only by so doing is it possible to lay a foundation for the apprehension of the perspectives of other cultures and to establish a basis for intercultural dialogue.

---

[62] Bénézet Bujo, "Afrikanische Anfrage an das europäische Menschenrechtsdenken", in: Hoffmann, *Begründung von Menschenrechten aus der Sicht unterschiedlicher Kulturen* (Frankfurt 1991), pp. 211 - 224; here: p. 216.
[63] *Ibid., p. 223.*

Globalisation: Implications for Africa

Peter Henriot, S.J.

When I left Zambia last week, one name was on everyone's lips: "El Nino." This climatic phenomenon originating in the middle of the Pacific Ocean is affecting the rainfall patterns in our land-locked African country many thousands of kilometres away. Drought is threatened, with consequent famine, disturbed social conditions, upset economic patterns, and unsettling political ramifications. "El Nino affects many parts of the world — perhaps also here in India — with heavy rains, but in our country its effect is just the opposite, with the halt of rains and resultant severe drought. The awareness that we live on a very small and very inter-related globe has come home in varied and dramatic fashion in recent years, but for us in Zambia, that awareness is heightened by the serious challenge facing the country in the weeks ahead arising from such a dramatic global phenomenon.

"El Nino," I suggest, is an example in the *natural* order of "globalisation", the interdependence of diverse activities occurring across the expansion of the globe. At this conference we are looking at examples in the *artificial*, human-made order of globalisation, in the economic, political and cultural spheres of life. Specifically, we are exploring in this session analyses of the phenomenon of *globalisation and its social consequences*. My task here is to offer some brief reflections on the implications of globalisation for Africa. (Having lived and worked for some years in Zambia, my examples will most often be from my experience there.)

I. Premises

In order to understand the significance of globalisation in the African context, there are two premises that I believe focus the debate more realistically.

A. The first premise is that it is important to understand that today's "globalisation is actually the *fourth stage* of outside penetration of Africa by forces which have negative social consequences for the African people's integral development. This outside penetration has occurred over the past five hundred years in a variety of forms.

The first stage was the period of *slavery*, during which the continent's most precious resources, African women and men, were stolen away by global traders, slavers, working for the benefit of Arab, European and North American countries. Estimates vary from two to ten million slaves extracted from the continent, with disastrous economic, social and psychological effects. I come originally from a country, the United States of America, whose industrial progress in the north during the eighteenth and nineteenth centuries depended upon agricultural progress built unjustly, inhumanely, on the backs of African slaves who toiled in the fields of the south.

The second stage was the period of *colonialism*, when British, French, Belgium, Portuguese, Italian and German interests dictated the way that map boundaries were drawn, transportation and communication lines established, agricultural and mineral resources exploited, religious and cultural patterns introduced. Whatever minimal benefits might have come to Africans because of colonialism were far outweighed by the many negative consequences of economic exploitation, environmental degradation, and social dependencies. Indeed, many of today's ethnic conflicts which attract international attention trace their origins back to colonial stratagems.

The third stage has been described a *neo-colonialism*, what Pope Paul VI called "the form of political pressures and economic suzerainty aimed at maintaining or acquiring dominance."[1] The independence struggles begun in the late 1950's may have brought local governmental rule to the many nations of the continent but did not break the ties — subtle and not so subtle — that bound Africa's future to outside influences. Trade patterns, investment policies, debt arrangements, etc., all reinforced earlier conditions that were

---

[1] Paul VI, *The Development of Peoples*, 1967, #52.

not beneficial to Africans. Another striking example was the political manipulation of African states as bargaining pawns during the Cold War, with the resulting legacies of armed conflicts, for example, in the Horn of Africa and in southern Africa.

We have now entered the fourth stage, the period of *globalisation*, characterised by an integration of the economies of the world through trade and financial flows, technology and information exchanges, and movement of people. The dominant actor in this stage is the free market. The globe is conceived as one market directed by profit motivations of private enterprises that know neither national boundaries nor local allegiances. In this stage, Africa experiences both minimal influence and maximum consequence.

B. The second premise is simply the statement of an obvious but not always acknowledged fact: *globalisation is not working for the benefit of the majority of Africans today*. While globalisation has increased opportunities for economic growth and development in some areas, there has been an increase in the disparities, and inequalities experienced especially in Africa. *The Least Developed Countries 1997 Report* (UNCTAD) notes that 33 of the 48 LDCs are in Africa; that the continent has the highest debt to exports ratio; that the average growth rate of these countries fell from 5.4% in 1995 to 4.6% in 1996; that the export primary commodity prices fell especially in tropical foods (e.g., coffee) and minerals (e.g., copper), areas of particular concern for Africa; and that aid flows have declined and foreign direct investment (FDI) flows have remained small.[2]

The process of globalisation in Africa is a driving force behind the imposition of severe economic reforms under the structural adjustment programme (SAP). The burden of the transition from state-centred economies to free market economies has been borne unequally by those who already are suffering, the poor majority. SAP has meant increased prices of basic necessities, service fees for health and education, retrenchment of the formal employment force, and dismantling of local economic structures in the face of

---

[2] See *Non-Governmental Liaison Service, (NGLS) Roundup*, November 1997.

liberalised trade patterns. While neo-liberal economists argue that there may be "short-term pain but long-term gain in the implementation of SAP, it is increasingly clear throughout Africa that the *sort-term* pain, for example, of social service cuts, ecological damages and industrial base erosion will in the *long-term* have truly disastrous effects upon any hope for an integral and sustainable human development.[3]

II. Realities

The reality of globalisation as it affects Africa can be seen from examples of the *structures* it takes and the *consequences* it induces.

A. Structures

1. *Ideological:* The basis for globalisation is the *neo-liberal* ideology (ideological structure) that many feel is the only alternative for the future, and some even argue marks "the end of history". This is an economic fundamentalism that puts an absolute value on the operation of the market and subordinates people's lives, the function of society, the policies of government and the role of the state to this unrestricted free market.[4] Throughout Africa, socialism is dead and it is now not only capitalism that is alive but a version of capitalism that Pope John Paul II has poignantly called "savage capitalism".

Neo-liberal policies support *economic growth* as an end in itself and use macro-economic indicators as the primary measurements of a healthy society. As will be noted below, this ideology governs not only economic structures but also political arrangements. It assumes almost a religious character, as greed becomes a virtue, competition a commandment, and profit a sign of salvation. Dissenters are dismissed as non-believers at best, and heretics at worst.[5]

---

[3] See Peter Henriot, "Zambia: Debt and Structural Adjustment," *The Month*, July/August 1997, pp. 268-273.

[4] For a clear explanation of this ideology with examples of its workings in Latin America, see "Neoliberalism in Latin America: A Letter from the Latin American Provincials of the Society of Jesus," in *The Month*, July/August 1997, pp. 281-184.

[5] For a well-developed analysis of this economic fundamentalism and its implications, see John Mihevc, *The Market Tells Them So: The World Bank and Economic Fundamentalism in Africa* (Penang, Malaysia: Third World Network, 1995), especially pp. 21-42.

2. *Commercial:* In Africa, the commercial structures of trade and investment are key factors in economic development. These were, of course, the major instruments of the colonialism that gripped the African continent for nearly a century. In recent times, the Uruguay Round of GATT agreements are implementations of a liberalised vision that free trade and unrestricted investment will solve development problems facing the continent. But a group of African non-governmental organisations (NGOs) meeting in South Africa in April 1996, prior to the UNCTAD-IX gathering, challenged this vision on the basis of recent experiences.[6] For example, poorer African countries have been opened up to foreign imports and firms which has led to the destruction of local enterprises. A process of deindustrialisation has taken place in many countries such as Zambia. Our once-flourishing textile industry has been wiped out by imports from Asia; several small industries such as tyre manufacturers and medical supply companies have folded in the face of competition from large South African firms.

The World Trade Organisation (WTO) is emerging as a very powerful actor in the globalisation process, but without much beneficial influence being exercised on its direction by African countries. The WTO is primarily an instrument of Northern governments and countries and its proposals for trade and investment are more in the interests of these elements. The promotion of foreign direct investment (FDI) is hailed as the new engine for development. But FDI flows to Africa are very small (under US$ 5 billion in 1996), are largely advantageous to only a few countries (such as South Africa), and tend to benefit the already privileged elite.

3. *Technological:* Africa is being affected in profound ways by the new electronic communication possibilities that bind together the globe in previously unimaginable ways. Personal computers, fiber electronics, satellites, cellular phones, networks of faxes, e-mail and the Internet: all of these structures make economic and political globalisation more and more a reality. Transfer of funds is almost as important as transfer of information and it is done instantaneously simply by punching keys and flipping switches. (AF1

---

[6] See Africa Faith and Justice Network (Washington, DC), *Around Africa*, January 1997.

opens, or closes, whole new worlds!) Human interface is frequently not necessary and often not desired. Throughout Africa, technological innovations are coming in rapidly and will be a major force in the future.

It is too early to say whether these technological innovations will truly benefit the majority of Africans. I know that I enjoy the advantages of e-mail and Internet connections and that it greatly enhances my work for social justice and peace in Zambia. But only a very small portion of the population of Africa presently have access to personal computers. Other technological structures are slow in developing on the continent.

4. Cultural: One commentator has called the process of globalisation the birth of the AMcWorld — a cultural integration and uniformity that mesmerises the world with fast music, fast computers, and fast food. This AMcWorld is the product of the influence of MTV, McIntosh and McDonald's.[7] Cultural imperialism is not a new phenomenon, but it assumes alarming proportions today when driven by the new technologies and profit propensities of the dynamics of globalisation.

In Africa, this cultural structure of globalisation presents specific problems. Traditional African cultures (there are many cultures in Africa, not simply one) emphasise values such as community, family, respect of life, hospitality. But these cultural values come into strong confrontation with the values communicated through Western music, movies, videos, cable and satellite television, advertisements, and the idolised figures of entertainment and sports. One analyst speaks of the predominance of geoculture over the geopolitical and the geoeconomic.[8] Culture is gaining ground over the traditional sources of economic and political power, and the dominant geoculture of the West is an overwhelming force against traditional African cultures.

5. Political: An important new factor in the process of globalisation is that there is a significant change in the geo-political

---

[7] See Benjamin Barber, "Jihad vs. McWorld," *The Atlantic Monthly*, March 1992.
[8] Xabier Gorostiaga, S.J., "Citizens of the Planet and of the 21st Century," *SEDOS Bulletin*, Vol. 28, No. 3, 15 March 1996, p. 92.

structures. There has been a breakdown of the bi-polar world. With the collapse at the end of the 1980's of the Soviet Empire and the end of the Cold War, there is no longer major political division along the economic lines of capitalist and socialist countries. The West reigns supreme, and if the "New World Order" proposed after the 1991 Gulf War is not yet a reality, at least there is no serious challenge to that supremacy. We in Africa experience that dynamic with the wane of the influence of competing Super Power interests in the local affairs, for example, of Ethiopia, Angola and Mozambique, and South Africa. Where outside interests do play a role — for example, in the current tragedies of the Great Lakes Region — they are French and English rather than East and West.

One significant political development of globalisation in Africa is the push toward *democratisation*. This includes a heightened emphasis on good governance and respect for human rights. But this development is not without serious questions. First, the West pushes for political reforms that it considers compatible with the neo-liberal economic order: free politics and free markets are too closely equated. And the understanding of state activity is minimist in the global neo-liberal vision.[9] Second, donors' demands and pressures for policy changes, even when guided by the best of humanitarian motivations, can be interpreted as yet another imperialist or neo colonialist imposition of African states. A "back-lash" can develop against this push toward democratisation. Recent events in Zambia have provided examples of these difficulties, when in 1996 donors suspended aid over disputes regarding constitutional and electoral issues, and when political crack-downs following the failed October 1997 coup attempt have brought increased international isolation to the country.

B. *Consequences*

1. Economy: One of the starkest consequences of globalisation in Africa today in economic terms is *the rendering redundant of the African people.* This may appear to be a harsh overstatement, but I believe its validity can be demonstrated. Last year I participated

---

[9] See Peter J. Henriot, S.J., "Retreat of the State: Political Consequences with Social Implications for Zambia," in *Trocaire Development Reveiw 1997*, upcoming.

in a major study done for the UNDP and the ILO, analysing the employment situation in the neo-liberal economic model being pursued in Zambia.[10] Our study noted that the Structural adjustment programme - driven governmental policy regarded the provision of people with meaningful work as a function mainly of sustained economic growth. Employment promotion was at best of secondary importance. As a consequence, formal employment of the labour force had dropped to as low as 14% in recent years, with no explicit employment generation policy included in government programmes.

The simple definition of economy that appeals to me is: *women and men working together with the earth to meet basic needs.* But there is neither cooperation nor progress when local people are ignored except as factors in profit maximisation by outside interests. Women especially feel the negative effects of economic reform.[11] Globalisation views Africa and Africans as components of a global free market, independent of considerations of livelihoods and integral human development.

2. *Ecology:* Globalisation has a two-fold ecological consequence in Africa. First, there is the climatic impact of global warming (the so-called "greenhouse effect"), caused by pollution levels in northern industrial countries, and the dangerous practice of toxic waste dumping. Environmental concerns at the global level tend to pay more attention to effects in the rich countries of the north. Again, Africa is marginalised.

Second, poverty conditions induced by the severe Structural adjustment programme approach means both less care of the environment by cash-strapped governments and more encroachment on nature by persons desperately struggling for survival. For example, in Zambia soil erosion and deforestation are serious problems today and will be even more serious tomorrow. Trees are cut down for

---

[10] Venkatesh Seshamani, John Milimo, Peter Henriot and Moses Banda, "Employment and Sustainable Livelihoods in Zambia," report prepared for UNDP and ILO, Lusaka, January 1997, p. 25.

[11] Among many studies critiquing gender-insensitive policies, see Busi Nhliziyo and Deprose Muchena, "The Impact of ESAP on Women," *African Agenda*, Vol. 1, No. 9, 1996.

charcoal manufacture (an income-generating activity of the poor), resultant negative changes in rainfall patterns are experienced (causing drought and famine), and response mechanisms of over-grazing and excessive use of chemical fertilisers spoil previously fertile soil (decreasing future productive capacities of peasant farmers). Poverty hurts the whole community of creation, the natural environment as well as the human population.

3. Equity: The gap between rich and poor on both the global level and on the national level increases with the spread of globalisation. The famous "champagne glass" figure of global wealth distribution was portrayed in the 1992 *Human Development Report of the United Nations Development Fund* (UNDP).[12] This *Report* documented that the richest 20% of the world's population receives 82.7% of global income, while the poorest 20% receives 1.4%. That gap is continuing to grow, having doubled over the past thirty years. Of the 45 countries listed in the "low human development" category in the 1997 *Report,* 33 are in sub-Saharan Africa.

The major beneficiary of globalisation in Africa, South Africa, already accounts for over 40% of the sub-Saharan GDP; its own GNP per capita of US$ 3010 contrasts sharply with Zambia's of US$ 350, Malawi's of US$ 145, and Tanzania's and Mozambique's of US$ 80. I know that India is described as a poor country, with GNP per capita of US$ 320 and over 50% of the population estimated to live below the poverty line. But the World Bank estimates more than 80% of Zambians are below the poverty line, living in households with inadequate income to meet basic daily needs.[13] Key to equity issues, of course, is the fact of what has been called the "feminisation of poverty", with the disproportionate numbers of the poor being women and those dependent on women.

---

[12] UNDP, *Human Development Report 1992* (New York: Oxford University Press, 1992), pp. 34 ff.
[13] For a helpful comparative study, see Venkatesh Seshamani, *Economic Policy Reforms, Economic Growth and Sustainable Human Development: A Comparative Study of India and Zambia,* Tokyo, Institute of Developing Economies, September 1997.

III. Responses

By way of conclusion, let me very briefly suggest three sets of responses that should be of concern for this conference as it addresses globalisation from the perspective of the victims of history.

A. *Analytical*

From the viewpoint of the countries of the so-called "developing world (the poor countries), keen analysis must be made of the operations and outcomes of globalisation. This analysis cannot, however, be restricted to purely economic considerations but must take account of the human dimensions of the phenomenon. This, of course, is the outlook of this present conference and it is increasingly emphasised by studies from both secular and religious sources.[14] One of the participants in the recent "Synod on Americas" noted that "globalisation is certainly not being driven by Christian principle of solidarity. It is being driven by the motive of financial profit and, every often, by just plain greed.[15] Our analysis should point out the root causes of the suffering experienced by the majority of the world's population, and should take as the analytical starting-point the "preferential option for the poor.

B. *Political*

Africa's response to globalisation must be political in the sense of coordinated efforts to stand up to dominant outside forces that work for the detriment of the people. But to be honest, efforts undertaken with prominence in Africa frequently are more self-serving critiques or unabashed acceptances — and more rhetoric than resolves. Genuine political action is not forth-coming. The NGO community that might be expected to speak more honestly for the majority of people is frequently excluded from key decision-making processes.

The pre-eminent African political leader, Nelson Mandela, appears cautious in any critique of a globalisation process that at least initially is offering benefits to key sectors of the economy of South

---

[14] See, for example, United Nations Research Institute for Social Development, *States of Disarray: The Social Effects of Globalization* (Geneva: UNRISD, 1995).
[15] Cardinal Edmund Casimir Szoka, President of the Pontifical Commission for Vatican City State, November 1997.

Africa. Robert Mugabe of Zimbabwe is reported to have urged the November 1997 meeting in Libreville, Gabon of APC nations (African, Pacific and Caribbean states bound together with European states through the Lome Treaties) that these nations should discuss and negotiate more as a single bloc in order to be strong in the face of the European Union. Frederick Chiluba of Zambia embraces the structural adjustment programme and all its components in a very uncritical fashion. Both Daniel Arap Moi of Kenya and General Sani Abacha of Nigeria speak critically of global forces more in their own self-defense of dictatorial policies than of concern for the majority of their own citizens.

C. Ethical

1. Globalisation of solidarity: A counter-emphasis — indeed, a "counter-cultural emphasis — to the driving force of globalisation that today so negatively affects Africa is offered by John Paul II's expression, a globalisation in solidarity, a globalisation without marginalisation.[16] The Pope asks key questions about the process: "Will *everyone* be able to take advantage of a global market?... Will relations between States become more equitable, or will economic competition and rivalries between peoples and nations lead humanity towards a situation of even greater instability?" Solidarity is the central theme of the 1987 encyclical, *The Social Concerns of the Church*, where John Paul II critiques the structures of sin that mark so much of a globalisation driven by profit and power.

2. Family of God: A distinctly African emphasis that provides an ethical critique of the present process of globalisation is found in the discussions of the African Synod (1994). Here a model of church was proposed that envisions the church as the "family of God. As such, the church must be an "instrument of universal solidarity for building a world-wide community of justice and peace.[17] An attractive approach to a human-friendly globalisation would be based on the familial values of respect and sharing that mark African traditions.

---

[16] John Paul II, *World Day of Peace Message*, 1 January 1998, #3.
[17] John Paul II, *The Church in Africa*, 14 September 1995, #114.

3. Globalisation from below: Integral human development, sustainable development, depends more on harmonious human relationships than on the organisation and operation of an unfettered free market. A fundamental fault with globalisation as experienced in Africa is that it is not rooted in community but structured from above according to abstract economic laws. To counter this situation in an ethically authentic and creative fashion calls for the promotion of local communities that work for integral human development and are effectively linked with similar groups across national boundaries. Much — but not all — of the recent worldwide explosion of non-governmental activity (NGOs) is an expression of this effort to build globalisation from below. Indeed, this very conference this week, as well as the conference coming up here early next month, "Colonialism to Globalisation," can be steps toward a qualitatively different globalisation that will have more positive implications for Africa.

Is The Answer in the South: A Latin American View

Xabier Gorostiaga S.J.

The dependence theory that had dominated our economic analysis twenty years ago was then blended with liberation theology, and it was those theoretical mediations that accompanied the profound political, social, and theological transformations of the 1960's and 1980's: the Cuban Revolution, the guerrilla movements, the military populism of Velasco Alvarado in Peru, the Latin American struggle to recover the Panama Canal with Torrijos, the socialist experience of Allende in Chile, the revolutionary insurrections in Nicaragua, El Salvador and Guatemala, the revolution in Grenada, the continuous struggle for democracy and equity throughout the hemisphere and the massive irruption of the poor in the life of the Church.

All this assumed a way of thinking, an outlook, a vision of the future, and new social subjects. Today we are suffering a crisis of paradigms, particularly following the collapse of Eastern European state socialism and the electoral defeat of the Sandinista Front. Furthermore, the involution of the hierarchical levels of both the Catholic and the Protestant Church have "religiously" accompanied these events, while poverty, unemployment, the marginalization of our countries and the exclusion of the majority of our people prevail as the principal developments of 1990's.

Today we must find the new theoretical mediations to meet the avalanche of the North upon the South, of Capital upon Labor, and to confront a profound crisis of civilization.

Who are the social subjects of this new era? What type of intermediation is called for to understand, analyze, and confront the rapid and extreme transformations of the turn of the century? What are the alternative proposals, given this avalanche? Perhaps the greatest challenge and the most urgent need 500 years after the so-called "discovery" of America and India is to know what to ask as well as how to find the new transforming subjects of our society and the new analytical, cultural, and theological mediations that will make it possible to offer a gospel-based response to our peoples' anguish and despair.

The twenty-first century has begun in the 1990's. There are ten dominant factors that distinguish the advent of the new millennium:

Crisis of paradigms and loss of international counterbalances

The fall of the Berlin Wall and the rapid and definitive collapse of state socialism have produced a crisis of paradigms and opened an era of perplexity and uncertainty. This phenomenon is accompanied by a world state of **unipolarity**, in which the United States no longer faces economic, political or military counterbalancing. In fact, the East has begun to compete with the South for the world's scarce financial resources and the West's political attention.

The technological revolution

The profound and rapid technological revolution during the last twenty years in electronics, space technology, biotechnology, and computer science has produced two phenomena that indicate a transformation in the axis of international accumulation. Today's accumulation is found more in the "intensity of knowledge" than in the intensity of productive or even financial capital. The accumulation of knowledge is the linchpin of modern accumulation.

Moreover, the revolution in management, the new methods of global administration through telecommunications, computer science and transportation, have made it possible to create an area of accumulation that has been classified as **flexible accumulation**. This flexible accumulation, which is the product of the concentration and centralization of economic, financial, and technological power, makes it possible to concentrate profits in those intersectoral links that serve as production crossovers: marketing, financing, and specialized services.

These global links of flexible accumulation are increasingly concentrated and centralized in fewer banks and multinational firms (which meanwhile tend to merge) and are controlled by highly speculative finance capital with a fast turnover (US$1000 trillion per day). The financial explosion of this flying capital has annual growth rates close to 100 percent, whereas the growth rates of the real economy range from 2 to 3 percent of the GDP.

Power concentration and centralization

The technological revolution and the axis of accumulation of knowledge have caused a new historical phenomenon: power concentration and centralization. Power tends to be concentrated in an increasingly smaller number of countries and population. This generates an unprecedented concentration of economic, financial, technological, political, and military power. Five hundred years after the conquest of Latin America and the Caribbean (LAC), the gap separating the North (20 percent of the world population) from the South (80 percent of humanity) is wider than the gap between the metropolis and the colonies had been at any time before.

The dematerialization of production, the **use of less material per unit of product**, is an outcome of the technological revolution that makes it possible to attain the same productive unit with less raw material, causing a permanent structural reduction of the value of raw materials and a structural disadvantage in the terms of trade between the North and the South, between countries with technology and countries without technology.

The technological revolution also produces the **growing automation of productive labor** and services, diminishing the value and need of human labor per unit of product. This leads to a loss of the negotiating capacity of labor as opposed to capital both in the North and in the South. Within labor itself, manual labor forfeits value to technical-scientific labor.

Therefore, the comparative advantages of the South (i.e., raw material and labor) become static before the dynamic of modern technological production. Even the thesis of "diminishing returns", which is the basis of the theory of perfect competition, is altered. With the new technologies, this is changed into "increasing returns". The technological revolution therefore increases the asymmetry and the obstacles to the weaker competitors with less technical know-how.

The centralization and concentration of knowledge and power are manifested in all the spaces of life (economic, military, and political) and in the new expansion areas of world accumulation, such as control of space and seabeds.

Growing poverty: the dominant fact of our age

Growing poverty and margination are logical and at the same time in contradiction with the technological revolution and modernity. Indeed, these have become the dominant social and political character of our era.

The recent UNDP report "Human Development 1992" asserts that throughout the world the last decade has been characterized by the rise in inequality between the rich and the poor, in terms of both countries and peoples. In 1989 the richest fifth (representing approximately 1,000 million persons) controlled 82.7 percent of the revenue; 81.2 percent of world trade; 94.6 percent of commercial loans; 80.6 percent of internal savings and 80.5 percent of investment. If in terms of distribution the panorama is untenable, it is equally so regarding resources: the rich countries possess approximately one-fifth of the world population, but consume 70 percent of world energy, 75 percent of the metals, 85 percent of the timber, and 60 percent of the food. Such a pattern of development, the UNDP concludes, is only viable in the degree to which the extreme inequality is maintained, as otherwise the world resources would be exhausted. Therefore, **inequality is not a distortion of the system. It is a systemic prerequisite for growth and permanence of the present system.**

What is significant is the acceleration of the gap. In 1960, the incomes for the wealthiest 20 percent were 30 times higher than those of the poorest 20 percent. In 1990, they were 60 times higher. Moreover, if one takes into account the unequal distribution within the countries of both the North and the South, the reported incomes for the richest 20 percent of the world population were 150 times higher than those of the poorest 20 percent.

(According to the report, Brazil is the country with the greatest income disparity)

Another important assertion of the UNDP report is that global markets do not operate freely. The unequal relationship between the North and South costs developing countries 500,000 million dollars annually; or ten times more than what is received as foreign aid. Furthermore, 20 of the 24 most industrialized nations are currently more protectionist than they were ten years ago, although total market liberalization is imposed on the less developed countries. According to the GATT (General Agreement on Tariffs and Trade), **only 7 percent of world trade is in conformity with the principles of free trade. The rest is under "administered market".**

Since 1970, the South's participation in international trade has been reduced drastically: from 3.8 percent to 1 percent for Sub-Saharan Africa and from 5.6 percent to 3.3 percent for Latin America and the Caribbean. The growing process of marginalization is affecting 1,700 million people who are increasingly excluded.

The most important reason for the environmental crisis has been the wasteful development system that benefits the 20 percent of humanity that devours world resources and discards their waste in a contaminating manner. The environmental crisis is also affected by the poverty of the three-fourths of the world population which causes "equal and at times even greater" stress upon the ecological systems.

The "environmental debt", together with the "social debt", and the unprecedented international emigration (some 75 million people move each year as refugees, displaced persons, or migrant workers) are the most important reasons for world instability in the post-Cold War era. Accordingly, the UN report recommends the creation of a Security Council of Development and the reform of the World Bank, the International Monetary Fund (IMF), GATT, and UN Programs with a view to ensuring better management of the world economy in the interests of all the countries and all the peoples.

In the midst of a technological revolution and in a world that has become closely integrated into a global village with a universal citizenship, the social, political, and military gap is wider today than it was 500 years ago.

In 1492 and 1498, Europe was discovering in LAC and India, that its interpretation and vision of the world were wrong. What was actually discovered was the historic unity of the world. Five hundred years later, that discovery has become reality in a world unified by technology and divided by power. This unity is polarizing, unstable, contradictory, false, and dangerous, causing an authentic crisis of political ungovernability, economic nonviability and environmental unsustainability.

The global elite and the world conservative revolution

There exists today a geoeconomic hierarchy which controls and manages the concentration and centralization of the economic, political, technological, financial and military power of the world. The restructuring of the transnational companies and banks has enabled them, on the basis of mergers, to diversify their activities and has ensured the flexibility of their accumulation. These new megaconglomerates, organized around technological structures and scientific matrices, allow them great flexibility in adapting to the new demands, created to a great extent by themselves through their control of the mass media. (Mitsubishi, for instance, has activities in ninety sectors of world economy.)

The "continentalization" of economies and the international division of labor in the service of these mega-groups, together with the increased integration of the countries of the East, have changed this geoeconomic hierarchy into an **organic elite of transnational capitalism.**

These global actors born out of alliances and intersystems of world economy grew with the support and the policies of the Governments of the Group of Seven and the countries of the North, with the aim of controlling international competition. Today these global elites are those who define the rules of the game in technology, production, marketing and finance. Meanwhile the Group of Seven has turned into a **Global Parallel State** in the service of these interests. The multilateral organizations and even the United Nations lack the financial and political space to control and implement democratic and equitable international development. The IMF and the World Bank, dependent to a great extent upon the Group of Seven, are part of the international bureaucracy that protects and preserves the logic of the dominant transnational capital and its global elite.

The global restructuring of the economic system taking place in the 1980's and 1990's has materialized from the North without any counterbalance or competitive capacity from either the East or the South.

The neoliberal revolution and neoconservative ideology constitute the legitimizing ideological project of this global elite. **Neoliberalism, therefore, is not an economic project but a project of society, of State, of international relations and of social relations within each society.** The so-called "end of history" conceals an authentic revolution of the world's right-wing given the collapse of the East, the deep crisis of the left, and the global weakening of the negotiating capacity of labor and of the South.

This conservative revolution makes a strong impact on the world of ideology and religion. The involution of the Catholic Church, with growing centralization and Vatican control, the limitation of space for the national and continental episcopates, the censure of the liberation theologians and of political theology in Europe, (Leonard Boff, Tissa Balasuriya and Hans Kung among others) are part of the same phenomenon. In the same sense, the rapid expansion of charismatic groups within Roman Catholicism and evangelical churches, promoting a sanctimonious religion and transcendental escapism, conform to this global phenomenon.

The opaque power

The systemic character of these phenomena create **power structures of low visibility**, yet with a real capacity of invisible domination. The Santa Fe Report's "metaphysical war", which the Reagan era ideologists were foretelling at the beginning of the 1980's, is a proven historical phenomenon today. Perhaps few conservative ideologists could have stated it with such clarity as Zbigniew Brzezinski himself, a founding member of the Trilateral Commission and permanent advisor to various subsequent U.S. administrations: "...In the technetronic society, the direction taken will apparently be marked by the individual support from millions of uncoordinated citizens who easily will fall within the range of magnetic personalities who will effectively exploit the most efficient techniques for manipulating emotion and controlling reason..."[1] Not only reason, but hope as well.

The restructuring of the axis of international accumulation conforms to and demands this **ideological recolonization of the New World Order**, just as 500 years ago the conquest of America (then called the New World) required papal legitimization. Neither the protests of the Dominican priests articulated in the "Cry of La Española" of Friar Antonio de Montesinos in 1511 nor the prophetic roles of Bartolomé de Las Casas and the first Bishop martyr of Latin America, Antonio Valdivieso in Nicaragua, together with "the majority of the friars of the Kingdom", whom the Viceroy Toledo of Peru denounced before His Majesty Philip the Second, were sufficient to arrest either the conquest or the colonial system. Nor will protest without alternative proposals be able to check the opaque neocolonization of this turn of the millennium.

The monopoly of planetary thinking

The creation of macroplanetary policies that authorize the global administration of the world in turn calls for a monopoly of planetary thinking that legitimizes the global monopoly of accumulation. **The control of the media, the images, the wishes, and demands is fundamental to guaranteeing the legitimacy needed to stabilize this global power.** The control of research, knowledge and even alternative thinking is a prerequisite for the new global restructuring. The crisis of the universities and the tribulations of the research centers and NGO's that do not yield to this logic of capital and market, is a recurrent phenomenon the world over, even within the churches.

The "economic Darwinism" engendered by neoliberalism, which the Pope himself classified as "savage capitalism," demands a **tech-**

---

[1] Brzezinski, Zbigniew, *The Technetronic Society*, quoted in Spanish by Erick Fromm in *Revolución de la Esperanza*, F.C.E., Mexico, 1987 (p. 13).

nological totalitarianism that maintains a system of technical apartheid in the South. The reduction of the budget for higher education, the political control of the universities, the emphasis on primary education promoted by the World Bank in the Third World cannot conceal the real purpose -- maintaining the great masses of population as technological and analytic invalids, incapable of understanding and changing the "technetronic society."

The great capacity of neoliberalism has not been one of creating efficiency and growth, but one of destroying any alternative that does not respond to its market logic, to profit as the driving force of society, and to the acceptance of the "opaque power" as an inevitability of the New Order.

The New World Order carries with it a New International Division of Knowledge in this era of technological revolution. **The democratization of knowledge, therefore, will be one of the fundamental demands of an alternative order.**

The geoculture of despair

Opaque power demands not only geoeconomic hegemony but geocultural hegemony as well. The market ideology and the market automatism that postulate the capacity for solving the problems of poverty, unemployment, and ecological destruction by their own dynamic, carry with them the *need for world homogenization and uniformity*. The multiple and varied brands of products found anywhere in the world respond to a *homogeneous productive and cultural system*. This modelling of the market dictates a modelling of the culture.

During the recent Week of Theology held in Nicaragua, Franz Hinkelammert, who has worked extensively on this theme, told the story of the international president of McDonalds inaugurating the McDonalds headquarters in Moscow. "...As part of the democratization process in the Eastern countries," he was reported to have said, "the people of Moscow will be able to eat the same hamburger that is eaten all over the world, with the same size, taste, and sauce..." This "Big Mac" democracy is also producing "Big Mac" Christianity and "Big Mac" culture.

This homogenization and automatism of the market leave a future full of promises but without any projects or prospects. Even concepts such as Development, Self-Determination, and Sovereignty disappear. **It is the culture of consumption and democracy based on the market, without a vision and project of society.**

Because they were breaking through this process of homogenization which started with the Reagan era, those countries which gave rise to new hopes, like Grenada, Nicaragua, and El Salvador in the 1980's, needed not only to be destroyed but also discredited and converted into a spurious hope of romantic peoples. Today **the geoculture of despair and the theology of inevitability** require global projection to facilitate homogenization of the new restructuring promoted by the global power elite.

Despair guarantees power for the dominator. The erosion of hope is a systemic necessity, as Brzezinski foretold. This nihilism of values has been carried by Franz Hinkelammert back to Nietzsche himself. The need to accept the inevitable has imposed itself on vast sectors of intellectuals and of the Latin American Church, including the political left itself. This may be the greatest achievement of neoliberalism. Deprived of hope, there is no reason for struggling for the quality of life, and daily survival is accepted as normal life.

This **culture of submission** enables the global project to be reserved exclusively for capital, not labor, and the transnational power elite, not peoples. With the end of the Cold War, the countries of the South and those Northern sectors sharing with the Southern poor an alternative horizon of hope for the 21st century no longer need to be stigmatized as the "evil empire". They may now be demonized as the "evil slum".

This geoculture of despair, born out of the inevitability and the submission caused by the metaphysical war, is part of the nihilism of Nietzsche and of a perverse dialectic which, in the face of poverty, underdevelopment, and growing unemployment, in times of cholera,[2] AIDS, and drug abuse, and facing the threat of a collective

---

[2] A play on words in Spanish, since the word *cólera* refers both to the epidemic disease now sweeping Latin America and also means rage or extreme anger. Also

suicide due to the environmental crisis, does not propose alternatives, much less solutions, thus allowing the "invisible hand" of the market (this time of death) to be the builder of life.

Apathetic democracy

The North, the richest 20 percent of the human race, may be considered democratic because two-thirds of its population have a chance to participate in the benefits of its system. Nevertheless, that Northern democracy has created a situation wherein two-thirds of the world's population do not have an adequate material basis for building their own democracy or meeting their minimum necessities. The world is divided into a Northern minority in which two-thirds enjoy "democracy" at the cost of the Southern majority, where only one-third experience it.

In Latin America, the masks of democracy have been falling one-by-one: "Low Intensity Democracy", which requires an interfering, authoritarian hand for its transition; "Restricted Democracy", which must limit not only economic but also participatory demands to avoid the risk of anarchy; "Facade Democracy", which offers the legal framework for democratic rights without the capacity to implement them; and "Guardianship Democracy", which requires a foreign power to protect and guide its construction. All these "ambiguous democracies" have democratic apathy as a prerequisite, as evidenced by growing electoral abstentionism in both the North and the South.

The new interventionism

The end of the Cold War has not yet reached the tropics. Be it due to the global unipolarity, or to the propensity of all hegemonic powers in decline to take recourse to intervention, or to the ungovernability of its Southern neighbors, or to all three tendencies at the same time, one notices a growing U.S. interference and intervention in Latin America and elsewhere (Haiti, Somalia, Persian Gulf). This humanitarian-philanthropic interventionism has been cloaked

---

a reference to Gabriel García Márquez' bestsellling novel, *Love in the Times of Cholera*.

by the legal mantle of the United Nations, thus affecting the credibility of that multinational organization.

The most subtle yet obvious of these tools of intervention are those utilized by the international financial institutions, which impose authentic strait jackets on domestic economic policies. Furthermore, the increasing protectionism of the major industrial countries interferes in the very rules of the market game imposed by these international financial organizations, maintaining and even exacerbating the classic deterioration of Latin America's terms of trade. Since the mid-1980's, debt management has involved a variety of swaps which have licensed intervention in environmental control, in industrial reconversion, and in the use of natural resources. Drug-trafficking, on the other hand, has served the United States -- the country which has created the world's principal demand for drugs -- as a pretext to militarily and commercially intervene in various countries of the region like Panama, Colombia, Mexico. (The Noriega case had an undertone of undisclosed interests: maintaining control over the Panama Canal and preventing Japan from dominating the Pacific-Atlantic trade bridge and platform.)

The most peculiar characteristics of this new interventionism are its "legal" and "democratic" aspects. The recent decision of the U.S. Supreme Court regarding the extradition of foreign nationals and the legal agreements regarding banking and trade laws -- without reaching the extremes of the Panamanian phenomenon[3] -- indicate a process of **imposed legal homogenization** without the input

---

[3] The MLAT (Mutual Legal Assistance Treaty) carries with it a set of treaties related to drug control, the interception and boarding of Panamanian ships on the high seas by U.S. warships, the patrolling of Panamanian waters by the U.S. Coast Guard, and tributary information to circumvent U.S. tax evasion and money laundering related to drug trafficking or other activities. One of these treaties that was imposed upon Panama under the threat of canceling an US$84 million loan, involved probes into Panama's conduct and procedures, thus affecting its legal and national sovereignty. These additional controls have affected the platform of international services established in Panama, which are progressively moving to Miami. This legal interference complements the military invasion of Panama and tries to induced the creation of the Centre, Multilateral Antidrugs (CMA) which will allow a permanent military USA base in Panama after the completion of the Panama Canal Treaties on the 31th. of December 1999.

of national legislators and without the required consensus among different nations.

This tendency toward legal interference must be analyzed among nations of the South, and proposals must be advanced for international legal collaboration and for guaranteeing the equitable application of international law. The United States' refusal to comply with the International Court of Justice's decision in the Nicaragua harbor-mining case jeopardizes the possibility of international coexistence under a state of law that encompasses all nations equally. The USA embargo and the Helms-Burton law against Cuba exemplify this unilateral interventionism against the unanimous position of all Latin American countries and a substantial majority of the World Community.

The manipulation of the democratization processes -- processes which were generalized throughout Latin America during the last decade -- is the most determinant aspect of this new interventionism. The implementation of an "induced neoliberal democracy" by the financing policies of the World Bank and the IMF and the practices of institutions created by AID and by the bilateral aid of the other industrialized countries demands a concerted analysis throughout the countries of the South.

The effects of these interventionist policies can be discerned in the manipulation of demilitarization processes, the creation of new police forces, and the education systems, as well as in the reduction of State structures. Thus, a "parallel State" of private institutions is created that make plans for the nation under the directives of an external scheme. The common norms imposed universally throughout the hemisphere, make it possible to classify this "democratic interventionism" as a "low-intensity democracy" which follows the low-intensity war strategy to control the processes of self-governing democracy.

The concept of "promoting democracy" has been used to manipulate political parties, finance electoral campaigns, define the content of human rights, and even administer the democratic processes emerging in various countries. Perhaps the most striking examples have been Panama, Nicaragua, Haiti, and Peru, where the same tendencies that have been managed more subtly in other countries have been carried to extremes. The neoliberal democracy project that is being forced has increased poverty, corruption, political polarization, loss of consensus and the lack of capacity to construct a national project.

The possibility of a consensus democracy in Latin America is seriously hindered by this new interference. This "introspection of neoliberal democracy" is essential to discovering the alternatives that exist for depending and **nationalizing democracy** without being deceived by the formalities of functional democracy.

In the long run, democratic interventionism only increases the pressure upon the social subjects looking for a democratic solution to the crisis. One of the greatest obstacles to genuine democracy in the South is the conditioning imposed by Northern interference.

THE HARVEST OF THE EIGHTIES

In economic terms, the so-called "lost decade" for the LAC signified three and even four lost decades for Central America, particularly in the case of Nicaragua, the only country in the world with the per capita income of 1945.

Nevertheless, the decade of the eighties was the decade of civil society. The irruption of the organized popular sectors in civil life, in a revolutionary manner in Nicaragua and El Salvador and to a certain extent in Guatemala as well, but particularly in a new civic presence of the impoverished and marginated masses, is a phenomenon that has definitively changed the region's social fabric. This experience, perhaps not so effervescent, is noticed in a new dynamic made evident through the growth of NGO's and the linkage and networking throughout Latin America of organizations formed by peasants, indigenous communities, women, environmentalists, urban dwellers, and the emerging student (particularly university) movement.

In spite of the crises of Haiti and Nicaragua, the harvest of the 80's has ripened in the 90's, turning into a crisis of ungovernability, demonstrating the irreducible force of civil society, despite the dominant pressures upon these peoples. The lack of an alternative project capable of constructively guiding the dynamic force of civil society breeds a culture of resistance and a "challenging force" to the neoliberal project, while accumulating alternative experiences at the local level which will lead to a project that will be functionally viable.

The search for a new democratic, social, political and economic power

A common tendency noted among these popular organizations is the search for a new social and political power with a self-managed economic basis, in a dynamic coming from below and within its own sectoral reality. The struggle to win state power -- often, in the past, through armed action -- has been largely supplanted by the struggle to construct a new social power. The State and control of the state do not appear so determinant to their objectives. Their objective seems to be the creation of an alternative social power capable of defining negotiating positions with capital, State, culture, and international relations.

The multipolarity and multiplicity of these new social subjects leads to a heterogeneous agenda, at times implicit and not formulated with precision, combining diverse identities and forms of struggle. Their organizational strategies are manifold; nevertheless, one notices in all of them a rejection of verticality and hierarchical vanguardism. Organizational Leninism collapsed in Latin America prior to the crisis of the East. The tendency to search for alliance, consensus, participation, and dialogue is a cultural as well as a democratic and economic phenomenon.

With varying levels of development, one notices the search to create a particular economic base, self-managed and as self-sufficient as possible. At the same time, in acknowledgement of limitations, national and international alliances are sought. In this sense, the horizontal ties between these organizations are Creating different kinds of coordinating bodies that begin to interlink at the international level as well, through NGO's, churches, trade unions, women's and ecologists' movements as well as small producers who are setting up alternative trade relations.

Furthermore, a Latin American integrationist vision, with increased participation of subregional blocks (MERCOSUR, Andian and the Association of Caribbean States which includes Central America, the Antillas, Mexico, Colombia and Venezuela), and the search for a proposal of selective global insertion in conjunction with other political movements of the South and the North, could be the beginning of a new political map for the end of the millennium, when elections will be held in some 15 countries of the region.

Organic autonomy of popular sectors

The most characteristic political phenomenon of these popular movements is their autonomy in relation to the institutions which adopted them in the past, whether the latter be political parties, churches, NGO's, or even private enterprise or the State itself.

The relationship with the political parties reflects a tendency towards "organic autonomy". That is to say, a clear autonomy decisively refusing to serve as the drive belt for any party or political elite. At the same time, there is a tendency to search for a broad political organicism based on alliance and consensus, creating a new specific political specter surpassing the old formations of Fronts with their specific vanguard. Similarly, an attempt is made to overcome State instrumentalism, so as to be a democratizing lever of the State, while surmounting the paternalistic culture and subsidization that created so much paralysis and dependence for many popular organizations in the past.

Self-criticism and the demand for internal democracy with accountability and ethical coherence, given the corruption that has penetrated the parties and even the NGOs, is also one of the identifying marks of the new emerging subjects.

This phenomenon coincides with the erosion of the traditional parties of the right and the left. A profound review and restructuring of what has been called " the new Latin American left" is underway. At the Forum of Sao Paulo, which has brought together more than 60 Latin American political parties, these diverse dynamics in the political parties are noted, although they still have not been able to consolidate a sufficiently coherent and planned platform. The bad habits of the past continue to weigh heavy. The lack of a clear and convergent analysis hinders the process. The dominant tendency is toward searching, overcoming defeatism, and attempting to link up with the new emerging social subjects.

Due to Latin America's heterogeneity, it is impossible to define with precision the character of this emerging civil society. However, in innumerable gatherings of these sectors (which are taking place in almost all the Latin America countries), the similarity among an array of factors is evident. The distinctions and identity of each sector, even their different cultural and political interests, retain their cultural integrity in an ever-more-convergent process of an emerging consensus. While there is an increasingly more Latin American projection, they remain open to the search for a joint global project with similar organizations in other continents, the so called *gloncal strategy* (global, national and local).

The failure of neoliberal dependent capitalism

There is an increasing awareness of the erosion of the neoliberal project and its political propellants in Latin America. The profound division and weakness of the governments of Doña Violeta Chamorro and Arnoldo Aleman in Nicaragua, as well as the inability of her Central American counterparts to consolidate democracy and begin economic recovery and regional integration, are manifested with their particular characteristics in most Latin American nations. The crises of the governments of ex-Presidents Carlos Andres Pérez and Collor, of Presidents Endara, Fujimori, Menem, Zedillo ect. indicate a **crisis of democratic ungovernability in the presence of neoliberal dependent capitalism**. The proceedings against Collar de Mello in Brazil Carlos Andrés Perez in Venezuela, Salinas in Mexico reflect a mature civil society that has taken into its own hands the defense of the rule of law, demanding an end to corruption and calling for transparency and accountability from politicians and governments, thereby definitively strengthening democracy.

Our countries have succeeded neither in opening competitive spaces in the international market, nor in redefining the terms of a more equitable insertion, nor in curbing growing impoverishment and the deterioration in the standard of living. Nor is an economic and political panorama of stability and human development for the turn of the century.

There are few Latin American countries that could be considered exceptions to this generalized erosion of the neoliberal project. Chile appears as the most notable exception, having a sufficiently ample domestic consensus for its government's economic achievements. The same cannot be said of Brasil, Colombia, Peru and Costa Rica, whose processes are considered successful internationally, but lack a domestic majority consensus.

No stable solution is possible with a foreign project

In spite of the concentration and centralization of power in the hands of the global elite, it is important to note the increasingly clearer and more numerous signs of collapse in the agenda of the North and the so-called New World Order. The crises in Eastern Europe, particularly that of Yugoslavia, and in the different republics of the Community of Independent States, in addition to the critical tension in the agreements of Maastrich, and the resurgence of neofascist groups in Germany, Austria, Italy, and France, all indicate that the new Europe is not consolidated. The three Europes -- Eastern, Common Market, and Muslim -- with the strong resurgence of popular nationalism on one hand and ultra-right and fundamentalist groups on the other, do not offer a hopeful prospect for the South.

The situation in the Pacific, with the phenomena of corruption and loss of financial impetus in Japan, plus the recent financial crisis among the "Asian Tigers", the suggested "model" for LAC, does not present the framework of stability the global elite has sought to offer.

The situation in the United States in spite of its economic recovery, has revealed the depth of its social instability, and the lack of a coherent vision and leadership.

Furthermore, the contradictions and commercial and financial tensions among the three mega-markets -- the U.S., Europe, and Japan/Asia do not lend themselves to a visualization of the coherent and homogenized world market that had been sought. The profound contradictions even within the power nucleus of the Group of Seven itself leads to inaction in relation to the global problems of environment, poverty, unemployment, debt and the increasing gap between North and South.

On the other hand, the Group of 77 and the Non-Aligned Nations continue postponing the Southern agenda, which is presented with increasing urgency in numerous fora, but which is not taken up by the governments and elite of these nations.

Latin America needs its own agenda, particularly given the most recent U.S. proposals, the Initiative for the Americas (IFA) and NAFTA (North American Free Trade Association). **The U.S. proposal could serve as a catalyst for diverse Latin American regional alternatives**, incorporating our proposals related to the debt, investment, and trade, and adding our own agenda points regarding the environment, drugs, security, jobs, and the fight against poverty and gender discrimination in order to consolidate democracy.

Previous points for and from the Southern agenda

(a) The crisis is abysmal. Its solution calls for serious proposals for decolonizing the imagination, the mind, and the heart. At 500 years, a review of the internalization of dependence and submission is a basic issue for this Latin American and Southern agenda. Without the recovery of hope and confidence in ourselves, there is no possibility of proffering viable alternatives.

(b) Historical dominations have been based on the control of our people's labor, nature, gender, and culture (identity-sovereignty). A Latin American and Southern agenda must be based on the resolution of these contradictions. A new perspective and logic based on labor, nature, women, and culture (identity-sovereignty) and the new generation (over 90% of new born are generated in the South) may be the source of our own project.

Democratization of international power

The current international setting and multilateral institutions thwart an agenda and program for and from the South. The United Nations, the World Bank, and the IMF must be democratized. These international institutions must become platforms and instruments for the defense of international law, for democratizing economic relations and promoting "democracy from below, from within", which is to say, from the sovereignty, culture, and national identity of each nation. That is to say, democracy open to all the citizens of the planet, to international relations that overcome the current anti-democratic order.

This democratic insertion in the world calls for an endogenous project that would be internationally complemented. Insertion in the world market would be defined selectively according to the phases and the prerequisites of the project itself. The neoliberal insertion imposed by IFIs (International Financial Institutions) causes an indiscriminate and asphyxiating opening for countries with less competitive capacity and instead of expanding the market, it reduces and co-opts the national markets. Neither the isolation of autarchy, nor indiscriminate, asymmetric neoliberal insertion, but rather the selective insertion that responds to one's own project.

Linking micro with macro

Linkage of the local with the national and of the national with the global (gloncal) is one of the major requirements of the new alternative projects. *Nations are too small for the immense problems of the future and too immense for the small problems of daily life.* The linkage of the "daily" with future development demands a participatory and consensual democracy that surpasses the central planning of state socialism, as well as the pure imposition of market forces. "Act locally and think globally," recommends a current slogan. The challenge includes accomplishing the macro-micro balance, the gloncal strategy that was never attained by the different currents of thought in the past.

State reform

State reform is needed to perfect the market and even generate markets where deformations in social and economic relations either block entrance or eliminate those subjects less capable of competing. The "economic Darwinism" prevailing today reduces markets. The balancing and generating role of State initiatives is particularly needed in poor and dependent countries to give impetus to the first phases of sustainable development.

State, market, and planning are not antagonistic, but complementary, concepts. It is impossible to create a national project backed by broad consensus when inserted in a submissive position in the dominant global market. The State is needed to bring different wills together and defend national space; to develop an open project of its own; to overcome technological apartheid with an adequate technological project; to create a Latin American scientific network that surpasses the current technological alignment that condemns us to remaining technological invalids; and to complement the market as a rational mechanism for the efficient use of resources, given that the market undervalues future needs. Neither ecology nor women, for example, are equitably and efficiently included in national accounts or market assessment. (The need for new social inclusive indicators.)

A new State that is democratic, efficient, participatory and transparent is a crucial element of the alternative proposals. Confronted by the neoliberal State, subjected to international conditionalities, with neither a national project nor popular space, and given the old oligarchic character of the State based on the dominant power group, a democratic State of Civil Society is imperative. We propose a global *Social Contract,* a national and international pact, a new deal to construct the global village induced by a globalization from below, from inside their own culture and open to the planetary citizenship of 21st Century.

Critical assessment of science and technology

Science and technology are a product of social relations and specifically of relations of power. Therefore, acceptance of the dominant technology is not the acceptance of a democratic or positive element, but of an imposed element. The **democratization of science and technology** is a prerequisite for equity and development. In this sense, the role of the universities and technical higher education is an undervalued factor in Latin American alternative thinking.

On the other hand, the neoliberal project seeks to privatize and commercialize higher education so that it responds to market trends, losing its capacity for more critical, long-term thinking. In this sense, the **recovery of universities as part of a democratic and popular project** is one of the prerequisites for the 1990's. In a world without an outlook and in a geoculture of despair, the need to democratize knowledge and technology is the new role of universities, which resume the prominent role they occupied during the most critical moments in Latin American history. At present the educational system is part of the problem not of the solution because it reproduces and amplifies the system which is creating this crisis of civilization.

Crisis of civilization

The social model and the civilization of the countries of the North cannot be universalized. Should the Northern norms of consumption and overdevelopment be taken up by the Southern majorities, it would lead to collective suicide. There exists an ecological limit and a democratic limit. The ecological limit is visualized more dramatically every day. Rigoberta Menchú, Nobel Peace Prize 1992, and daughter of a culture, the Mayan, closely tied to the earth, said in one of her first statements after receiving the peace prize, *If we do not make peace with our Mother Earth, we will not live very long; for humans do not rule Nature, but rather Nature governs the life of humanity.* The current social model demands economic Darwinism, which indicates the exclusion of a substantial majority of the world population, who become superfluous. Some nations become unviable because, due to the present capacity of their human or natural resources, they do not have the potential to compete under the terms set by the world market.

This civilization cannot be democratic, as it demands a democracy that excludes the majority of humankind. In this kind of "second-hand democracy", peace will continue to appear as a chimera, because "development, the new name of peace" (Pope Paul VI), is becoming just a dream and not the fundamental right for all proclaimed by the United Nations. Peace and development have become increasingly less accessible to the majority, as the latest reports of the United Nations and the World Bank itself have statistically shown.

The current civilization is also **an antagonistic civilization.** It confronts the North with the South; Development against Nature; Science against Culture; Men against Women; the Present against the Future. It sets the races in opposition to each other, and the uniformity induced by the market against genetic and cultural biodiversity, thus making competition a polarizing and alienating principle that hinders the realization of an integrated project of society and harmonious civilization. **An antagonistic civilization cannot be the civilization of the future in a global village.** The alliance of interests and common values to meet the common threats against planetary citizens of the world **demands a participatory and consensual civilization and culture, and the integration of diversity in an awareness of global democracy.** "The human afflictions of the North and the human privations of the South" that the UNDP 1992 report mentions, are part of this crisis of civilization.

Will it be possible for this world of cultural and political diversity and of economic urgencies affecting survival, to think and act globally from the different local realities, to jointly build a new world community? Are growth, capital, and its logic the only component with the capacity to transcend these differences and propose and create a world system? Is there no other logic capable of inspiring and summoning humanity at large to a more humane community project?

Faced by this civilizational challenge, two contradictory logics and cultures are confronted, as trenchantly summarized by Marcos Arruda: The logic that **he who has, is** and the logic that **he who is, has.** The logic of having and the logic of being, an ancient contradiction that is resurrected again with a fundamental radicalness due to the severity of the crisis.

The tragedy of our generation is that we have no proposal with which to respond to this question. Perhaps our contribution will be to raise this question and reclaim with it the historic query of December 21, 1511, in the "Cry of La Española," issued by the Dominican friar Antonio de Montesinos: *With what authority, with what justice?* Montesinos questioned the legitimacy of the Conquest, even confronting the Papal Bull. Today we must question the legitimacy of a system established 500 years ago that reproduces the asymmetry and violation of the fundamental right to life. *Are they [the Indians] not also humans?* Montesinos demanded of the Spanish authorities. This question, on behalf of the 1,000 million human beings living in a state of misery and another 2000 million living under poverty, is the fundamental question which the South must reclaim at the end of the millennium in the midst of a Technological Revolution.

Recover the culture of resistance

We must reclaim the queries of 1511 and the poorly-answered questions of 1917. State socialism did not know how to and could not respond to the genuine inquiry that sought economic democracy, equality among the citizenry, and equity in relations between peoples and nations. The current avalanche of North against the South, Capital against Labor, and Present against the Future, tends to deepen the abyss and widen the gap between the citizens of the global city which forms the world in 1992, at the same time that it attempts to eliminate any questions about the system. Therefore, what is needed is a **culture of questioning and resistance** to face this geoculture of despair and Theology of inevitability.

The culture of resistance was transmitted in the *Popol Vuh*, the holy book of the Maya-Quiche people:

> They ripped off our fruit,
> cut down our branches,
> burned our trunks,
> *but they never could kill our roots.*
>
> (Popol Vuh)

This culture of resistance also implies a culture of shame. On few occasions in history should humanity have felt more ashamed that now, given the growing poverty in a world of abundance and in full technological revolution.

The recovery of historical memory and of the culture of resistance accumulated in human history is part of the root of an alternative to this geocultural crisis.

PART 1 : GLOBALIZATION: ITS SOCIAL CONSEQUENCES 101

The vision of the future, the current historic need for an alternative, struck me, as I was walking through the streets of Old Havana, distressed by the dramatic situation of the Cuban people due to the relentless harassment violating all rights to which the North American empire submits the island. An anti-democratic aggression that does no more than heighten the intolerant stance of the Cuban government. On the wall of a colonial convent, I found a line, from José Martí, that struck me like a prophetic psalm: *Through love we see, with love we see, love is who sees. Soul without love cannot see.*

This capacity for seeing, for radically questioning, down to the root, is the indispensable attitude for thinking alternatively. Questioning as has Eduardo Galeano: *The West has sacrificed justice in the name of freedom upon the altar of divine productivity. The East has sacrificed freedom in the name of justice on the same altar. The South wonders whether such a god deserves the sacrifice of our lives.*

The type of questions which the genius Albert Einstein posed to us when he characterized our civilization as *the civilization that perfected the means, but could not get the objective straight*. This capacity for questioning lead to the assassination of my brother and colleague Ignacio Ellacuría, S.J in the Universidad Centroamericana (UCA) of El Salvador, who stated that, *the oppressor is incapable of discovering oppression; it is the oppressed who discovers the oppressor. The true reality of the oppressor can only be seen by the oppressed.* Is the geoculture of the South the only universally-applicable civilizing root in a global world? Is the **International of Life** the only civilizing international?

Five hundred years following the conquest of LAC, indigenous and African-American movements, women's, ecological, and urban dwellers' organizations, the Christian Base communities, the student and university movements, carry this query hoisted upon their diverse hopes. The expansion of cultural, social, economic, and intellectual movements has created a **new social fabric** in Latin America and in other places of this "Global South", even in these times of cholera, AIDS, drugs, and ecological disasters. How to channel this protest in pragmatically audacious alternative proposals is the challenge in Latin America. Also, I hope, worthy of the commemoration of 500 years of the arrival of Vasco de Gama to India, and of 50 years of Indian Independence, in order to confront jointly the imposed Globalization with an alternative Globalization from below, from the victims crucified by a history of colonialism and also domination of its domestic elites.

PART 2 :

Globalization:
Its Cultural Bases

Globalization and Its Cultural Underpinnings

Léon Diouf

Introduction

A first analysis of globalization has outlined its social consequences. At this second stage we have to discover its cultural bases from the point of view of the Victims of History. Who are the Victims of History? Speaking of globalization from their point of view spontaneously evokes in my mind the situation of the Third-world in front of the Euro-American world. The Third-world being vast, I shall focus on the Black People as a type of the Victims of History. This will be my first point. Secondly, in this historical field I shall try to discern the cultural bases of globalization.[1]

1. Black Africa and the Victims of History

The reason for choosing the Black People as a type of the victims of history is, first of all, to speak of what I know. But it is also because, they suffer from **three great ruptures** in its history which makes them victims of history three times. I would like to speak of the **Treaty of the Slaves**, of **Colonization** and of **Globalization**. A similar examination of the history of the other regions of the Third-world will allow us to explore the fate of other victims of history.

---

[1]For the historical overview as well as for the discernment of the cultural bases of globalization in the North, I refer to David J. Bosch, *Transforming Mission* (Maryknoll, Orbis Books, 1991) For African history as a type of the Third World, I refer to the following African historians. Cheik-Anta Diop, *Histoire de l'Afrique précoloniale*, (Paris, Présence Africaine, 1966) For the discernment of the cultural bases of globalization I have used Ka Mana, *Foi chrétienne, crise africaine et reconstruction de l'Afrique* (CETA/HAHO/CLE, 1992)

Let us be sure of what we are going to do. After thirty years of independence, it will be infantile on the part of the Africans to accuse only the others. We have also to be critical of ourselves and we are. But it will also be unjust to hide the consequences of history in the actual situation of Africa. Besides, there is no spirit of vengeance or revenge in this recall of these consequences nor in the discernment of their evil effects in Africa today. For us Christians such a reflection must summon us all, the oppressors and the oppressed, to the foot of the Cross. It is there that we find our common healing and shared happiness. Such is the spirit that animates this reflection.

1.1. Victims of Slavery

The Treaty of slaves has profoundly wounded Black Africa. Its people have been affected both in soul and body by one of the most serious dramas of history. It has changed the course of its history by putting an end to the processes which were preparing its unity and increasing its chances of development.[2] Like other peoples, Black Africans also unfortunately practised the old institution of slavery. The African slaves were sold even in Spain and Portugal. It is not Europe that had invented black slavery. It invented the **Treaty of the Africans**, as it will invent the treaties of groundnuts, of coffee or of cacao. Hardly had it arrested the Moslem onslaught at the end of the 15th century, it starts the colonization of Africa, Asia and the Americas. Such an enterprise required workers, slaves as much as was possible. The Blacks had to pay the price. This

---

[2]There were movements towards big geographical groupings which would have led to unity. For example, the *Sudanese empires* that succeeded each other from the 8th to the 15th centuries; the empire of *Ghana* (8th to 11th centuries); the empire of *Mali* (11th to 14th centuries) and the empire of *Sanghay* (15th to 16th centuries). This last empire had the first contacts with Europe in the 15th century. These empires are known to us both by African oral tradition and by Arab writers like Ibn Hawkal (10th C.), El Bekri (11th C.), Ibn Khaldoun (14th C.) and Abderrahman Saadi (17th C.), both of whom were from Tombouctou, in the present Mali. They report the history, the socio-economic political, cultural and religious life of the empires of Ghana, Mali and Songhay. We learn that the Sudanese empire brought together many countries like the British and French empires in Africa, which will replace them. A central dynasty maintained the unity of the empire through a strong but *decentralized government*. The economy was based on agriculture, cattle breeding and trade, specially in iron, copper, gold, salt and slaves.

is the **first great rupture** of African history. As a matter of fact, Europeans decided exactly at this time that only "coloured" peoples, as "inferior" beings, could be slaves.[3] One should say that they decided to consider them as inferior in order to reduce them to slavery. Oppression had to find a justification. The Spanish and the Portughese who started the Treaty were quickly joined by other colonial powers, among whom the British took the lion's share. No one, not even the institutional Church, protested.[4]

There were all sorts of consequences of the Treaty.[5] For our purpose I shall limit myself to the psychological consequences, which relate to the cultural bases of globalization.

1.2. Victims of Colonization

The Europeans yielded to the pressures of those who demanded the abolition of the Treaty of Slavery only when they could replace them with machines. At the same time it did not abandon its hold on Africa. The Treaty was not yet abolished before it started a

---

[3] For the unhappiness of the Black people the old institution of slavery, unfortunately as old as it was universal, had taken, precisely at this moment, another direction.
 In the ancient Roman Empire as well as medieval Europe slavery had little to do with race. After the "discovery" of the non-Western world beyond the Muslim territories this changed; henceforth slaves could only be people of color. The fact that they were different made it possible for the victorious Westerners to regard them as inferior. (Bosch, op.cit., p.227)

[4] Bosch notes that between 1783 and 1793 not less that 880 ships left Liverpool carrying 300,000 slaves to the Americas. The institutional Church had not protested at this time certainly because, in 1537 the Pope authorized the opening of a slave market in Lisbon, where up to 1000 Africans were sold every year to be transported to the Antilles. (Cf. Bosch, op.cit., p.227) There were besides two different measures. Since the missionaries like *Bartolomé las Casas* had taken up the defence of the American Indians, the colonial powers turn towards the Blacks of Africa. The Church forbade the slavery of the Indians, but authorized the Treaty of the Blacks.

[5] According to Bosch, the estimates of the number of black slaves sold to European colonies vary between 20 to 40 million individuals. (Bosch, op.cit.; p.227) Other estimates speak of a number between 100 and 150 millions. Whatever it be, such an important bleeding of the population, at this time, could only have weakened black Africa for a long time. This is so much more the case since the Treaty, because of commercial interests, focussed on the most robust and most dynamic groups of people.

second **colonization**, which was defined as follows at that time (1912):

> To colonize is to relate to new countries in order to profit by their resources of every kind, value them highly in the national interest and, at the same time, bring to the primitive peoples the advantages of the intellectual, social, scientific, moral, artistic, commercial and industrial culture of the superior races.[6]

This is was **the second great rupture** of African history: the confiscation of their riches and their initiative by people who refused to recognize in them all that made them human. This is the spirit that constitutes **colonialism**.[7]

---

[6]Merignhac (1912), cited by Borella (1958), cited by Gerti Hesseling, *Histoire politique du Sénégal. Institutions, Droit, er Société*. (Karthala/Asc?, 1985), p. 128.

[7] We should look closely at the colonial spirit. Coming from far, it emerges always in some attitudes, more or less unconsciously in those who adopt it. We should know first of all that it has its roots in the *presumed superiority* which feudal Christian Europe deduced, in the Middle Ages, from the superiority of the Christian religion. This presumed superiority will be one of the rare heritages which the AEnlightenment will keep from the Middle Ages. It is the same colonial spirit which justified the Treaty of the Blacks and will justify colonization declaring that the Blacks are inferior beings. Even a great thinker like Hegel betrays the same spirit, sorrounded by a large consensus. He attributes gratuitously to Africa all the evils that he experienced in his own society. In history, he writes, "Africa is characterised by concentrated sensuality, immediacy of the will, absolute inflexibility, and an inability to develop." Quoted by Bosch, *op.cit.*, p. 292 from Hegel, *Lectures on the Philosophy of World History. Introduction: Reason in History.*

The same colonial spirit was also shown by some missionaries who felt that they were sent in the name of the Gospel and of *culture* (their's, certainly), to root out the defects of the Apagan world, which they themselves listed. This knowledge resembles strangely that which one has of oneself standing before a mirror. Bosch quotes, the American Presbyterian James Dennis in Christian *Christian Mission and Social Progress,* who enumerates: "gambling, witchcraft, cruel customs, lack of public spirit, caste, corruption and bribery, commercial deceit and fraud, idolatry, superstition, and many more." (*Ibid.*, 293)

Finally it is the same spirit which, even in the Church, leads some people to question the capacity of African to be celibate. It is always the same spirit which underlies, more or less consciously, the *afro-pessimism* which is only a demoralization in the face of the challenges faced by Africa, when it is not unacknowledged racism.

There were people in the Third-world in general and in Africa in particular who denounced and opposed colonialism.[8] But the situation was not such that the conquered peoples could change it under favourable circumstances. With the scientific and technical fruits of the era of the "Enlightenment" (17th-18th centuries) and with the capital amassed with four centuries of the Treaty of the Blacks (16th to 19th centuries), the Europeans enjoyed knowledge and wealth which guaranteed their power. They show it in the treaty of Berlin (1884-1885) in which the British and the French divide Africa among themselves. The Germans, the Belgians, the Portughese and the Spanish satisfy themselves with "crumbs," though they are "very" nourishing.[9] Conquered one after the other, the various black African countries are grouped, disrespecting every natural frontier, in new colonial empires, which forestalled Africa's own processes of constituting bigger units. The consequences of colonialism are many. But I shall focus only on the socio-cultural ones.

1.3. Victim of Globalization

Colonization has not and could not have prepared Independence. It is, on the contrary, a handicap at birth for the African nations. Directed towards various European capitals, as a matter of fact, Africa, torn to pieces, suffers from a lack of unity and of common destiny from the beginning of independence. This is the **third great rupture** in its history, still present. The facts show that political independence does not always guarantee freedom, nor does it solve all the problems. It is even driven to the wall more than once by globalization, the more easily because the lack of unity and common destiny leaves the multiplicity of little African States weakened. The colonizers have, as a matter of fact, tied the individual African States to themselves. Some have even broken up the colonial groupings, which may have proved an interesting fall out of colonialism. It is known that division

---

[8] The movements in the Black world prove this abundantly, from those of the American Blacks in the beginning of the 20th C. .to contemporary African theology, passing through all the identity claims coming out of the "Negritude" movement in the 30s.

[9] Gerti Hesseling, *Histoire politique du Sénégal*, p.124.

facilitates domination. It facilitates this new domination which is globalization.

The reason for not speaking about the positive fall outs of colonialism is not to ignore them. But what interests us is globalization as the logical outcome of colonization thanks to the cultural bases provided by the latter.[10]

2. The Cultural Bases of Globalization.

In the context of all that we have seen above what are the cultural bases of globalization that we can discern among its protagonists both in the North and in the South?

Let us call them:
1. the strong bases of domination from the North; and
2. the weak bases of the victims from the South

2.1. The Strong Bases of Domination

If we look at history, the most visible seem to be attached to the European period of the "Enlightenment" (17th - 18th centuries).

---

[10] It is not a question of denying the benefits, or rather fall out, of colonialism, very often mediated by Christian mission. It will be unjust. Some however seem to accuse us of ingratitude and injustice in recalling to us these "benefits."

> The missionary movement made a prime contribution to the abolition of slavery; spread better methods of agriculture; established and maintained unnumbered schools; gave medical care to millions; elevated the status of women; created bonds between people of different countries, which war could not sever; trained a significant segment of leadership of the nations now newly independent.

Quoted by Bosch, *op.cit.*, p. 294 from Eugene L. Smith, *Mandate for Mission*, New York, Friendship Press, 1968, p. 71. If it is unust not to recognize these benefits, it wil be equally unjust to hide the consequences of History in the actual situation of Africa. The final message of the Synod for Africa (n.32) makes a vigorous denial.

> The Synod demands greater justice between North and South. There should be an end to presenting us in a ridiculous and insignificant light on the world scene, after having brought about and maintained a structural inequality and while upholding unjust terms of trade! The unjust price system brings in its wake an accumulation of the external debt which humilates our nations and gives them a regrettable sense of culpability which is imposed on us. But at the same time *we appeal to all our African brothers who have embezzled public funds that they are bound in justice to redress the wrong done to our peoples.*

There is however another basis that we should not forget. It is the *new politico-religious order* started by the integration of Christianity with the Roman empire and by the idea of society that emerged from it, namely *feudalism*. These are the roots of western hegemony. Let us recall them briefly to start with.

2.1.1. The Cultural Roots of Western Hegemony

Though the roots of its hegemony go way back in its history (to the Middle Ages [7th to 15th centuries], and even beyond to St. Augustin of Hippo [354-430]), Europe acquires this hegemony only at the end of the Middle Ages. It is therefore undoubtedly *Christian*. Its States are constituted on the basis of the feudal system in which God, who is at the top of the social pyramid, legitimates the place of each one in society: of the Church, first of all, then of the King and the Nobles, thirdly of the people and finally of the animals, plants and material objects. It is the feudal Christian Europe[11] which derives from its proclamation of the superiority of the Christian religion the superiority of its civilization. This presumed superiority will always more or less underlie their attitudes to non-European peoples. It belongs to the cultural bases of globalization.

2.1.2. The Fruits of the Enlightenment Era.

In the 17th-18th centuries, there was an extraordinary effervescence of thought in Europe. That is why this era is known as the period of the Enlightenment and starts the modern era. In its critique of the past in keeping with its options, it is particularly critical of feudal Christian Europe, but keeps its presumed superiority. The period of the Enlightenment also makes a certain number cultural options which have been decisive in the progress of Europe. They constitute the set of the cultural bases of globalization. Their

---

[11]Bosch, marking the limits of the Middle Ages with reference to the events and persons who have made a particular impression, places the emergence of feudal Christian Europe exactly at the end of the Middle Ages. These start with the papacy of *Gregory the Great* (590-604) and the successful emergence of *Islam*. It ends with the taking of *Constantinople* by the Moslems, in 1453, and the *great expeditions* of the Portughese and the Spanish. Starting with Gregory the Great and the elan of the christianization of Europe which he gave to the Church, one can conclude that by the end of the Middle Ages, nearly six centuries later, "*Europe had become indubitably Christian.*"

weakness appears today and demands rethinking. Here are some of the options of this line of thought: they are briefly formulated in relation to globalization.[12]

2.1.2.1. The Promotion of Reason

The Enlightenment is linked to Reason. It is presented as the obligatory and only path to all forms of knowledge. This option has provided the West with the arms to conquer the world. It is one of the first cultural bases of globalization in the West. Today, its narrow rationality needs to be widened.

2.1.2.2. Domination of Nature

With Reason, the Enlightenment assigns potentially unlimited power over nature to man and opts for its total exploitation. This option has given rise to western industry and its consequent cultural effects. These effects constitute a set of uncontestable cultural bases of globalization. They can be summarised in terms of a civilization of cosumerism in which the rich continue to amass more riches in order to satisfy their needs which are created by advertisements which are always one step ahead of their desires. The perverse effect of this option requires us to think of it again.

2.1.2.3. Planning its Action

In keeping with its manner of treating nature, the period of the Enlightenment opts for immediate causality instead of final causality. The west has learnt from this to foresee and plan its action. The spirit of foresight and planning is one of the essential cultural bases of globalization which works with longtime projects. The perverse effects of planning without a superior goal lead to review such an option.

2.1.2.4. Belief in Progress

The discovery of human potentialities and the option for immediate causality have lead the Enlightenment to opt for progress, not limited by any superior consideration. This option has activated and still activates the creativity of the West. By its cultural effects,

---

[12]Bosch, *op.cit.*, p. 264-267 and 351-362.

which one can summarize as the civilization of progress it also constitutes one of the essential cultural bases of globalization whose successes are more often starting points rather than points of arrival. The perverse effects of such a progress demands that it be rethought.

2.1.2.5. Being Efficient.

With its way of looking at reality, the period of the Enlightenment has opted for rational knowledge, considered objective, as opposed to belief, considered subjective and without any hold on reality. This option has enabled the West to lead the game of the world. Its spirit of efficiency certainly constitutes one of the essential cultural bases of globalization. This latter has to remain on top in order to survive. But this position is not attained once for all. It has to be defended efficiently. Lacking a superior finality, this efficiency proves too short and deprives people of a wisdom which is indispensable for their greatness. This option therefore need to be rethought.

2.1.2.6. Believing in Science and Technology

For the people of the Enlightenment, every problem seems soluble by science and technology. They opt therefore for their freedom from any higher regulating authority. This option has lead the West to conquest that support its hegemony. It constitutes therefore a cultural basis of globalization which is hegemonic in the spirit of domination.[13] Its defeats, serious as they are in the field of true human knowledge, require such an option to be revised.

2.1.2.7. Being Competitive

For the people of the Enlightenment, the human individual is emancipated and autonomous from every one and every thing. So they opt for complete individual freedom. This is a factor for success in

---

[13]Globalization and hegemony are partly related because in both a minority confiscates the initiative from the majority among the protoganists of a common action. It does so in the name of a supposedly superior interest which is in fact its own. Or again it does so in the same of supposedly superior laws from which no one can escape, but which actually are its own and which it changes when there is need.

a competitive society. The spirit of competition to which this gives rise is one of the cultural bases of globalization in the West. The perverse effects of individualism and competition demand the rethinking of this option. These cultural bases (the presumed superiority of Europe and the fruits of the Enlightenment) can be found in the phenomena of globalization. In addition, their game is facilitated by the cultural bases which are the weaknesses of the victims of globalization, which crosses over to the South in order to integrate them in its own cultural framework.

2.2. Cultural Bases - Weaknesses of the Victims

As I had said earlier, I would like to seek to discern the cultural bases of Globalization on the side of the victims of history in Black Africa, as a typical region of the Third World. One can find similar historical situations with similar cultural bases of globalization in other parts of the Third World. This Black Africa is plural. Its ethno-cultures are many. However all share common cultural elements that history has always confirmed, especially the ruptures of African history. These ruptures play a determining role in the globalization of Africa. As a mater of fact they are responsible for the cultural bases of Africa. But they find accomplices in the limits of the common cultural elements of Africa. Let us begin with these.

2.2.1. Negro-African Culture and Globalization

The Church in Africa makes a special contribution today to think and live the African situation. All over the continent, it analyses the different national situations, discerns its causes and proposes remedies. The number and quality of its documents are a good illustration of its contribution.[14] What emerges from this is that, in the eyes of the Church, Africa is in crisis. It is not the crisis of

---

[14]In his *Foi chrétienne, crise africaine et reconstruction de l'Afrique*, Ka Mana indicates, in note 57, the list of documents on whcih he himself has worked. We would add to this list two letters written by the Bishops of Sénégal in 1982 and 1994

Lettre pastorale de la Conférence Episcopale du Cameroun sur la crise économique dont souffre le pays, Pentecost 1990;

La politique au service du pays, regard de foi et d'espéranace, Pastoral letter of the Bishops of Ivory Coast, in *La documentation catholique,* n.2021, 2-16 Sept. 1990, pp. 820-826;

growth of which people often speak who only see "young Churches" and "young States" in Africa. The crisis has to do with thinking in terms of direction and meaning. Our countries do not seem to have any more "clear guidelines for thinking, living and acting in the modern world."[15] Such direction would be "linked, not only to the defeat which our people have sustained with reference to the West, but especially to the way in which, longer than one would imagine, we have made a certain number of metaphysical and social choices which are inoperative and sterile."

These choices could be summarized with reference to God, to the humans and to nature as follows:
1. Omnipresence of the invisible,
2. An unlimited significance for the communitarian and the collective,
3. The cult of life and its fecundity.

Le Mémorandum du Comité Permanent de la Conférence Episcopale du Zaire adressé au président Mobutu lors de la consultation nationale sur la situation générale du pays et le fonctionnement des institutions, published by *Jeune Afrique*, n.1527, April 9, 1990, pp. 20-25;

Lettre pastorale du Comité Exécutif national de l"Eglise du Christ au Zaire au peuple de Dieu face a la situation socio-politique du Zaire, mimeographed;

Ethique chrétienne et politique dans le Bénin d'aujourd'hui, Declaration of the Interconfessional Council of the Protestant Churches of Benin folowing the Consultation in Porto-Novo, February 12-13, 1990;

Maseru declaration on the debt crisis as it affects human rights, Document published afte the meeting organized under the auspices of the Conference of the Churches of All Africa, September 26-30, at Lesotho Maseru; the Report of the debates at the meeting of the leaders of the Protestant Churches of Central Africa at Kinshasa-N'Sele, August 12-21, 1990, CETA 1991;

Libérer la Démocratie. Déclaration des Eveques du zaire aux chrétiens catholiques et aus hommes de bonne volonté, Lent 1991;

Le 35e. Synode général de l'Eglise Evangelique du Cameroun prend position sur le contexte socio-politique du pays, March 1991;

Le temps propice pour le changement, CETA 1991;

Que faisons-nous de notre pays?, Pastoral letter of the Bishops of Central Africa, Bangui, 1991;

"Respecter et promouvoir le Bien commun," Pastoral letter of the Bishop of Sénégal, 1982;

Batir ensemble un Sénégal du justice et du paix, Pastoral Letter of the Bishops of Sénégal, 1994.

[15] Kä Mana, *op.cit.*, p.124. On this topic the author refers us to his book *Destiné négro-africaine. Expérience de la dérive et énergétique du sens* (Kinshasa-Bruxelles, Ed. de l'Archipel, 1987)

As the European fruits of the Enlightenment, and, more generally, as all human phenomena, these "metaphysical and social choices" of Africa sin by exaggeration, as others sin by downplaying them. Still to qualify them as inoperative and sterile would be an error.[16] That Africa has been the victim of its uncontrolled generosity before a calculating Europe does not invalidate in an absolute way its cultural options. As for the options of Europe of the Enlightenment, one should not "throw away the baby with the bath water."[17]

The exhortation **Church in Africa** takes up these options, which for John Paul II as for the Synod Fathers, are far from being sterile and inoperative. After having recalled them, he invites the people to see also the "positive accomplishments of the people of the

---

[16] This error appears in *L'Afrique noire va-t-elle mourir?* (Paris, Cerf, 1991) The author says that the African crisis is basically a crisis of the African social imagination touching our very capacity for developing ourselves. For proof he appeals Ato what the Africans say about themselves which shows a globally negative perception which the negro-Africans have of their society and its future. Cf. Kä Mana, *op.cit.*, p.128.

This African discourse is rather recent and reflects the ruptures of African history rather than the cultural bases of the negro-Africans. On the contrary, the error that underlies the perception of the African crisis as a crisis of its social imagination is a condemnation of the cultual bases of negro-African culture which is mistaken. Such a condemnation can go very far. It is certainly evident in the way the author speaks, sometimes too negatively, about the African peoples and persons, particularly religious leaders, to the point of being inhuman in the way he sees the Christian sense of the human. Such a misconception of the cultual bases of negro-Africans and a consequent lack of Aafricanness betray a lack of justice and charity. Cf. *Christ d'Afrique. Enjeux éthiques de la foi africaine en Jesus-Christ* (Karthala/Ceta/Cle/Haho, 1994), ch.6, AFrom the ecclesial structures to the individual imagination", pp. 151-181.

[17] Even in the dynamic of *reconstruction*, justifiably dear to the author (Kä Mana, *op.cit.*) the common negro afican riches would not disappear. It is important to Africans, as to every people, that their choices have deep roots in the past. Africa cannot be reconstructed if these are ignored. The figure of Christ that one has to promote in this reconstruction has to be *incarnated* in the cultural bases of Africa. It is in this way that they will be assumed, purified and placed in the tension of the Aalready and Anot yet of the Kingdom. This is true of the whole of creation.

[18] The Exhortation declares: "Africans have a profound religious sense, a sense of the sacred, of the existence of God the Creator and of a spiritual world." (42)
"In African culture and tradition the role of the family is everywhere held to be fundamental. Open to this sense of the family, of love and respect for life, the African loves children, who are joyfully welcomed as gifts of God." (43) Linked to

continent" (nn.42-45).[18] But these accomplishments have their roots particularly on the African sense of human dignity, of peace and of shared happiness, which are values, besides others, that are rooted in the black-African culture. Let us be careful then not to abandon these riches. They represent an opportunity for universal communion. They are sources of high human values: spiritual values that raise the humans above themselves and values of fellowship which save them from hatred. They are also sources of a certain significance for nature, which makes it a sharer in our happiness. But let us remember our historical defeats in order to rethink these cultural riches. It is in complicity with its limits, as a matter fact, that the psychological consequences of the ruptures of African history join the field of the cultural bases of globalization.

2.2.2. African History and Globalization.

As I have pointed out above, the three great ruptures of African history involve consequent cultural effects which meet globalization to make its cultural bases. These are the effects of the Treaty of the Slaves and of Colonization.

2.2.2.1. Effects consequent on the Black Treaty.

I discern two of them: the complex of "forgetfulness" and that of "self justification."

---

this love and this respect for life one can evoke here the respect of the negro-african for nature.

"African cultures have an acute sense of solidarity and community life." (43)

The exhortation is particularly relevant with regard to the "positive achievements".

"While the shadows and the dark side of the African situation... can in no way be minimized, it is worth recalling here a number of positive achievements of the people of the continent which deserve to be praised and encouraged." (44)

"The 'winds of change' are blowing strongly in many parts of Africa, and people are demanding even more insistently the recognition and promotion of human rights and freedoms." (44)

"In spite of its poverty and the meager means at its disposal, the church in Africa plays a leading role in what touches upon integral human developement... I feel it my duty to express heartfelt thanks to the church in Africa for the role which it has played over the years as a promoter of peace and reconciliation in many situations of conflict, political turmoil and civil war." (45)

2.2.2.1.1. The Complex of "Forgetfulness."

This is a clumsy defensive reflex, born from the drama of the Black Treaty, which one can qualify as the complex of forgetfulness. The preparatory committee for a consultation having for its theme "Memory of Black Slavery: Towards its Christian Management" speaks of it as follows: "Mechanisms of censure and psychological and socio-cultural inhibition function, unknown to us, in order to keep in forgetfulness a reality that oppresses us."[19] Torturers and their victims suffer from the same complex, though for different reasons: one group to hide their responsibility and the other for seeming only to be innocent victims. The Africans add to this a persecution complex, forgetting that in the drama they have a double role: they are the torturers as the sellers and victims as the sold. Every one adopts the same politics of the ostrich: they think that there is no danger since they do not see it. Globalization finds in it a double cultural base. Everywhere, the complex of forgetfulness gives rise to modern forms of slavery. The persecution complex facilitates the emergence of these new forms of slavery. Globalization takes care to integrate among its cultural bases the spirit underlying these phenomena.

2.2.2.1.2. The Complex of "Self-justification."

The complex of forgetfulness goes together with that of "self-justification."[20] One excuses oneself by accusing the other. Self-justification provides a double cultural base for globalization in Africa. On the one hand it excuses the Africans faced with the consequences of the ruptures of their history. On the other hand, it leads them to undergo, with a kind of fatality, the presumed superiority of the West and its more or less unconscious, but not less active, racism.

---

[19] The preparatory comittee of the Consultation continues: "Thus, inorder to survive, our memory is made an accomplice. Faced with the terible horror, the spontaneous reaction has been one of self-justification that accuses the other. It is not the tormentor that prevents us from remembering; it is ourselves." Cf. Institut Catholique de l'Afrique de l'Ouest (Abidjan, Ivory Coast), Consultation on *"Route de l"Esclave."*

[20] See the previous note.

2.2.2.2. Effects induced by Colonization.

I see three of them: the complex of "inferiority," that of "borrowed personal identity" and that of "borrowed national identity."

2.2.2.2.1. The Complex of "inferiority."

One of the consequences that one could expect from the Treaty and from Colonization is the complex of "inferiority" of the "black person" in front of the "white person." One could have expected it and avoided it. Unfortunately, it is there. The complex of "expecting help" is one of its forms, from the top to the bottom of the State. Evidently, it is one of the important cultural bases of globalization in Africa, which functions under the form of a confidence that makes one inactive and open to hidden exploitation. This complex is important since it is as prevalent among the elite as among the masses of the people.

2.2.2.2.2. The Complex of "borrowed personal identity."

The complex of "borrowed personal identity" seems linked to the complex of inferiority. Born out of certain types of colonial government, it comes from the impossible identification with the colonizer, whose identity the colonized adopt in vain.[21] This is also, evidently, an African cultural base of globalization. It makes us accept the proposals of the West the more easily since we recognize ourselves in them since we have borrowed its identity.

---

[21] To speak only of French colonization this complex is linked to the politics of *assimilation*, whether it has to do with *political and administrative assimilation, personal assimilation or cultural assimilation: The Gauls are our ancestors!* Cf. G. Hesseling, *op.cit.*, pp. 129-137. This way of governing intended to bring civilization, French, obviously, to the colonized. It aimed at making them Western, French in fact. The school and the town have been the privileged locations of such progress.

The assimilation has not achieved its aim, except to declare the inhabitants of such or such a colonial area *"French citizens."* However it has had a profound impact on the mentality of the people. It has left a *western imprint*, which is now an ally of globalization. What will not one do, at the suggestion of the "white man," to resemble his image? It is a trap of globalization. More or less harmless practices show the existence of this complex. Starting with food habits and consequent heavy imports from the West to a phenomenon like *xeesal* (in wolof/Sénégal: to make white), in a vain search for identity as "white."

PART 2 : GLOBALIZATION: ITS CULTURAL BASES

2.2.2.2.3. The Complex of "borrowed national identity."

This is a situation that has come about at the time of independence. One could call it the complex of "borrowed national identity." Born out of colonization and managed by a westernized elite, the African States have been obliged to adopt western institutions.[22] Inspite of the efforts to adapt them to the African context, these remain borrowals. This complex constitutes a cultural base of globalization in Africa through the very borrowal of the western institutions. It facilitates the game of western interests among those who have abandoned their own juridical language to adopt that of the West. It is a "mafia of the spirit,"[23] more perhaps in the hands of the multinationals than of the governments. Any way, globalization can continue to give birth to its own cultural bases among its supporters whether from the South or from the North. It creates a sort of universal legal system to which every one is obliged to conform under pain of being losers in their undertakings. Is the situation then hopeless for Africa, and for the Third-World? The following piece of advice, satirical but relevant, given by one of the heroes of a Senagalese novel shows a way. Go to the West, says our hero, to know "how to win without justification."[24]

2.2.3. Towards an African Response to Globalization

Faced with the hegemony of the West and faced with the many cultural bases connected to globalization, the Africans search for a solution. Some have started to ask themselves if the solution is,

---

[22]The reasons for such adoption are many. Apart from the fact that those who were responsible were the westernized people or technical counselors from the West, it is also necessary to appreciate the need to give oneself a Constitution that will find immediate acceptance in the West, whose partnership was compulsary. Any attempts at going back to traditional juridical systems were considered misdirected in the modern world. The western juridical system was taken over in Africa, replacing the traditional systems, at least at the top levels of the State apparatus. Thus the African governments themselves find it difficult sometimes to reach out to the depths of the country. But, even if borrowed, the western institutions were seen as inevitable for our nations. They were the necessary conditions of living in the modern world, in harmony with the Organisms of the United Nations, and of access to international aid.

[23]Lester Coutinho, S.J. (India), "The Global against the Local, Environment against Development" in *Promotio Justitiae*, n.58 (November 1994).

[24] Chekh-Hamidou Kane, *L'aventure ambiguë* (Ed. 10/18, 1994).

after all, to enter into the dynamic of "economy-world," which is nothing else but the present world order in which the North is in control.[25] They maintain that it is possible that Africa, and the Third-World in general, can develop themselves in the framework of an "economy-world."[26]

The ways and the technical means that these researchers propose should certainly be taken into account. But it is not enough. The North and the South must rethink their own cultural options and accept, with appropriate reservations, their options. In other words, the battle between the North and the South is not fatal. The quality of our cultural options have a determining role. This is in our hands. It is the responsibility of the humans to make this world in which they are going to live. It is more a human problem than a scientific or technological one.

---

[25] Mamadou-Lamine Diallo, *Les Africains sauveront-ils l'Afrique?* (Karthala, 1996) This author from Sénégal, polytechnician and civil engineer from the *L'Ecole des Mines* of Paris, had worked in the World Bank in Washington, before joining the BCEAO (The Central Bank of the States of West Africa) at Dakar, in 1993. He knows what he is talking about. His major concern is to refuse the condemnation of Africa to marginalization and poverty, while respecting its cultural roots which, to him, seem indispensable because very essential. He says that he has borrowed the notion of AEconomy-world from Fernand Braudel, *Le temps du monde* (Paris, 1980) This socio-economic notion indicates, to start with, a Azone in which exchanges with the outside is very negligible. Such a zone is made up of a *centre* which appropriates to itself the best benefits of the system, a *semi-periphery* which is made up of the countries who are candidates to become the centre and a *periphery* still farther away from development. Before the western hegemony, there could have been many Aeconomy-worlds in the world. Today, there is but one which covers the whole planet under the full control of globalization. In this global Aeconomy-world the fight to be at the centre is fierce. This centre has been successively occupied by the *City-States* (Venice, Geneva, Amsterdam), then by the *Nation States* (England followed by the USA). After the fall of the Soviet Union which attempted to supplant the USA, if not to share the centre with it, there seem to be two conditates to be the centre today: *Europe* and *Japan*.

[26] M.L. Diallo offers two arguments to support his affirmation. First of all "one does not quit easily the economy-world, especially if one is at the bottom of the periphery. The attempt of the Soviet Union failed even though it had many more possibilities. Secondly, as it has been shown, first of all by Japan and then by other Newly Industrialized Countries in the course of recent years, it is possible to progress in the context of economy-world, briefly to develop oneself, to improve the level of life of the people and to reduce poverty." Cf. *op. cit.,* p. 127. p.11.

Conclusion: "Behold the Man"

The humans are made for happiness and there is no happiness that is not shared. Unfortunately one of their major weaknesses is egoism. That is why the Church in Africa proposes everywhere the same basic remedy: conversion.[27] Conversion from each one of their options which are not in favour of the human, either in oneself or in the others, in order to bring-in the human everywhere. Such conversion is for the oppressors as well as for the oppressed.

For us Christians, this conversion takes the form of "following Christ, who Acomes not to be served," but to serve (Mt 20:26). The triple temptation at the beginning of his ministry shows that this renunciation pervades his whole life. He refuses to make use of God; on contrary God's Word is his nourishment. He refuses to tempt God even to manifest God's glory. This will be blackmail. He refuses finally to exchange the absoluteness of God with any one or any thing.[28] The following of Christ should also pervade the whole of our lives.

"**Behold the Man!**" (Jn 19:5), says Pilate to the crowd, pointing to Jesus. He is the Human we should all become so that there will be neither globalization nor victims of history.

---

[27]Cf. *Bâtir ensemble in Sénégal de Justice et de Paix*. Pastoral Letter of the Bishops on Sénégal, "A Call to Conversion," p. 11 (Dakar, 1994)

[28]R. Beraudy, *Sacrifice et Eucharistie* (Paris, Cerf, 1997), p. 72.

Beyond the Fatal Impact Theory

Frans Wijsen

I was asked to give some cultural underpinnings of the phenomenon of globalization from an European perspective. I allowed myself the freedom to interpret this request in such a way that I could not only speak as an European about my experiences in my own culture, but also about my experience as an European in Africa and Asia. However, I will limit myself to the cultural perspective.

The theses that I want to defend are that economic globalization does not necessarily lead to cultural unification, that globalization is accompanied by cultural revival, and that the remaining cultural identity contains the seeds of resistance, as many examples in the past and the present show.[1]

Recently there was a resurgence of African and Indian religions in Latin America, ancestor belief being recognized as an official religion in Benin, the chiefs being reinstalled in Uganda and Ghana.[2] Of course, these chiefs - such as Ronald Mutebi II of Uganda, are not very powerful in political and economic affairs. Yet they represent a 'symbolic capital' which can be transformed into material power.[3]

---

[1] The Third World Centre of the University of Nijmegen, The Netherlands, did some excellent studies on globalization and diversification. See H. Siebers, *Creolization and Modernization. The Case of the Q'eqchi'es of Guatemala*, Nijmegen 1996.

[2] In Sukumaland, the area where I lived and worked in North West Tanzania, the 'sungusungu' represent such a revival movement. See R. Abrahams, "Sungusungu. Village vigilante groups in Tanzania", *African Affairs* 86(1989)179-196.

[3] For the concept of 'symbolic capital' see P. Bourdieu, Outline of a Theory of Praxis, London 1977; Id., "Symbolic Power", *Critique of Anthropology* 4(1978)13-14, 77-85.

For this reason I hesitate to speak about 'victims of history'. In no way do I wish to deny that there were and are many victims. Unfortunately, there are too many proofs for that. But by formulating the theme of this consultation in this way we emphasize too much that people at the underside of society underwent historical developments. We tend to forget that in many cases these people played an active and creative role.[4] Too much victimization is historically untrue and pedagogically unwise. We need to move beyond the 'fatal impact theory', which interprets colonial history only in terms of colonial rulers bending colonised peoples to their will.

But first let me explain what I mean by 'culture'. By culture I understand the meaning system that is learned and shared by the members of a group and that is used by them to interpret experiences and to organize behaviour.[5] In a culture there are two levels. The first level is that of the 'inconsequential beliefs and values', which the people easily change if they find it profitable to do so. The second level is that of the 'root paradigms', which are the unquestioned presuppositions about the nature of the world and of human beings.[6]

My experience with adult education in Europe, Africa and Asia makes me believe that a lot of globalization occurs at the first level of culture, but little at the second level. Root paradigms do not change easily. These root paradigms make 'contrast experiences' possible. People at the underside of society suffer from economic, political, psychological, cultural and religious oppression. But deep inside they know that their situation should not be like that.[7]

---

[4] The Afro-American medium-religions are an example of this. See also G. Huizer, "Religion and struggle for land in Zimbabwe," in: G. Peperkamp, C. Remie (Eds.), *The Struggle for Land World-wide*, Saarbrücken 1989, 87-107; Id., *Folk Spirituality and Liberation in Southern Africa*, Bordeaux 1991.
[5] I favour a cognitive understanding of culture. See J. Spradley (Ed.), *Culture and Cognition. Rules, Maps and Plans*, San Francisco, 1972.
[6] For the concept of 'root paradigms' see V. Turner, *Dramas, Fields and Metaphors*. Ithaca, 1974.
[7] I borrow the concept of 'contrast experiences' from E. Schillebeeckx, *Jesus. An Experiment in Christology*. New York, 1979, pp. 619-622; Id., *Church. The Human Story of God*. London, 1990, pp. 5-6.

1. Experiences of a European in his own culture

I was born in the city of Maastricht in the southern part of The Netherlands, a city that since the outbreak of the Eighty Years' War (1568 - 1648) was dominated by Spanish (1579 - 1632), Dutch (1632 - 1673) and French (1673 - 1678; 1748 -1749; 1794 - 1814) invaders.[8] Local sources say that during the Spanish rule the population of the city decreased from 35.000 to 400 people. This seems an exaggeration, but the repression must have been terrible.

After the fall of Napoleon the United Kingdom of The Netherlands was formed, comprising Holland and Belgium. In the Belgian Revolt, the city was kept by the Dutch king; all other cities West of the river Meuse that gave the city its name and formed a natural border became Belgian in 1839.

People in my region feel that they were colonized by 'the Dutch', that they are being oppressed as a developing country within The Netherlands and kept backward. Saying to them that they come from 'Holland' is a big insult. Holland is just one part of The Netherlands, which is the official name of our country. From the perspective of a globalizing world this feeling of being oppressed seems ridiculous, but it has deep historical roots.

My town is widely known by the fact that it was there that the 'Maastricht Treaty' was signed in which European nation states decided to build a European Community, was signed. However, the fact is that with the enlargement that is brought by the European Community, regionalism grows and local cultures and languages regain popularity.[9] As chairperson of the European Commission, Jacques Delors already spoke about *"l'Europe dés regions, pas des nations"*. An 'Embassy of the Frisians', an ethnic group in the northern part of The Netherlands, was recently opened in The Hague. The region is 'in'.

---

[8] On January 30, 1998, it will be 350 years since the 'Peace of Münster' was signed. This 'peace' finished the eigthy years struggle of the Dutch against the Spanish, in which the Catholic and Protestant religions were the driving forces. It was the beginning of The Netherlands as a nation state and also of an international legal system in Europe.

[9] For example, new books on Celtic culture are numerous. It is believed that Celtic culture is more important for understanding the European identity than Roman and Greek cultures. See, among others, I. Bradley, *The Celtic Way*. London, 1996.

This has also shady sides. Think of the ethnic conflicts among the Irish, the Basque and the Bosnian people, or the ethnic conflict between the Wallonian and the Flemish people, just 10 kilometres from where I live. Some people there would claim the end of the nation state by dividing Belgium into a French and a Dutch part.[10]

If people think that the animosities I refer to are just minor ones compared to the ethnic conflicts in Central Africa, I would remind them of the anthropological insight that between tolerance and intolerance there is a difference of degree, not of kind. Both tolerance and intolerance presuppose a negative attitude towards 'the other'.[11] That is why tolerance can turn into intolerance under certain historic conditions. The ethnic conflict in Bosnia makes this clear.

In the past ten years I have been doing participatory research in a suburb of Maastricht, while doing urban mission work.[12] Here mainly working-class people live. However, at present many people are unemployed.[13] This suburb started in the beginning of this century as the first housing area outside the ancient city walls, for people who were driven away from their slums in the inner city.[14] There was an attempt to socialize them and to integrate them into 'civilized' society.[15]

Concrete housing blocks were built as temporary shelters, as well as a huge Catholic church. The Government and the church

---

[10] Just recently nationalist movements in Corsica and Cyprus emerged again; also in Scotland and Catalonia nationalist movements remain active.

[11] The only difference is that in the attitude of tolerance the other is accepted (passive) whereas in the attitude of intolorance the other is persecuted (active).

[12] The results of this research have been published in F. Wijsen, *Geloven bij het leven. Missionaire presentie in een volkswijk*. Baarn, 1997.

[13] Globalization causes problems not only in the southern countries. In The Netherlands, the so called 'polder-model' in which social partners (government, employers and trade-unions) cooperate to cope with economic problems caused a breakdown of the social security system. It is estimated that out of the 6 million households in The Netherlands some 830.000 live at or under the social minimum, and some 200.000 live in poverty.

[14] Maastricht started to be industrialized in 1825, as one of the first towns in The Netherlands. Porcelain factories were situated in the inner town. Here there was a massive support for the socialist movement. In Maastricht in the predominantly Roman Catholic southern part of The Netherlands. The first branch of the present-day Dutch 'Labour Party' was founded.

worked together to 're-educate' these people. However, these attempts failed and the people have largely remained themselves.

Liberalism as the most important features of the globalized mind (freedom of the individual) and secularism (the abolishment of all transcendental boundaries that limit this freedom) are mentioned. However, these features are not found among the people. Here community life is still important and popular devotions flourish as never before. According to statistics, The Netherlands are one of the most secularized countries in the world, after the former East Germany. But I did not find much secularization in my suburb, nor do other urban mission workers working in similar suburbs in different parts of The Netherlands. This shows the conflict between the 'official image' of a society and what is really going on.[16]

My case study gives an interesting example of how the ruling classes within a society try to determine the lives and the world views of people at the underside of the society, and how these people succeed in escaping the control of the bourgeois people and their mentality.[17] Domination and dependence qualify the relationship not only between rich countries and poor countries, but also between rich and poor people everywhere.[18] This has always been

---

[15] In the fifties a sociologist diagnosed that Maastricht was oneof the towns with the highest 'anti-social' population in The Netherlands, and within Maastricht this was situated in the suburb that I studied. As a thereby he proposed special housing areas (referred to as 'schools') where people could learn to live in a 'decent' way. See H. Litjens, *Onmaatschappelijke gezinnen. Sociologisch onderzoek naar de onmaatschappelijkheid in Maastricht.* Assen, 1953.

[16] As most surveys use questionnaires which presuppose a certain level of education and literacy, people at the underside of society are not well represented in this kind of research.

[17] It is a merit of the subaltern approach that it corrected the classical Marxist approach by showing that popular cultures can provide one of the few resources of identity and thus contain the seeds of resistance. See A. Gramsci, *Prison Notebooks.* New York, 1991.

[18] The exploitation of people in the colonies was closely linked to the exploitation in Europe. In my own region, the villages of miners are called 'colonies' till today. Directors of mining companies in the Dutch East Indies often had a long record in the State Mines at home, where the same methods of exploitation were employed. In an unpublished manuscript, one of those directors advises the church officials about their faithful: "if you keep them ignorant, I will keep them poor". See H. Schaapveld, *Cultuurondernemingen als steunpunten voor de missionering,* n.p., 1928.

the case, also during the European expansion in Africa and Asia. In many cases local chiefs and sultans were as exploitative as the European traders and colonizers, with whom they were eager to collaborate. Colonial history cannot be understood completely within a framework that primarily distinguishes between central and peripheral economies.[19]

2. Experiences of a European in Africa and Asia

From these experiences in my own culture, please allow me to comment on what I as a European observed in Africa and Asia.[20] The Forum for African and Asian Spirituality asked its members and friends to study five hundred years of colonial history from the point of view of the colonised people in order to prepare the Vasco da Gama Year.[21] Most responses that I have seen are not really from within and from below. They analyse the situation in macro-economic terms and they ignore the deep-rooted ambiguity of colonial and neo-colonial history.[22] We are in need of a new theoretical orientation towards colonialism and neo-colonialism.[23]

---

[19] The so-called 'European expansion' in Africa and Asia was only possible by seeking allies with local rulers and by conducting a policy of divide and rule. The struggle for slaves, gold and spices was mainly a struggle of the rich among themselves.

[20] After I worked in Sukumaland as a missionary, I did 8 extensive periods of fieldwork there between 1985 and 1995. Since 1995 I have been a guest lecturer of practical theology at the Duta Wacana Christian University at Yogyakarta, Indonesia. I visit this country twice a year. For what I say about Indonesia I depend very much on papers written by my students there.

[21] Jubilee 1998 Coordinating Secretariat, "Framework for the Study of Five Hundred Years of Coloninial History from the Point of View of the Colonised People," in: *Quest* 137 (April 1995), pp. 11-19.

[22] History is a complex whole in which good deeds can have evil consequences. By defending the human rights of the 'Indians', Bartolomé de las Casas contributed to the atlantic slave trade. While writing the present presentation I watched the inquiries of the South African Truth and Reconciliation Commission on television. An example of the ambiguity of history is Winnie Mandela, a symbol of the liberation movement in South Africa, who simply denied all her alleged crimes, regardless of the evidence.

[23] See G. Prakash (Ed.), *After Colonialism. Imperial Histories and Postcolonial Displacements*. Princeton, 1995.

It is often said that the voyages of discovery of Columbus and Vasco da Gama were the beginning of globalization and Europeanization. Maybe it holds true for the European discovery of the Americas. But it is inappropriate to interpret the European expansion in Africa and Asia in terms of invasion and domination.[24] There was much trade going on between (East) Africa and Asia long before the Europeans came.[25] And even after the Europeans came they did not dominate the markets, at least not before the 18th century.[26] Sri Lanka and the Philippines are the major exceptions to this rule. To interpret the voyages of discovery as the beginning of Europeanisation exaggerates the European influence in this part of the world.[27]

Talking about five hundred years of European expansion in the world is not only too Eurocentric, it is also too elitist. In no way can it be denied that much Europeanisation was going on, and that Africans and Asians did interiorize European values. But this is largely true for the upper classes, for those who were socialized into the Western educational and medical systems. People at the underside of society, however, largely remained outside these

---

[24] When Europeans 'discovered' Latin America this continent was thinly populated and local cultures were weakened. Here European exploitation was much easier than in Asia where the density of the population was much higher and where the Europeans met well-organized civilizations. Even in Africa at that time Europeans were not superior but severely beaten, either by Arab traders or by African kings See L. Ofosu-Appiah, *Slavery. A Brief Survey.* Accra, 1969, pp. 26-28.

[25] The word 'globalization' may be new, but the phenomenon it refers to is not and this phenomenon did not start with the European discoveries! The idea that 'globalization' started with the European voyages of discovery is an expression of the European superiority complex. It is sad that the 'European success story' was interiorized by some Asian and African intellectuals.

[26] For a long time the Portuguese, the Dutch, the English and the French did not occupy countries, but established trading posts, mainly in coastal areas. In many cases it was difficult for them to secure their settlements, as they met strong competition from Muslim powers, both in Africa and Asia. By exploiting the rivalries between local rulers they were able to maintain their foothold on the coasts. It was only in the 19th century that colonization became possible.

[27] Even today it may be questioned if we really live in a uni-polar world. Most markets in the South East Asian region are dominated by the Chinese. And the Chinese will form the major economic force in the 21st century. See also S. Huntington, *The Clash of Civilizations and the Remaking of the World Order.* New York, 1996.

systems.[28] A large majority of people in Africa and Asia did not receive higher education. Most people in this world did not join the information super highway; more than half of the world's population never even made a phone call! Many people continue to make use of indigenous medicine and customary law, and most economic activities of African subsistence farmers remain outside official statistics.[29]

Moreover, many studies about the European expansion in the world are too superficial. Some scholars speak about the 'McDonaldization' of society.[30] Here again, I do not deny that much 'McDonaldization' is going on. However, this 'McDonaldization' remains largely at surface of the culture. Beneath the surface there remains a large reservoir of 'root paradigms'. In Javanese language, for example, there is an old saying 'tuno bathak, bathi sanak', which means: a loss of wealth is a gain of friendship. This saying reflects a reality, especially at the underside of society.[31] The same holds true for Africa.[32]

Consequently I think that there is too much talk of victimization in studies of colonization and globalization. Very often these studies present colonized people as objects of change or victims of history. This view largely neglects the massive rejection of oppres-

---

[28] In the 19th century already several hundreds of millions of people lived in India. Some thousands of British colonial administrators were not able to have a major impact on this huge population. The same applies to Tanzania.

[29] Peasants in Africa devote aproximately 60 to 70 per cent of their labour time to subsistence farming. See G. Hyden, *Beyond Ujamaa in Tanzania. Underdevelopment and an Uncaptured Peasantry.* London, 1980, p. 13. See also T. Maliyamkono and V.M. Bagachwa, *The Second Economy in Tanzania.* London, 1990.

[30] See G. Ritzer, *The McDonaldization of Society.* New York, 1993. It is said that globalization leads to a 'McWorld', a world-wide homogeneous culture dominated by multi-nationals such as Coca Cola, Disney, Nike, Microsoft, MTV. However, there is also the trend of 'Jihad', the 'tribalization' by which groups of people stick to their own identity and make a 'holy war' against other 'tribes' and against a world-wide culture, which absorbs cultural identity. See B. Barber, *Jihad vs. McWorld,* New York, 1995.

[31] See F. Wijsen, "In the very first place Javanese. Contextualization and church development in Indonesia," in: H. Hoeben, R. Fornet-Betancourt (Eds.), *Yearbook of Contextual Theologies 1997.* Aachen, 1997, pp. 83-98.

[32] See J. Healy, D. Sybertz, *Towards an African Narrative Theology,* Maryknoll 1997; see also L. Magesa, *African Religion. The Moral Traditions of Abundant Life,* Maryknoll 1997.

sive policies of colonial authorities, for example by slowing down projects or civil disobedience campaigns.[33] To victimize Africans means depriving them of their 'symbolic capital', namely their spiritual power by which people who are written off economically are able to survive.[34]

Some African theologians tend to speak about the consequences of European expansion in terms of 'anthropological poverty' or 'cultural death'.[35] Without playing down their own personal experiences, being trained in the seminary system, I am afraid that by doing so they do not serve the interests of the ordinary people. An analysis from within and from below shows the African power of positive thinking. According to most Africans, all evils have a personal cause. Therefore they can be changed! There is little place for fatalism or despair in the African paradigm of the Good Life. Africans always look for a solution to their problems, regardless of the cost. I experienced Africans as extremely proud people, proud of their language, proud of their history, proud of their culture. So we need to move beyond "Afro-pessimism".

Epilogue

Speaking from a cultural perspective the big question is of course to what extent are local cultures determined by the 'laws' of neo-liberalism. Have national governments anything to say? Is the world economy ruled by the powers of the free market? Or does economy follow culture? Studies of 'McDonaldization' show that attempts to manipulate consumers only succeed if they leave room for cultural identity.[36] And the symbol of McDonalds does not refer to a world-

---

[33] In Sukumaland, for example, the multi-racial district council introduced by the British administration was effectively resisted. It became a symbol for the nationalist struggle everywhere in Tanzania. See G.Maguire, *Toward "Uhuru" in Tanzania*. Cambridge, 1969, pp. 196-234.

[34] The post-colonial government in Tanzania was much more oppressive than the British colonial administration was, for example by enforcing villagization or cotton growing upon the people. Here again these programs were effectively resisted by indigenous people. See G. Hyden, *op.cit.*; Id., *No Shortcuts to Progress*. London, 1983.

[35] See A. Ngindu Mushete, *Les thèmes majeurs de la théologie Africaine*. Paris, 1989, pp. 97; 102-105; and L. Magesa, "Overview of 100 years of Catholicism in Kenya," in: *African Ecclesial Review* 32(1990), pp. 42-50.

[36] See M. Waters, "McDonaldization and the Global culture of Consumption," in *Sociale Wetenschappen* 39(1996)4. 17-30.

wide homogenous culture, but to a world of difference. In Europe, 'McDonalds' stands for 'junkfood'; in Indonesia it symbolises the lifestyle of the rising middle classes.[37]

My conclusions are that we may not ignore the deep-rooted complexity and ambiguity of globalization and that the fatal impact theory needs to be completed by a multi-perspective approach. Many studies view colonization and globalization from the perspective of the development of a world-system and analyse this development in purely economic terms. This macro-economic perspective needs to be completed by an approach that pays attention to local power relations and to cultural factors that facilitate or reject globalization. Colonization and globalization need to be studied within the framework of the interrelationship between global and local processes of change, and of the interrelationship between economic and cultural factors that determine these processes.

In this contribution I have spoken not only about my observations and reflections as an European in my own culture, but also about my observations and reflections in Africa and Asia. Is it not arrogant to do so? Is it legitimate for an European to speak about African and Asian realities? It is my conviction that we are so much part of our own culture that it is difficult to take a distance from it. Outsiders to a culture often see it in a fresh and distinctive way.[38] In this sense there is an ongoing need of intercultural communication and international consultations like the one we are participating in here.[39]

---

[37] Also S. Huntington, op.cit. holds that economy follows culture, not the other way round. I do not follow this author in everything. Especially his fear of Islam reaches a xenophobic level. Yet he makes some interesting points which are worthwhile considering further.

[38] This was a conclusion from the project "Mission in The Netherlands" in which colleagues from Third World countries were asked to analyse our Dutch society. Their insights and reflections was an eye-opener to many missiologists in The Netherlands, including myself, Our guests really observed things which we did not see anymore.

[39] One of the challenges for the church is that it is itself an agent and product of globalization, being the largest 'multi-national' in the world. It can bring people of different cultures together as we experienced in this consultation. In this way the world-wide church can counter-balance the negative consequences of globalization, while promoting the positive sides of this process.

Globalization and Counter-Culture: Liberation Movements in Asia

Michael Amaladoss, S.J.

Though it may have taken new economic and commercial forms in a politically post-colonial situation, globalization is not a new phenomenon. Its cultural message has remained constant, though it is projected with more vigour and perhaps with wider impact through the modern media. People in Asia have not been its helpless or passive victims as the history of its various liberation movements show. Even the movements for political liberation had their economic dimensions. People like Mahatma Gandhi in India, Bhikku Buddhadasa in Thailand, Ali Shariati in Iran stand out, among many others, for their holistic approach to liberation. They have been particularly critical of the immanentist materialism and secularism and egoistic individualism and consumerism of the scientific-industrial-economic-commercial complex that has been trying to impose itself globally. As early as 1908, much before he took over the leadership of the political liberation movement in India, Gandhi wrote *Hind Swaraj*, which not only affirmed nationalism against all forms of foreign domination but also criticized the materialistic industrial civilization of the West, contrasting it with the spirituality and simple living of the Indian tradition. The contemporary feminist and ecological movements in Asia continue such counter-cultural approaches. Given the constraints of time, I will have to limit myself to a few general remarks.[1]

Asia is a continent nourished by many great religions. This world and life in it have never been given an ultimate value by any

---

[1] For a more detailed account and a detailed bibliography one may consult my *Life in Freedom. Liberation Theologies from Asia.* (Anand, Gujarat Sahitya Prakash, 1997)

of these religions. Secularism, as the absolute autonomy of the 'secular' over the 'sacred', has never had much of an impact in Asia. Buddhism relativizes the reality of the life-world as we experience it in the context of Nirvana. Hinduism searches for an experience of the Absolute beyond name and form. Islam affirms the absolute sovereignty of God who is Lord over all. The ideology of secularism has not been attractive to the majority of Asians. This does not mean that Asians are not interested in physical and material well being. The economies of Asia, though in temporary difficulties just now, bear sufficient witness to that. But they refuse to absolutize it and make it the sole goal of their lives. They keep alive a spirit of transcendence as providing a dimension of ultimate meaning to their lives and efforts. Many visitors to Asia are surprised by the cheerfulness and hospitality of the poor. I think that the secret is the refusal to idolize the secular and the attachment to transcendent humanist and spiritual values, which relativizes even their poverty. Even the poor have their dignity.

Asia is also a continent of great and rich cultures that have built up the identity of their peoples over many thousands of years. Asians are proud of their cultural roots. This identity may not necessarily take the form of nationalism. National boundaries are often artificial colonial consequences. People may identify themselves in ethnic/linguistic/cultural terms. This identity is supported by a historical tradition and solidarity. I do not think that a superficial global culture is any threat to this tradition. This does not mean that Asian cultural tradition will remain unaffected by the impact of science and technology. But it will integrate this impact in its own way rather than simply imitate foreign models. Sociologists analyzing the phenomena of modernization and social change point to a distinction between categorical and instrumental values. In Asia, while the instrumental values do change, the categorical values seem to hold fast. Apart from exceptions that prove the rule, we do not see reasons to doubt this either in Asia or among Asians living in the West. Social and religious reformers in Asia will also point out to the need of changing some of the traditional categorical values, as, for instance, those that are oppressive of women and of other subaltern groups. But it is not the modern global culture that is going to bring about this transformation. It rather brings additional forms of oppression and discrimination. What is needed is a renewal from within the cultural tradition. Some movements, branded fundamentalist, may have counter-cultural elements that are not appreciated. The liberation movement in Iran, for example, was a reaction against the secularizing modernity imposed by the Shah, as a stooge of American economic and political interests. The Western media are not always the best guides in interpreting cultural movements in Asia. In India, for instance, there is some rethinking regarding a secularism that ignores religion.

Modern leaders have affirmed the basic humanism of Asian religions. Both Hinduism and Buddhism affirm the humans as the masters of their destiny. In the midst of a karmic cycle of births the humans are invited to liberate themselves, with or without the help of the divine, though a radical distinction between the human and the divine may be problematic in Asia. Gandhi defined the goal of life as the pursuit of Truth - *Satyagraha*. Gandhi's main complaint about modern industrial culture is its tendency to make the humans slaves of the machine. Today one can also become the slave to market forces. Gandhi was not opposed to industrial progress. But he wanted the humans to be masters of the machine and of the market forces. As a matter of fact, the autonomy of the technological and economic machine is a carefully cultivated myth. The "free market" is not really free. It is controlled politically, with the support of military might when necessary, by the richer nations, helped by such 'international' organizations like the International Monetary Fund, the World Bank and the World Trade Organization.

The modern market survives on the promotion of consumeristic needs and desires. The Asian religions and cultures have always encouraged 'being' rather than 'having'. The control of needs and desires is the first step in human search for fulfillment. The goal sought after is the quality of life rather than the quantity of things that one might accumulate. In spiritual and liberative practice this control of needs and desires takes the form of an ideal of *being poor* in order to liberate the poor from their poverty.

Asian traditions see egoism as the source of all evil. Modern individualism and competition is nothing but a manifestation of egoism. Various traditions propose various ways of opposing egoism. Buddhadasa speaks of reality as a network of beings that are interdependent. To get rid of the ego is to become aware of one's dependence on others. Such an egoless attitude gives rise to an ethic of sharing and mutuality which Buddhadasa develops as *dhammic socialism*. One must produce not only for oneself. One must produce enough to be able to share with others. Nirvana itself is interpreted as inter-being opposed to egoism. Gandhi is critical of private property and speaks rather of trusteeship. The world's goods are for the whole of humanity and are to be shared. We do not own what we have; we are only trustees who hold them for the benefit of all. The Islamic tradition too sees the world as a gift of God to all peoples, who are not masters but only vice-gerants of the world's goods. The Confucian tradition sees the human community as a network of relationships of various kinds.

It is in this context of community that Asian traditions speak of duties rather than of rights. Rights protect the individual from an authoritarian State. But in a community reciprocity is not understood in terms of rights that one demands, but in terms of gifts that one can expect from others who have a duty to offer them. Sometimes the collectivity may be over-emphasized to the detriment of the individual. But competitive individualism is no solution. It is discriminative and divisive.

This sense of community also provides the ideal context for the protection, promotion and equitable sharing of the earth's resources that is the concern of ecological movements that protest against the unjust exploitation and destruction of the earth by the few to the detriment of the many. In Asia ecology is closely linked to feminism as the defence of the producers of life in its various forms. Women are in the forefront of the defence of nature, of seas, forests and water resources, not merely as fruits for enjoyment, but as sources of life. Feminism in Asia also focuses on basic issues of life and production of life which make women proud of their identity and role in society.

Following Gandhi there is also a tradition of active non-violence that offers an alternative to the growing militarization represented by the forces of globalization. Asian theologians have recently highlighted the fact that harmony is a basic value promoted by all Asian religions and can serve as the horizon in which the Asian religions can engage in liberative dialogue.

All across Asia, subaltern groups like minority ethnic groups in many countries, the Dalits in India and the women everywhere are becoming aware of their oppression and their quest for identity and freedom. These groups within Asia as well as Asians in general in the global market place may be having an uphill task in the face of dominant social and economic forces. But they cannot be characterized as victims. Till last year East Asia was supposed to become a third economic pole in the world, side by side the USA and Europe. The East Asian economies are going through a bad phase at the moment. But when the hard lessons have been learnt, Asia will stand up. It may be economically weak. But the Asians believe that economics and politics are not every thing. The power of the human spirit, both in quality and numbers, is to their advantage. Recent history may have been unfair to it. But it may be a passing phase in our millennial march towards wholeness in harmony seen variously as *purnam* (fullness), *nirvana* (inter-being), *tao* (way), *umma* (community) *or the Kingdom of God*. We need not equate these. But they serve as a horizon for our common march.

Many decades ago, Gandhi spoke of the responsibility of Asia, as the cradle of all the world's great religions including Christianity, for humanizing and spiritualizing the world. That mission may be grandiose, though necessary. But we shall not be passive victims of globalization of whatever kind.

Globalization and Culture: A View from Oceania

Mikaele N. Paunga, S.M.

Preamble

I have been asked to reflect on the cultural underpinnings of globalization from the point of view of Oceania. It must be clearly stated from the start that New Zealand and Australia, though they are part of Oceania, are completely different from the rest of the Island nations. It is important therefore, to clearly distinguish between them and countries covered by the Episcopal Conferences of the Pacific (CEPAC) and by the Episcopal Conference of Papua New Guinea and Solomon Islands. In spite of that, it is interesting to note that the recent LINEAMENTA for the Synod of Bishops, special Assembly for Oceania, has lumped them altogether.

According to Dr. Michael E. Costigan: "Australia and New Zealand are "First World" countries, where the colonial settlers who began to arrive 200 years ago soon outnumbered (and unjustly exploited) the indigenous inhabitants, while the Church was established on a European or Irish model".[1] In the case of Australia, it was almost a genocidal attempt to wipe out an entire people, the Aborignials.

For the Maori, the native people of New Zealand, the treaty of Waitangi, signed in 1840 by a majority of chiefs, ceded sovereignty

---

[1] Cf. MICHAEL E. COSTIGAN, Ethics and Economics in the Teaching of the Bishops of Oceania", a paper delivered at an International Conference on *Ethics, Economics and Development: Episcopal Teaching from Five Continents*. This was organised by the Institute International Jacques Maritain and the Moral Theology Institute of the University of Friboug, Switzerland, April 1-3, 1993. Costigan is the Executive Secretary, Bishops' Committee for Justice, Development and Peace, Australia.

to Queen Victoria in the presence of representatives of three missions: the Anglicans of the CMS, the Wesleyans and the Roman Catholics. This was the official take over of the land by the white people. It is reported that one of the Maori chiefs, who refused to condone that European act told the other chiefs: "Do not sign the paper.... If you do you will be reduced to the condition of slaves and be compelled to break stones on the roads. Your land will be taken from you and your dignity as chiefs will be destroyed."[2] Indeed, that Maori chief was a prophet.

This article is an attempt to uncover the cultural underpinning of this phenomenon. It will consider the question from three angles: its characteristics and aim, its cultural underpinning with specific references to Pacific societies, and finally, its devastating consequences on the Pacific peoples and their cultures.

Characteristics and Aim of Globalisation

Haraka Gaudi, in a Pacific Consultation on the same topic stated that globalisation refers to: "the forces that make the Pacific region part and parcel of the world global community economically, politically, socially, culturally and spiritually".[3] Its first ideological orientation is capitalism. Individualism is promoted as it champions self-reliance and self-sufficiency, where one becomes a master of one's own destiny. The rights of the individual are seen as more important than anything else. Everything sinks or swims alone.[4]

Michael Amaladoss describes this modern culture in terms of: a materialistic outlook on life and reality: a spirit of individualism and competition; an approach of autonomy in the name of science from the ethical and the religious; an attitude of consumerism; a profit-oriented commercial activity; an ideal of unity as uniformity

---

[2] See JOHN GARRET, *To Live Among the Stars*, WCC Publications Geneva: 1982, pp. 65-66
[3] Cf. HARAKA GAUDI, "One Gospel: Globalisation and Pacific Regional Theology", in *The Pacific Journal of Theology*, Series II, Issue 17, 1997, p. 54. He is currently Head of Department of Anthropology and Sociology in the University of PNG. He has assisted the Pacific Conference of Churches in a Consultation on "Church and Tourism", and a research project on "Militarisation, Economic Penetration and Human Rights in the Pacific".
[4] *Ibid.*, p.55

and intolerance of pluralism; life is mechanised; and finally, there is no sense of the common good and people are expendable.[5]

Felix Wilfred sees globalisation as a mechanistic economic process happening out there to which all nations and all people's have to conform. A mechanism whereby all must fall in line, and thus, there is no choice. Its hub is liberal capitalist economy.[6] According to him, its most insidious aspect is its claim to inevitability and absoluteness. Its aim is to serve profit, the market and consumerism. It is an instrument of gain and profit, thus, divorced from its humanistic objectives.[7] Its ultimate concern is FREE MARKET and not FREE PEOPLE. It is a system where economy grows without the poor. Technology has become its handmaid. Furthermore, it exploits nature and its resources for the purpose of quick profit. In this sense, technology is used to destroy the life support system of nature on which the poor depend very much. It is thus an instrument of slavery rather than freedom.[8] There is hardly an iota of solidarity in it for suffering humans. What reigns supreme is the worst brand of individualism and self-seeking which wants to exclude the weaker ones. Globalisation as it takes place today leads to amnesia-forgetfulness-of the local: "The local is called upon to be sacrificed on the altar of the global".[9] Finally, economy, technology, capital and market all constitute the linchpin of globalisation.

Writing on the effects of the global economy market model on charitable organisation, David de Carvalho states: "there is no place for solidarity in the market model... the relationship is reduced to the status of a commercial transaction between a supplier and a consumer. *Transacting* is the primary mode of the market model... [It] focuses only on individuals, not on broad social groups or the causes of disadvantage. It not only works against the development of community identity, but also undermines the political strength

---

[5] Cf. Michael Amaladoss, S.J., "Globalisation from the Perspective of the Victim of History: A Project for the Seminar", May 12, 1997, p.1.
[6] See FELIX WILFRED, "No Salvation Outside Globalisation?", in FABC OHD Info. Vol. 23, Nos. 3-4, March - April, 1997, p. 2.
[7] *Ibid.*, p.4
[8] *Ibid.*, pp. 4-5.
[9] *Ibid.*, p.5

that community identity can generate for the purpose of structural and institutional change."[10]

Thompson sees this modern culture as: "the universalisation of the cultural values of the middle-class".[11] It is a process that he calls the *enbourgeoisierung* of Europe. It is an autonomous culture which grew out of The Enlightenment. It was based on faith in a trinity of powers - radical individualism, *laissez faire* economics, and science and technology to solve the problems of mankind and to build a new Utopia. It endorses the life-style and values of the middle classes. Education above all else is the passport to economic prosperity and self-sufficiency. It believes in the combination of "white-hot technology, education for autonomy and state capitalism as the panacea for economic and social ills." Hopes and aspirations of people in this process appear to be most fundamentally determined by a liberal humanist vision of humanity.[12] The emphasis of this vision is on radical individualism, personal autonomy and 'privatised' morality; a prevailing economic 'liberalism' which is the basis of 'economic rationalism'; the uncritical faith in 'enterprise capitalism' and the ideal of economic self-sufficiency; a divorce of business, law, science, medicine and politics from ethics; the decline of faith in the common, or, use of our common wealth for the commonweal; faith in science, medicine and technology to provide a technological fix for everything; the individualistic pattern of religious faith and pietistic devotion; and finally, the increasing secularisation of the society despite nominal belief in God.[13]

---

[10] Cf. DAVID DE CAVALHO, "To Market, to Market... The Changing face of Church Charitable Organsations", in *The Australasian Catholic Record*, Vol. LXXIV, July 1997, No. 3, p. 274. He is the Deputy Director, Australian Catholic Social Welfare Commission. He cautioned that the "Church and community-based welfare agencies are now being remodelled into little more than competitive players in a welfare industry. This 'marketisation' while it has made community agencies more efficient, has provided a serious threat to their unique role in society. They were never created to be profit-generating business ventures though business-like professionalism has its place within them", see, p. 275.

[11] Cf. IAN THOMPSON, "Opening up Discussion on the Theology of Culture", in *The Australasian Catholic Record*, Vol. LXXIV, July 1997, No. 1, p. 9.

[12] *Ibid.*, p.10

[13] *Ibid*. In Australia, he thinks that there appear to be powerful forces favouring the development of that middle-class monoculture everywhere.

PART 2 : GLOBALIZATION: ITS CULTURAL BASES   141

Along the same line, William Greider asserts that the principles of global capital economy are transparent and pure: "maximising the return on capital without regard to national identity or political and social consequences. Global finance collectively acts as the disinterested enforcer of these imperatives, like a Committee of Public Safety presiding over the Terror".[14] Moreover, global economy is underpinned by technology, unlimited geography and politics. The new technology has the capacity to amplify human intellect rather than muscle. In those terms, the new technology "is more individualistic and anti-egalitarian: it restores a premium for the higher technical skills held by the best-educated people."[15] Its most important breakthrough is the decontrol of capital movement itself. In the 1980's when Germany, France and Japan abandoned financial controls and open their financial system to foreigners, the process was largely complete: "capital is free to cross and recross the major borders".[16] Global capitalism degrades law. It also undermines legal protection for workers in some advanced economies. Concern for human rights, including freedom of assembly for workers wishing to speak for themselves, has been pushed aside by commercial opportunity.[17]

It appears from the above views that globalisation as an economic process is concerned mainly with optimum profit at the expense of everything else: human beings, cultural, political and social values. Therefore, there is a need to challenge: "the laissez-faire presumptions of the global system, pretensions of free trade that are largely fraudulent in any case".[18] But in spite of its negative

---

[14] See WILLIAM GREIDER, *One World Ready or Not: The Manic Logic of Global Capitalism*, Allen Lane, The Penguin Press, London: 1997, p. 24. Interestingly, he further notes that: "financial investors monitor and punish corporations or whole industrial sectors if their returns weaken. Finance disciplines governments or even entire regions of the globe if those places appear to be creating impediments to profitable enterprise or unpleasant surprises for capital. If this sounds doctrinal, the global financiers also adhere to their own rough version of egalitarian values: they will turn on anyone, even their own home country's industry and goverment, if the defence of free capital seems to require it". *Ibid.*
[15] *Ibid.*, p.28
[16] *Ibid.*, p.33
[17] *Ibid.*, p.37
[18] *Ibid.*, p. 471.

consequences on human life and nature, who is responsible for its existence? Why is it allowed to continue? First, its cultural underpinning must be understood inside out.

The Cultural Underpinning of Globalisation

It was necessary to present some of the salient features of globalisation first, because it helps to highlight some of its cultural underpinning which will now be examined.

From the context of India, Felix Wilfred tells us that globalisation has generated a kind of global sub-culture whose representatives in India are the 'yuppies'. Their basic attitude to life is shot through with a crass pragmatism centred on money, consumer goods, career, etc. He noted that in the institutes of higher education the one-time political and social ideals are replaced by pragmatic considerations of competing for avenues with prospects for money-making and career advancement.[19] It would seem that its cultural underpinning with regards to India lies in the upper and middle classes. Transactional connections, new instruments, goods and services go to reenforce their attitude of superiority vis-a-vis the poor classes and castes. Unfortunately, this ugly individualism is soaked in and nourished by the caste system. "Social ideals and idealism are being replaced by the philosophy of comfort, money, careerism and so on."[20]

In Oceania, there are two factors that appear to indicate a repetition of the same pattern. Firstly, it has occurred because most of the social structures are highly stratified, especially that of the Polynesian societies. And secondly, because of their oppressive dimensions.

In Tonga itself, already back in 1985, Bishop Patelisio Finau had noted the existence of this trend as it is clearly demonstrated in this text:

> Are our leaders and economic planners aware of the large number of families in Tonga?... In Tonga today at the top of our values is money. And this comes from our leaders. The welfare of the

---
[19]FELIX WILFRED, p. 5.
[20]*Ibid.*, p.5.

people and the Christian faith are well down on the list. If we look at the wages paid to workers in Tonga it is obvious that we have lost the fraternal spirit, the dedicated people, the giving of ourselves for others. Our values flounder on the big wages and the various ways of becoming rich. The disease is infectious. The scripture is right.. 'The love of money is the root of all evil' (1 Tim 6:10). We have many examples of this and economic planning which makes one's heart throb for many families of Tonga in the future, since they are already poor. The plan runs according to the wishes of the wide wild world. But it is Tonga in which we live, Tonga boasts of its soul, and rejoices in its love, its feeling for each other, its brotherhood, its concern for people, and its christian beliefs.[21]

This bold statement contains themes which epitomises the notion of globalisation in its cultural underpinnings, its sub-culture and its devastating consequences on the local people. Although this text is about Tonga, one can generally conclude that it is basically true for the rest of the South Pacific nations.

The first theme calls attention to the leaders and economic planners of Tonga. Finau has noted a dramatic change in the value system of the people due to the importance given to riches. Consequently, money has become the most important value. He thinks that the leaders are responsible for this. The relationship between the government and the people of Tonga is, "... money-oriented. Money or the economy is the important thing. The personal touch has largely gone."[22] He further observed that Tonga was becoming known as a nation where favouritism in public affairs has become a tradition. Some of the leaders are easily bought with money.[23] Since 1986, due to some revelations of financial mismanagement that were leaked to the public, most parliamentarians have been accused of misusing their power, a fact that greatly shocked the people of Tonga. In 1990 both the Honourable Ministers of Finance

---

[21]PATELISIO FINAU, "The Family in Tonga Today", in the Diocesan Newspaer, *Taumu'a Lelei*, October 1985, p. 2; see also DAVID MULLINS, (ed), *He Spoke the Truth in Love*, Catholic Publications Centre, Auckland: 1994, pp. 35-36. This book publishes a selection of the late bishop Patelisio Finau's writings.
[22]See PATELISIO FINAU, "

and of Police have been asked to be accountable for their involvement in secret selling of passports, with big finance involved.

The recent introduction of squash growing in Tonga to supply the Japanese market, has given great hope to everyone, especially the poor farmers. The government and the bank of Tonga gave loans in order to help growers. This wonderful opportunity was crushed by some selfish nobles, one of the Kings's sons and some middle class business men. The latter belong to the elite class and they are also the most successful business people in the country. Shamefully, they procured enormous profits through misappropriation of money that belonged to the farmers. Several of the growers never received or were given only a portion of their money. Sadly, today, many of them are still trying to pay their loans.

These local examples have already indicated the type of people and the system underpinning globalisation in Tonga. They are the nobles, some of the political leaders, the economic planners and the rich and educated business people; in other words, the elite of society. They are those who mostly benefit from the global market economy. Thus, they withhold the economic plans that run according to the big world. It serves only to further consolidate their wealth, their superiority and domination over the rest of the people. Moreover, they do not tolerate any change in the present structure, and they resist any attempt at a more democratic type of government. One such case took place in 1992. A convention on the Tongan Constitution and Democracy was organised by distinguished concerned leaders. The King, the nobles and the government were invited to participate. However, they not only refused to take part, but the Minister of police also banned overseas participants.[24] In Tonga then, it seems obvious that the principal defender of globalisation is the established system and the rich entrepreneurs. That conclusion is supported by this statement of Bishop Finau: "Is the life in Tonga today still manipulated for the benefits of the nobles, the educated and the well offs? And, of course, they them-

---

[23]PATELISIO FINAU, "God and Tonga Are My Inheritance - Curse or Blessing?" in the *Taumu'a Lelei*, September 1993, p. 2; see also DAVID MULLINS: p. 73.
[24]PATELISIO FINAU, "King and Government Badly dvised", in the *Taumu'a Lelei*, November 1992, p.2.

selves are the leaders making the rules. Despite having many years of education, too many of our people are still weak and poor. Still too many are refugees in their own land. The social structure of the land robs them of their dignity as adults and mature men and women".[25]

In Melanesia, the best example of how globalisation has exploited the rich minerals and raw materials of a country and torn its people apart, is the Bougainville crisis, which is now into its eighth year.[26] The authority over the rich Bougainville Copper Mine Limited (BCL), as it came to be called from 1972-1989, an evolution from Conzinc Rio-Tinto Australia Exploration (CRAE), rested with the Australian Government in Canberra, most notably the Minister for Territories. During its seventeen years of operation, i.e., from April 1972 until the end of May 1989, when hostile actions by some local residents forced it to shut down, the mine produced and shipped to overseas buyers (mainly Japan and Germany) nearly three million tonnes of copper, 304, 412 kilograms of gold, and 780,875 kilograms of silver, for a net sales revenue of about 1900 million kina. Up to 1988, a total of about K851 million had been payed to the PNG government, K75 million to the North Solomon Province, and K22 million to the land owners.27

The direct, large-scale and more or less detrimental effects that mining has had on the people of Bougainvillea range from: relocations of households, removing them from houses and style of life in an urban community; change of diet from rich local food to canned fish rations; continuous round the clock mining noises which have proved to be a painful change from the quietness of village life; inconvenience caused by blasting; deforestation, subsequent flooding, dumping of waste, noise and dust; destruction and loss of water supplies; loss of garden land and disturbances of sacred burial grounds. Finally, the physical and psychological hardships which cannot be expressed in figures.[28]

---
[25]PATELISIO FINAU, "Why Do People Leave Tonga?", in the *Taumu'a Lelei*, September 1984, p. 2; see also DAVID MULLINS, p. 168.
[26]For more details on the history of the mine and the crises, cf. DOUGLAS OLIVER, *Black Islanders: A Personal Perspective of Bougainville 1937-1991*, Hyland House, Melbourne: 1991.
[27]*Ibid.*, p. 121
[28]*Ibid.*, pp. 137-8

The cultural underpinning of this venture is the Company itself, the Australian Government in collaboration with the Government of PNG. All of them benefited from this operation, while the local people were being appallingly treated. That fact is clearly demonstrated in this most powerful letter:

> The fundamental truth is that BCL has colonised our people, it has taken their land, it has reduced them to passive dependence... The BCL mine has forever changed the perceptions, the hopes and fears of the people of Bougainvillea. You are the invaders. You have invaded the soil and the places of our ancestors, but above all, your mind has invaded our minds... You have been determined to take our earth and send it to Europe and Japan as quickly as possible, that you have created an operation on a scale which makes it overwhelming. Because of that massive scale you pour fifty million tons of our earth into the Jaba River every year. Because of that massive scale, you have made such massive profits that our economy has been reduced to colonial dependence.. Not only does BCL have almost nothing to offer that is relevant to assisting the self-reliance and dignity of our people, it actually saps the confidence, reducing our people to dependent wage slaves, cogs in a wheel... The modern corporation does not obey the natural rise and fall of life and death, as does our Melanesian tradition, which distributes a leader's wealth when he dies. The modern corporation obeys the ideology of the cancer cell, to ever grow and grow, without ceasing".[29]

From these two examples, it seems obvious that the cultural underpinning of globalisation in Oceania is no doubt in the hands of the local government in co-operation with the multi-national companies.[30] Perhaps it can be added that the classification of the world into economic categories such as : advanced and less advanced, developed and underdeveloped, independent and dependent

---

[29]FR. JOHN MOMIS, "Letter to Paul Quodling, the managing director of BCL", May 4, 1987, see Douglass Oliver, pp. 196-7.

[30]The territories of New Caledonia, Wallis et Futuna and Tahiti, are still very much within the control of France. The Northern Pacific Islands and territories, especially in Micronesia, are still largely influenced by North America, the initiator and proclaimer of this super global machine.

by the IMF, the UN and the World Bank, have perpetuated this situation. In their evaluation, the Third World countries including those of the Pacific Island regions are still considered underdeveloped. PNG for instance, in 1994 was : "branded by the World Bank as a Mineral rich Poor Country".[31] Thus, the Pacific Island countries are referred to as politically independent but economically dependent. This dependency theory could well be a deceptive mantle that acts as a supportive vehicle for the continual exploitation of the powerless nations by the powerful ones.

The Devastating Consequences of Globalisation on the Pacific Peoples and their Cultures.

So far, the meaning of globalisation and some of its cultural underpinnings has been presented. A close look at some of its destructive aftermaths on the Pacific peoples, may also assist the effort to understand its roots.

The earlier text from Bishop Patelisio Finau has already highlighted how this phenomenon has drastically altered some of the most basic values of the Tongan people. Speaking on how the global market has affected the Tongan family and moral values, he added: "The former protection given us by our families and extended families, given by the close village life, by Tongan society at large and the Church are weakening all the time. We are now more and more called to stand on our own two feet..." [32] Moreover, changes are inevitable. There is the ready availability of liquor everywhere. There is an increasing number of video tape shops, a growing number of videos in the homes and a wide range of violent and pornographic films available. [33] Sadly, money has become the most important value in Tonga today as people have become more and more greedy. The dignity of people and the Christian faith are secondary.[34] Closely related to this is the tourism industry, which is

---
[31] HARAKA GAUDAI, p. 61.
[32] DAVID MULLINS, p. 34.
[33] Moreover, he added, Tonga is: "controlled by videos, self-indulgence and materialism. The cheap things have become important in our lives; what was considered evil yesterday, is today okay. The change has hit us too quickly and it is too much for many of our families", *ibid*, p. 36.
[34] He further noted that: "We are seeing some people doing well in the modern social system imposed on Pacific people but so many are like sheep without a shepherd", *ibid*., pp. 20-21.

a "mixed blessing". While it brings benefits financially, unfortunately, it also encourages prostitution and greater risks of AIDS. Eventually, it hastens the breaking down of moral forces because it fosters moral promiscuity: free market economy, free travel, free and beautiful islands and free sex, but not free people.

The letter of Fr. John Momis quoted above illustrates vividly the destructive dimensions of mining, carried out in the name of economic progress, supported by the national government. Today, similar exploitations are carried out in many parts of PNG. In these unfortunate circumstances, the lamentations of Haraka Gaudi strike home: "What will happen to the big holes they dig in mining sites, the rivers they pollute and erosion caused by mass felling of our trees? Who will represent our vulnerable, uneducated, powerless land owners and fight for their rightful share in these economic ventures or stop developers destroying the environment when politicians argue that, "... we need the dollars to develop the country so don't stop progress?"[35]

There is a continual exploitation of the pacific natural resources both renewable and non-renewable.[36] Foreign resource developers see the land and other natural resources as commodities with money value attached to them. Their interests is to exploit the resources in the shortest possible time and to move on leaving nothing behind. To the Pacific peoples, the land, sea, the air, the birds and flowers all represent the universe and their heritage. Native people (PNG, Aboriginals of Australia, Maori of New Zealand) refer to 'Mother earth' as a provider. People are temporary tenants and stewards who live off what she provides. Whatever remains is for future generations.[37] In both Fiji and in PNG for instance, there is an unscrupulous exploitation of timber by Asian Companies operating in the region. A recent report from Japan on its logging activities remarked that "One of the main causes of destruction of tropical rain forests is Japan's appetite for South Sea logs. Fifty

---

[35] HARAKA GAUDI, p. 63.
[36] Non-renewable resources such as oil, natural gas, copper, nickel, gold are taken out in their natural form will never be replaced. This is mainly true for PNG, New Caledonia and Fiji.
[37] HARAKA GAUDI, p. 63.

percent of South Sea logs (' logs from tropical rain forests) have been imported to Japan."[38] Japan started logging in the Solomon Islands in 1966, and in Papua New Guinea from the 1970s. At the peak year (1985) the amount imported from the Solomon Islands reached 296,000 m3. In 1990, exports from PNG reached an amount of 1,278,000 m3 annually. Speaking on the devastating effects of logging in PNG, a Japanese forest engineer said: "The beauty of virgin forests in PNG is beyond words. It is extremely delicate and shining... I should say that logging activities in such forests are equivalent to an act of `rape' and clear felling is the equivalent of `genocide' of an eco-system.. When I realised how logging and deforestations was so destructive, I came back to Japan".[39] One of the reports revealed the entire mechanism of this timber industry in PNG. There has been corruption and abuse of privilege among PNG government politicians and officials. They have participated in the unjust activities by foreign companies. Hidden profits due to the systematic cheating of the government and landowners of PNG by foreign companies are easily used for bribing politicians.[40]

There is also the free-lance and uncontrolled harvesting of the sea resources in the Pacific by Japanese and Korean fishing boats. Many fish have been unnecessarily killed by the method of long "drifting nets".

Perhaps the most insidious of all is the loss of traditional human cultural values; the change of the basic communal cultural heritage of Oceania, be it the Wantok system in Melanesia or the Kainga, Ainga or Mataqali in Polynesia. For a knowledge of how the same process has taken place in Micronesia, Bernadita Camacho-Dungca of Chamoru from the Mariana Islands writes: "Once a free spirited people and in control of its own destiny, the Chamorus, however, for the last 400 years, have been politically, economically,

---

[38]See YASUKO SHIMIZU, "The Destruction of Tropical Rain Forests by Logging and Reafforestation", a paper delivered at the Assembly of the Pacific Partnership for Human Development (PPHD) in Saipan, northern Marianas, 1992, p. 1. She reported also that in a recent statistics by FAO, 17 million hectares of rainforests per year have been destroyed.
[39]*Ibid.*, p.4
[40]*Ibid.*, p.5

and socially oppressed by all three of its colonisers - Spanish, Americans, the Japanese and then the Americans again".[41] The Chamorus have been exposed to the outside world by the Spanish, confused by the Americans, brutally mistreated by the Japanese, and now being inhumanly and unjustly handled by the Americans. More over, according to Bernadita, they were made second-class rather than full naturalised citizens of the United States just so the coloniser can take their lands away and limit their rights. People were uprooted from their places and put in villages to make place for the military domain and naval base, thus removing them from the best farming and fishing places. For the Chamorus: "the lack of respect, at least the way they know it, is one of their strongest contentions about the Americans who came and took their land and subjugated them. The Americans have no sense of awe/respect for a peoplehood who because of their generosity allowed them to go almost unchecked".[42]

In Polynesia, the communal dimension of the culture is swiftly replaced by the individualistic philosophy of globalisation. Pacific societies from time immemorial valued sharing, communal living, caring for the sick and elderly, and hospitality to all strangers, or what is normally referred to as 'The Pacific Way'. The custom where my relatives (Kainga) help me to stand tall in any situation of lack in life, has become fragile in the face of capitalism.[43] According to Penisimani Tupouniua, the money impact has accelerated the break-up of the extended family, and changed the relative status of people. The reduced importance of the extended family follows the individualistic approach required by cash economy.[44] The Western mentality of borrowing and paying back at a high interest rate, has created a 'paying back' attitude. This change may have largely contributed to the economic exploitation added on to the traditional PNG "pay back" system of compensation.

---

[41] See BERNADITA CAMACHO-DUNGCA, "The Birth of a Pacific Culture for Human Development and Pacific Solidarity: A Chamoru Perspective", paper presented in the PPHD Assembly 1992, p.3.
[42] *Ibid.*, p.9
[43] That is what is normally called the principle of reciprocity.
[44] PENISIMANI TUPOUNIUA, *A Polynesian Village: the Process of Change*, South Pacific Social Science Association, Suva: 1977, pp. 34-35.

There is a lack of consideration for the environment. The nuclear tests conducted in French Polynesia have affected the livelihood of people and will continue to be life-threatening to them despite the continuous denial from the French government. Since the Churches in Tahiti have remained neutral, some independent groups have been very strong against the French Nuclear tests. The post nuclear period is very much a struggle in Tahiti now, trying to get France to pay for the damage that she has done.[45] On March 25, 1996, the three Western nuclear powers, USA, France and England at last signed the South Pacific Nuclear Free Zone Treaty disdained by them for 11 years. And with the apparently successful detonation of the sixth nuclear bomb in the current series on 25 January, 1996, at Fangataufa, the Government brought to an end 36 years of French testing in which some 180 nuclear devices were exploded in the Pacific region.[46] France conducted its tests with scant regard for the repeated statements of governments, churches and other related agencies, and with no respect for prayers, petitions and protests of the Pacific people.[47]

The United States of America and its nuclear history in the Marshal Islands is another big scandal. Being the administrator of the Island as part of the UN Trust Territory of Micronesia, it saw these scattered atolls as distant and therefore suitable location for nuclear testing. The story of the Island of Bikini is a well known one.[48] The US military conducted 66 nuclear tests on Bikini and

---

[45] See the "Plenary Discussion" following the article of Haraka Gaudi, in *The Pacific Journal of Theology*, Series II, Issue 17, 1997, p.78.

[46] See PCCNEWS, "France Announces an End to Pacific Testing" in *Journal of the Pacific Conference of Churches*, First Quarter, 1996, pp. 11-13.

[47] *Ibid.*, p. 13. With a note of triumphalism in his speech, and in the face of international concern, the President suggested that his resolution had never faltered. His first duty for France had been achieved. Its independence and security were assured by the possession of a lasting, modern and efficient defence system. If the history of the present century is any precedent, such a prediction for the security of France as a soverign state may not be necessarily guaranteed. Is peace, which is based on international and sustained dialogue and trust, truly established by testing a weapon that is the ultimate deterrent to war?

[48] Cf. PETER SALAMONSEN, *To Turn the Tide: Pacific Churches and Climate Change*, Star Printery Limited, Suva: 1995, pp. 21-22. It is reported that the US Military Governor of the Territory went to the Island in 1946 and told the people that the US Government wanted their Island to test a new weapon which was for

Enewetak between 1946 and 1958. On the first of March 1954, the US detonated its largest hydrogen bomb to date of 15 megatons, code-named BRAVO. It was the equivalent of 1, 200 Hiroshima bombs. People of Rongelap could see their footprints in the 2-3 inches of grey-yellow powder that descended from the sky on the Island. The truth of this was admitted only in 1994 with the release of classified information some 40 years after the event. There it became apparent, that not only had the US mislead the people about the extent of the contamination, but that they had deliberately exposed the Marshallese people to radiation as part of a medical experiment to study this unknown phenomenon.[49] There is also the shocking missile story on the Island of Kwajalein.

America also continually tried to persuade some South Pacific governments to allow the dumping of toxic wastes in their territories. Unfortunately, some 'civilised' countries regard the untouched islands as backyard for dumping toxic wastes. The long term prospects, especially, of dumping are alarming. One such enticing business venture had been proposed to Princess Pilolevu of Tonga. Fortunately, the Pacific Conference of Churches (PCC) and delegates to the World Council of Churches (WCC) meeting in Honiara, Solomon Islands successfully intervened. In a telefax addressed to His Majesty, the King of Tonga, the meeting aired the following concerns about the toxic wastes incineration project.

> We believe it a hazard to the environment and the health of the people. No monetary value from this kind of project can compensate for the dangers to the environment and the lives of the people. We, therefore, strongly urge a complete ban on this proposal. We believe people and their health to be more important than any of this kind of development. God's creation must be considered high priority and any effort to endanger the safety of the people's health must be stopped immediately. Our con-

---

the good of all mankind and was designed to end all wars. The chief and his people were shifted to the Island of Kili. Two weeks later after having departed from the shores that their ancestors had lived on since 2000 BC, the US exploded their first nuclear bomb. Some of the small islets that made up the atoll simply disappeared forever. Because the island was so radioactive and contaminated, the US military moved to Enewetak island.

[49] Ibid., p. 22.

cern and prayers are for a Pacific and Tonga free from technological dangers.[50]

This intervention, according to Bishop Finau, "reminds our political leaders and all of us that people must be our first concern. People have to be placed before money and profit".[51]

One of the sad consequences of globalisation is economic aid. The connection with Western cultures has made island nations dependent both in terms of financial resources and human expertise. The consequences are: waiting for white experts to provide support, and a standard of living higher than the local resources. Attached to this is a psychological sense of dependency and powerlessness.

Apart from that, some of the aid given to the islands have not been helpful to the local people. Speaking on social justice issues in the pacific, the late Bishop Patelisio Finau called on the Australian Government to think again about their military aid to pacific nations like Tonga and Papua New Guinea: "Military aid to Tonga gives employment to some of our youth in the armed forces," he said. "But who is Tonga going to war with? It is better that we be given money for boats in which we can harvest the seas, rather than boats in which to patrol them".[52]

These examples indicate that the Pacific region is no longer the romanticised paradise on earth. Today, the Pacific is part of the 'global network' greatly affected by the forces of industrialisation in the northern hemisphere, thus, susceptible to the depletion of the ozone layer and global warming which contributes to the rise of sea level. In a Conference Statement, the Justice, Peace and Development Programme of PCC asked all nations, especially industrialised countries to strengthen their commitments to the reduction of green-

---

[50]Cf. PATELISIO FINAU, "Concern for People and God's Creation", in David Mullins, *op.cit.*, p.62; cf., PATELISIO FINAU, "Becoming involved -- for the Sake of the People", in *POINT*, Series No. 18, Melanesian Institute, Goroka, Papua New Guinea, 1994.

[51]*Ibid.*, p. 64.

[52]Reported by RAY OWEN, "Give us fishing boats not gunboats", in *The Catholic Leader*, Septemebr 29, 1993, p.5. Finau further pointed out that what is needed is: "aid which will help the people at the grassroots, which will meet their real needs through community projects.. And there should be wider consultation with the Tongan people about their needs".

house gas emissions as agreed by the Earth Summit in Rio de Janeiro, 1992. If work is not done to turn back the tide of economic competitiveness and profit motivation, the Pacific could well be confronted with an ocean tide that it cannot turn back. The ocean which has been a source of life to countless generations of Pacific people could so alter the landscapes of island nations that future generations will be powerless victims of our intransigence based purely on a failure to put the concept of environment before the concept of economy in our thinking.[53]

Some hopeful Signs

In spite of all, it is comforting to know that already, there are concerned people in Oceania. A good example of this new consciousness is the recent Pacific consultation on globalisation, reported in the latest *Pacific Journal of Theology*. It is a sign of hope that the Pacific theologians are beginning to seriously consider the centrality of the economy to the livelihood of the Pacific peoples, and hence, its relevancy to theological reflection.

It is also encouraging to note that the **LINEAMENTA** for the Synod of Bishops Special Assembly for Oceania, is aware of international agreements which leave smaller or weaker nations at an economic and political disadvantage.[54] It has called also for responsibility towards creation. For instance, all economic activities such as mining, exploitation for oil, logging, farming, etc., can, if left unchecked, harm, if not destroy, whole parts of the environment.[55]

It is also a great sign of hope that various Episcopal Conferences and individual bishops, plus many Commissions of Justice and Peace, have recently spoken out in defence of the poor against exploitation by the global market economy.[56] The Catholic Bishops

---

[53]See PETER SALAMONSEN, To Turn the Tide: *Pacific Churches and Climate Change*, Report of the Pacific Conference of Churches Ecumenical Regional Consulation, Majuro, Republic of the Marshal Islands, 13-16 November, 1994, p.1.
[54]*Op.cit*, 39-40
[55]*Ibid.*, p. 40.
[56]Cf. A Statement by the CATHOLIC BISHOPS' CONFERENCE OF ENGLAND & WALES, *The Common Good*, Gabriel Communications Ltd., Manchester: 1996. See also, AUSTRALIAN CATHOLIC BISHOPS' CONFERENCE, *Common Wealth for the Common Good: A Pastoral Statement on the Distribution of Wealth in Australia*, Collins Dove, Melbourne: 1992.

of Australia (CBA) are to be commended for their recent effort in this field.[57]

In New Zealand, Cardinal Thomas Williams of Wellington has been a leading figure in calling for solidarity in the Pacific, in order to counter dominant political, social and economic ideology and behaviour patterns that worsen the plight of the poor.[58]

The Pacific Conference of Churches (PCC) has always been more vocal than the bishops of CEPAC regarding social, political and economic issues. Apart from very committed individual bishops such as Bishop Patelisio Finau of Tonga, Bishop Matin Neylon of the Carolines-Marshalls, and Bishop Paul Mea of Tarawa and Nauru, the bishops of CEPAC as a body need to get their act together.[59] Since the real challenge against globalisation is to confront the internationalists of commerce and finance on their own ground and compel them to accept larger social values, international and local corporate effort is needed. A strong national stand in the form of political control over global capital in order to defend work and wages, as well as social protection against assaults by the marketplace is required.

Such concerted effort is absolutely necessary, because as Greider has suggested: "this wondrous machine... is too awesome and self-

---

[57] See ACBC, "Sharing the Country throgh Understanding and Respect", statement issued for the Aboriginal Sunday, 2 September, 1990, in the *Catholic International*, Vol. 2, N.1 (1-15 January 1991), pp. 23-26; Bishop's Secretariat for Justice and Peace, "Bishops Rule on Justice and Peace", ACBC Press Release, 7 May 1987; BISHOP W. BRENNAN, "Bishops Decisions on Justice and Peace Initiatives", in *Justice Trends*, No. 47, June 1987; ACBC Commission for Justice Development and Peace (JDP), *Just Reading* No. 1, "Sharing the Country, the Real Truth about Mabo", Melbourne, 1993; *Just Reading* No. 2, "The Church and East Timor", Melbourne, 1993; *Just Reading* No. 2, "The Church and East Timor", Melbourne Archdiocess, 1993; DON BROWNING, "Re-Building the Nest: Families and the Need for a New Social Agenda," *Just Reading* No.3, Melbourne, 1994; Pastoral Letter of the Australian Catholic Bishop Conference, "Year 2000 will be time for Holiness, Christian Unity and Work of Justice", *L'OSSERVATORE ROMANO*, N.39, 24 September, 1997, p. 9; ACBC Pastoral Statement, "A New Beginning Eradicting Poverty in our World", A Dove Publication, Blackburn, Vic.: 1996.

[58] WILLIMS, THOMAS (Cardinal), *A Call to Solidarity in the Pacific*, ACSJC Occasional Paper No. 4, Sydney, 1991, p.5.

[59] The recent formation of its Commission for Justice, Peace and Development is an important step and a great sign of promise.

confident to yield to mere facts or gentle persuasion. In the history of revolutionary eras, when moderate voices come forward to plead for moderate reforms, they are typically brushed aside. Eventually, more radical solutions arise and advance because the reigning system would not pause to listen to dissenting voices".[60]

Conclusion:

The Scriptures report that when Jesus and the disciples arrived in Jerusalem, he entered the temple and began to drive out those who were selling and those who were buying in it. He overturned the tables of the money changers and the seats of those who sold doves. He would not allow anyone to carry anything through the temple. He was teaching and saying: "It is written, `my house shall be called a house of prayer for all the nations'? But you have made it a den of robbers" [Mk 11:17].

God's temple i.e., God's world, his nature and people created in his own image, have been turned by the global market economy into a "den of robbers". What a wretched situation! Who will rescue us from this man-made death machine?

People of the island nations must cherish their God-given heritage, the beautiful Pacific Way, as they try to come to terms with changes brought about by globalisation. It is a marvellous way, which did not escape the attention of a Marist Missionary Father, forty-three years ago when he said:

> Be faithful to your good Tongan customs and language. Be faithful to God and religion. Be faithful to your traditions. In Tonga you have no silver or gold mines, as some countries have. But you have a far more precious treasure, *fe'ofo'ofa ni*, brotherly love. You have that wonderful family spirit, that willingness to help each other. That is your God-given gold and silver. That is your treasure.. Cherish your God-given heritage. Don't lose it by a silly and servile imitation of the white man and his customs and manners. Remember, each nation has its own customs, its own traditions, its own lan-

---

[60] WILLIAM GREIDER, p. 472.

guage, keep yours, love them. They are part of God's plan for our happiness."[61]

BIBLIOGRAPHY

1. Episcopal Conferences:

AUSTRALIAN CATHOLIC BISHOPS' CONFERENCE, Common Wealth for the Common Good: *A Pastoral Statement on the Distribution of Wealth in Australia*, MekviyrbeL Collins Dove, 1992.

CATHOLIC BISHOPS' CONFERENCE OF ENGLAND AND WALES, *The Common Good*, Manchester: Gabriel Communications Ltd., 1996.

SYNOD OF BISHOPS SPECIAL ASSEMBLY FOR OCEANIA, *LINEAMENTA*: *Jesus Christ and The Peoples of Oceania : Walking His Way, Telling His Truth, Living His Life*, Vatican City: Libreria Editrice Vaticana, 1997.

2. Other References:

PCCNEWS, *Journal of the Pacific Conference of Churches*, First Quarter 1996, pp. 10-13.

AMALADOSS, MICHAEL, "Globalisation from the Perspective of the Victim of History: A Project for the Seminar", May 12, 1997.

CAMACHO-DUNGCA, "The Birth of a Pacific Culture for Human Development and Pacific Solidarity: A Chamoru Perspective", paper delivered at the PPHD Assembly, July 1992, Majuro, Republic of the Marshall Islands.

COSTIGAN, MICHAEL E. "Ethics and Economics in the Teaching of the Bishops of Oceania", a paper delivered at an International Conference organised by the Instiut International Jacques Maritain and the Moral Theology Institute of the University of Friboug, Switzerland, April 1-3, 1993.

DE CAVALHO, DAVID, "To Market, to Market... The Changing face of Church Charitable Organisations", in *The Australasian Catholic Record*, Vol. LXXIV. July 1997, No. 3, pp. 265-277.

FINAU, PATELISIO, (Bishop), "Why Do People Leave Tonga?", in the Diocesan Newspaper, *Taumu'a Lelei*, September 1984.

_____ "The Family in Tonga Today", *Taumu'a Lelei*, October 1985.

---

[61] EDWARD A. TREMBLAY,S.M. *When You Go to Tonga*, Daughters of St. Paul, 1954, pp. 211-212.

_____ "Concern for People and God's Creation", *Taumu'a Lelei*, July 1988

_____ "Tension Between States and People", *Taumu'a Lelei*, May 1990.

_____ "King and Government Badly Advised", *Taumu'a Lelei*, November 1992

_____ "God and Tonga are my Inheritance - Curse or Blessing?", *Taumu'a Lelei*, September 1993.

_____ "Becoming Involved - for the Sake of the People", in *POINT*, Series No. 18, 1994, pp. 109-113.

GARRETT, JOHN, *To Live Among the Stars*, Geneva: WCC Publications, 1982.

GAUDI, HARAKA, "One Gospel: Globalisation and Pacific Regional Theology", in *The Pacific Journal of Theology*, Series II, Issue 17, 1997, pp. 54-80.

GREIDER, WILLIAM, One World Ready or Not: *The Manic Logic of Global Capitalism*, Allen Lane, London: The Penguin Press, 1997.

MULLINS, DAVID, (ed), He Spoke the Truth in Love: *A Selection of Bishop Patelisio Finau's Writings and Speeches*, Auckland: Catholic Publications Centre, 1994.

OLIVER, DOUGLAS, *Black Islanders: A Personal Perspective of Bougainville 1937-1991*, Melbourne: Hyland House, 1991.

OWEN, RAY, "Give us Fishing Boats not Gunboats", in *The Catholic Leader*, September 29, 1993, p.5.

SALAMONSEN, PETER, *To Turn the Tide: Pacific Churches and Climate Change*, Suva :Star Printery Limited, 1995.

SHIMIZU YASUKO, "The Destruction of Tropical Rain Forests by Logging and Deforestation", paper delivered at the PPHD Assembly, July 1992, Majuro, Republic of the Marshall Islands.

THOMPSON, IAN, "Opening up Discussion on the Theology of Culture", in *The Australasian Catholic Record*, Vol. LXXIV, January 1997, No. 1, pp. 5-14.

TREMBLAY, EDWARD A. *When You Go to Tonga*, Daughters of St. Paul, 1954.

TUPOUNIUA, PENISIMANI, *A Polynesian Village: the process of change*, South Pacific Social Science Association, Suva: 1977.

WILFRED, FELIX, "No Salvation Outside Globalisation?", in *Federation of Asian Bishops' Conferences*, (FABC) OHD Info, Vol. 23, Nos. 3-4, March-April, 1997, p. 2-7.

PART 3 :
The Global and the Local: Theological Perspectives

Theology in the Global and the Local

Diego Irarrazaval

Pilgrimage is a basic symbolic activity, in Hinduism, Islam, Buddhism, Christianity and also in small religious traditions throughout the world. With our hearts and feet we search for a better life, for enlightenment, for joy. In modern times, the rich symbol of pilgrimage shows, among other things, how common people are moving within and beyond globalization[1]. Concerning the global reality, I offer a theological commentary, that seeks dialogue with other points of view.

Christian theology is not a mental-doctrinal activity; rather it is a loving relationship with God that implies celebration, transformation, understanding (an "intellectus amoris", according to J. Sobrino). A modern theological agenda begins with a critique of the signs of the times (in the spirit of *Gaudium et Spes* 4-10). Let us consider globalization in local, ordinary people's "lo cotidiano"[2]; where we lovingly search for human well-being within mother earth. Let us examine faith/hope/love from the underside of history, in communion with all the excluded who cry for life.

My point of view arises from an indigenous community in the Americas: their strong desires and daily struggle for modern progress

---

[1] See S. Coleman, Elsner, J., *Pilgrimage, Past and Present in the World Religins*, Cambridge: Harvard, 1995. In today's world, on the one travel, tourism and other secular activities have some elements of pilgrimage; and on the other hand, religious pilgrimages are " gaining in symbolic significance in some societies" and they "resonate with social processes... in the increasingly globalised, plural societies of the world" (p.213).

[2] Women rediscover "lo cotidiano" as a theological category; it refers to "processes of people's lives", "we as liberation theologians appreciate... how the poor and oppressed see realities in a different way from the way it is seen by the rich and powerful", Ada Maria Isasi-Diaz, "The present-future of EATWOT: a mujerista perspective", *Voices* XIX/1 (1996), 96-97.

(is it for globalization?), their pain and hope, shape my focus on macro-realities. Moreover people's inter-religious features demand a genuinely ecumenical theology. This essay is conditioned by my being among the poor, in ecclesial and professional work, and a masculine and socio-political status. My input is also shaped by a model of inculturation "from below" that is part of a tradition of church reform and refoundation that I assume wholeheartedly.

Hopeless and Hopeful Signs

The leading global factors are a test on christian hope; but these factors are counter balanced by emerging, alternative forms of globalization. Briefly, what are the major theological concerns?

On one part, hegemonic global guidelines are a test of faith in the living God, since modern absolutes (in spite of their secular claim) are really polytheistic. They also confront hope in a future life, since the so called end of history allows for no qualitative transformation of today's world order. Furthermore, they undermine the foundations of love; since two thirds of humanity is condemned to poverty. As they test faith-hope-love, leading forms of globalization are questioned and show themselves as hopeless.

This does not mean that globalization is an evil and demonic reality. The key problem is an inadequate capitalist world economy[3]. It reduces and consumes everything. So, seeing that human fulfillment is not to be expected from global factors, one can join others who build a sustainable, just world order. People acknowledge values in modern sciences and technologies, global communications, politics of participation, democratic consumption of economic production, migration, and other global processes. These are ambivalent and limited goods (these are not Gods!). At the same time, one seeks new paths.

Yes. There are emerging and plural alternatives. Some of them are: day to day resistance to cultural-military confrontations; accep-

---

[3] B. Kearn says it bluntly: capitalist economy "systematically leaves fundamental reality out of account", "natural resources... the social field, the political instiutions and the cultural world are also systematically `consumed'" ("A Colossus with clay feet", *Concilium* 1997/2, pp. 11-12.

tance of differences; destruct towards manicheistic patterns (such as: modernity is good, tradition is bad); plural religious products and meanings; local experiences of the sacred that sustain local theology and church; efficient new social movements (that are not yet linked together); all kinds of small economic initiatives, that underline solidarity instead of private success; wisdoms of the marginalized, for example, a new vision of the global as expressed by Rosa Khuno (teacher of Bolivia): "all for everybody and with everybody"[4], that is, a genuine global reality includes every person and is produced by all.

We may not sacralize each of these alternatives, in them we find weeds and also good wheat. However, they are small and powerful signs of human hope that have a transcendent thrust[5]. Here we are nurtured by the gospel imagery of tiny seeds, of the non-important (non-invited to the kingdom banquet), of unnoticed compassionate behavior, of hunger and thirst for justice, of these and so many other small signs of the unlimited *Basileia* of God. These signs of hope promote an alternative globalization.

Thus, we face, on one side, symbolic forces of destruction that have idolatrous elements, and on another side, symbols of life-for-all due to God's gracious salvation. In other words, globalization is not the object of our theological discourse; nor do we place the global versus the local. Rather, the task is to assess realities full of contradictory symbols. Our major concerns are to uncover masked Gods present in the midst of positive global factors, and to acknowledge life-bearing tiny seeds of universal salvation.

For this task we turn to resources in the Gospel of John. Salvation is seen through ordinary earthly and human realities. Jesus Christ is presented as water, light, vine, bread, door, road, shepherd[6]. We can say that these symbols of salvation are not anthropo-

---

[4] Rosa Khuno, in a dialogue in Corpa, Bolivia, 12/11/97.

[5] Julio Lois comments: today we focus on "small utopias" linked to global alternatives and to the final utopia of new heavens and new earth (J. Lois in *Utopias y esperanza cristiana*, Estella: Verbo Divino, 1997, pp. 240-241).

[6] This is John's language. There is no clear evidence on how Jesus called himself, except "human being" in the galilean expression *bar nasha* Son of man), Other titles: Messiah, Son of God, etc., belong to the post-resurrection community. The church creates thoelogy. The Johannine tradition made powerful symbolic contributions.

PART 3 : THE GLOBAL AND THE LOCAL 163

logo-centric; rather they are concrete-holistic. Moreover, in John's so called book of signs (2:1-12:50), seven ways of explaining Jesus' significance for believers rely on corporal, festive, social imagery.[7] These representations are in opposition to dehumanizing forces, poverty and hunger, sickness and lack of faith in salvation, stealing and injustice. So, today we may discern what is evil and what is life giving throughout "lo cotidiano," people's historical pilgrimage. In reading the "signs of our times", particularly the global and the local in ordinary existence, we find signs of hope and also denials of life. For example, success stories (highlighted in education and in means of communication) show social and racial discrimination and the material as absolute, and the gamut of fundamentalism, where the condemnation of others is sacralised. The other side of reality shows, for example, gender reciprocity, systematic and very democratic healing through natural means, strength of marginalized identities, and so on. Each of these are local/global realities. The local is not holy; nor is the global satanic. We rather look at different signs in each dimension of reality.

Thus, a theology of signs and symbols, in the context of global/local ordinary existence, offers a deep understanding of faith-hope-love. I consider incomplete and unilateral a theology that is mainly analytical (however critical of global evils) and centered on a western *logos*.[8] Theology that pays attention to symbols in today's world, and dialogues with human sciences and philosophies, does allow a radical critique and may name realistic alternatives. Moreover, an

---

[7] Seven events hold concrete signs of the Glory of God, present through Jesus' ministry: John 2:1-11 (marriage feast in Cana, water becomes wine), 4:46-54 (healing of the son of an official), 5:1-15 (the paralitic in Betzaida), 6:1-15 and 6:16-21 (needy multitude is fed, Jesus Walks on water: both events refer to the jewish history of liberation), 9:1-41 (blind person is healed, by Jesus light of the world), 11:1-44 (the resurrection of Lazarus).

[8] A crucial question today is the role of symbols and of concepts in theological discourse. Juan Carlos Scannona favors analogy "that assumes the structure of symbolic mediation... and places it in the speculative field of the philosophical logos" (*Nuevo punto de partida da la filosofia latinoamericana*, Buenos Aires: Guadalupe, 1990, 239). Thus symbol is subordinated to logos. It seems to me that these-symbol, logos-are different and complementary modes of understanding (and relating to) reality. One is not superior to the other.

understanding of symbols in today's global and local processes is like a framework for inculturation. Within and beyond such processes we have the interaction between christian faith and human cultures.

In this World and not of this World

Basic christian communities that are reading the word and being led by the Spirit, constantly ask if today's world can be a good place for all. I listen attentively to their answers. With realistic *sensus fidei* they usually affirm that creation and historical progress are good. At the same time, corruption, forms of violence, unjust social conditions, lack of opportunities for the youth, etc. are seen as opposed to God's plan. Most persons disagree with a "spiritual abstention" from this world. Moreover, a christian is neither optimistic nor pessimistic about globalization. This implies that inculturation does not consecrate each mode of living, but rather transform it.

Concerning these issues, many biblical resources are relevant, and in a special way John's message about the world.[9] In a sense it is positive: God loved the world... all who believe in Christ have eternal life (Jn 3:16; the world is saved, cf. 1:29; 4:42; 6:33; 51, 10:36, 12:47; 17:21). Yet, in the context of Jewish and then gentile disbelief towards Jesus and opposition against the christian community, the "world" is theologically seen as a negative reality. John emphasizes that *kosmos* (not in a cosmic and historical sense) is opposed to Jesus and the community of disciples, it is the realm of sin and Satan.[10] What can be done? The disciples are *in* but not *of*,

---

[9] I draw from R. Brown's *The Gospel according to John 13-21* (New York: Doubleday, 1970, pp.763-765) and *The Community of the Beloved Disciple* (New York: Paulist press, 1979, pp. 63ff). For Latinamerican insights on the "world", according to the New Testament, see essays by Elisa Estevez and Raul Lugo in *Revista de interpretacao biblica Latinoamericana*, 21 (1995) 89-90, 108-120 (Petropolis: Vozes); and Pablo Richard, "Critica teologica a la globalizacion neoliberal", *Pasos*, 71 (1997) 31-34.

[10] Mostly in John (and Paul; but not so in the synoptic gospels) it is a matter of fallen humanity, that is against God. The "world" is incompatible with Jesus, the Spirit, and the disciples (14:17, 16:8-11, 20, 17:14-16, 18:36). It hates Jesus and his followers (7:7, 15:18-21). So, Jesus judges the world, does not pray for it, overcomes it (9:39, 12:31, 16:33, 17:9); it belongs to Satan (12:31, 14:30).

and sent to the world (15:19; 17:11; 14-16; 17:18). I do not intend to examine these texts. Rather the question is their importance for the debate over globalization.

Obviously John's message regarding *kosmos* cannot be translated into a rejection of this century's global phenomena. Nor does it move us to take refuge in a christian oasis, nor to be irresponsible regarding modern history. Rather, it warns us not to be naive theologically, being aware of opposition to the Church's message of liberation and to Jesus' saving presence. It also gives theological criteria (and not a political programme) for action. Believers are within a sinful realm that is saved by God. This implies, in a hermeneutic of today's signs of the times, that global/local factors (the dominant ones, and the alternatives) have to be questioned and challenged. As a follower of Jesus one is not owned by, nor belong to, these factors, since they tend to become absolutes. One can affirm a missionary praxis in this global/local world of today, so that humanity and the cosmos continue responding to God's loving salvation of all. Thus, we are in, not of, and sent to, the world. We say this symbolically, in a theological language about the world.

Throughout Latin America and the Caribbean, theology is deeply involved with history, confronts the status quo, and works for a new society and humanity. However, we have shortcomings. One is the issue of a holistic project. Both some internal evaluations and some who claim liberation theology has died, say that we lack a human alternative (after the fall of a type of socialism). But theology may not be reduced to those European events. A holistic project is within and transcends human history and cosmic reality. Another crucial issue is the micro and macro dimensions. Both are significant for liberation; and it starts with small everyday events as well as with global concerns. However we have been perceived as if only structures and radical changes are important. The tiny hope, organization, tenderness, alliances, and so on, in ordinary lives are most important in latinamerican theology.

Different strands of a liberational understanding of faith/hope/love have in common a critique of today's reality and also a commitment to life. Each has its own accents and contributions; but I underline that these reflections are in/into this world although not belonging to this world.

Allow me to briefly mention basic insights in each theological strand. Work done by Latinamerican women focus on ordinary/holistic events, symbols, relationships; drawing a line between what is life-giving (concrete signs of Mystery) and what has to be transformed (since one is not owned by patriarchy and other evil structures). Afro-American theologians confront this world -- slavery, modern discrimination, etc.; reflect on God in terms of black sacredness, pray and struggle for the land of milk and honey. Indigenous theologies, in the midst of a garden of flowers, the challenge the modern poison - materialism and so on -, affirm true change and construction of a global house where all peoples may live, and acknowledge God as the only owner of a garden that is cared for by women and men.[12] Grass-roots biblical theology is a "caminhada" (journey); it critiques principalities and idols within our world, it reads and worships the word with the eyes of the poor, with historical and transcendent hope. Moreover, systematic liberation discourse is rooted in conditions of dehumanizing sin, and in struggle for justice and joy, where the music of God reveals the human paths towards life. So, all our theologies are within and beyond this world.

Since divine creation and human history are good, however damaged and wounded by local/global realities, christian inculturation and its theology are carried out *within* and *transcending* work, love, thinking, celebration. Inculturation corresponds to each people's journey and spirituality. It is not a socio-cultural conquest nor an alienation from one's roots and utopias. As churches: is that done with evangelical zeal and courage?

Community of Hope Today

We are members of local churches, and part of a universal *oikumene*. How, as a community of hope, do we deal with global/local reali-

---

[11] See systematic essays by R. Oliveros, C. Boff, G. Gutierrez, I. Eliacuria, J.L. Segundo, P. Trigo, J.B. Libanio, in *Mysterium Salutis*, two volumes, Madrid: Trotta, 1990.

[12] Excerpts of *Final Message*, III Latinamerican Workshop of Indian Theologies, Vinto, Bolivia, August 1997.

ties? Primarily by being a community; and thus a sign of communition that defies global inequality and exclusions; and by daily, hopefully, transforming the earth and enjoying heaven. This is a way of defining church; not as a ghetto of truth and righteousness, but rather as a faithful, ecumenical community dedicated to love and hope in today's world. May I now comment on urgent church responsibilities.

First, specific contribution to a global/local alternative. We are not called to be sectarians, building a christian space or reconstructing it (as planned by nostalgic Europeans and Latinamericans). The specific task is public witness of human alternatives; that is, of tiny and large, different and complementary, planned and marvelous, plants and flowers of a new humanity. This political task questions a world-order that denies qualitative change (and naively expects "the end of history"). Such a political witness is urgent, since planetary means of communication cont ol everyone's mind and heart.

For example, in tiny Central America, victim of imperial interventions, a christian network has drawn up their local/global options.[13] It heralds economic, socio-political, cultural possibilities vis a vis globalization; it also greets a human history (not centered in Europe); and underlines the personal qualities needed by those who build a new world.

Such a witness implies, theologically, that as church we are a humble and most meaningful sacrament of God's universal salvation. Not the spiritual center of world events, nor a moral caretaker of victims. We rather give witness and worship to the livir God, present in the midst of ambivalent events, and among all peoples and religions who seek peace and justice. Thus, our discipleship of Christ, the unique sacrament, becomes Good news with no boundaries.

Second, inter-religious dialogue and action, for the sake of humanization, ecological well-being, and spiritual growth. Here I touch only on christian responsibilities (as we interact with other

---

[13] "Compromiso hacia una nueva sociedad. Opoion en tiempos de globalizacion", workshop in the Jesuit *Centro de investiagcion y accion social para centro America*, CIASCA; published in *Pasos* 71(1997) 1-10.

faiths and religions, a pluriform agenda is drawn up). In today's world, some ideological and inter-christian barriers are lowered, but between world religions -- and inside each of these, between the ruling structure and "people's religion" -- barriers and non-communication are increasing. Some of us draw a clear line between universal salvation by Christ, and christendom's series of biases and at times destruction of other religions (especially of colonized or subordinated groups).

I place an accent on dialogue with ordinary religion. In Asian contexts, for example, one can share Hindu feeling and understanding of *shakti*, "energy... awe that people have towards the universe"[14]. One can also interact with peoples' faith, that Felix Wilfred characterizes as "open to pluriformity and diversity in experiencing God, to the language of symbols, signs and icons, and to diversified ways of worship" (instead of naming it polytheism, due to ethnocentric and political biases).[15] It seems to me that this dialogue is urgent, within the global dynamics of cultural differences and plural spiritual languages of liberation. These and other inter-religious bonds strengthen a community of hope in today's world.

This second responsibility entails an ecclesial re-visioning of her relationships and commitments. Brazil's Pedro Casaldáliga and other visionaries call it macro-ecumenism: it involves churches and different religions, and intertwines ecology, culture, politics, spirituality. In a local catholic context, I show how people bring together different religions when they do healing, celebrations, etc.; it seems that a pluri-religious church has christo-pneumatic foundations.[16] Many presuppose that the church is mono-religious. Since its origins, the christian church has included jewish, samaritan, gentile

---

[14] A.M. Abraham Ayrookuzhiel, *The Sacred in Popular Hinduism*, Madras: Christian Literature Society, 1983, p. 23.
[15] F. Wilfred, "Faith witout `faith'? Popular religon: a challenge to elitist theology and liturgy", in P. Puthanangady (ed.), *Popular Devotions*, Bangalore: NBCLC, 1986, 606. In this Seminar, a workshop concluded that in India's socio-political context, popular devotion is alienation, it does not "elicit creative power in people" (op.cit., 695). Wilfred places the problem not on the side of people's alienation, but rather on elitist, rational discourse that is alienated from symbolic language (op.cit., pp. 598-601).
[16] See my "Trenzado de religiones", *Allpanchis* 48(1996), 81-106.

factors; and during two thousand years we acknowledge many processes of in-culturation and what may be called in-religionation.

Third, community of women and men. This is also an urgent responsibility. Both women and men have their own ways of experiencing and naming God, of being humanly faithful and constructive. When we link together these different inputs, the world is transformed and all grow in holiness. Since the church continues to be androcentric, and denies the different contributions of men and women, all remain spiritually and personally deprived. As we build an alternative globalization of life, the gender perspective and action is the cornerstone. (Take note that this presentation is particularly masculine; it does not speak out of every human experience.) It is urgent that the voice and work of one gender be not imposed over the other. In positive terms, everything and everyone is renewed when as men and as women we join hands and take care of the earth, our common house.

Holistic action and thinking offer images of hope. For example, African theologies done by women and men have a moving mystique. Anne Nasimiya-Wasike says: "as christians and as women who have seen the liberating power of Christ, we have two functions to fulfill: first of all to witness to God's love and care for the universe; and secondly to give testimony to the continued human responsibility of creating a new world".[17] It is a global, alternative power, in communication with God-creator and in discipleship of Christ-liberator. However, principalities and dominions in our times make us re-read the gospel message. Kwame Bediako says: "the Cross desacralises all the powers, institutions and structures that rule human existence and history... stripping them all of any pretensions to ultimacy".[18] In so far as men and women continue to develop each one's theological insights and place them in the common thrust towards life, a new humanity becomes possible and desirable.

---

[17] A. Nasimiyu-Wasika in *Jesus in African Christianity*. Ed. by J.N.K. Mugambi and Laurenti Magesa. Nairobi: Initiative Publishers, 1989, p. 133.

[18] Kwame Bediako, *Christianity in Africa*. Maryknoll: Orbis Books, 1995. His hermeneutics: it is "by paying attention to the resonances of the biblical categories into the African primal world-view that the desacralising impact of the Gospel is experienced afresh." p. 245.

Conclusion

We read the signs of the times: hegemonic global factors that test our faith, and emerging alternatives that kindle cautious hope. We interpret global/local realities, experienced from the underside of history, from the perspective of victims who are wise and joyful. Inspired by John's gospel, christian discipleship and mission today is seen in/into the world, but not belonging to the status quo. Latinamerican, Asian, African theologies draw lines in the human quest for life. According to these theologies, the church has urgent responsibilities, work and worship are inter-religious, and women and men offer holistic, spiritual proposals.

In terms of inculturation, it can no longer be reduced to an ethnocentric concern; since it is globally/locally contextualized. The task of inculturation acknowledges that the Spirit is moving events, religions, human structures and hearts in the direction of life. But, cautiously we allow the development of evil plants and of wheat (cf Mt 13:24-30), that grow together in the fields of history. One can say that some other global/local realities are shared and enjoyed by all. Evil is not replaced magically (in a revolutionary way!) by goodness. Rather, good realities are in the midst of evil ones.

We are moving through the crisis of modern civilization. Some of its global factors are challenged and replaced by new seeds and plants, by small and realistic utopias that need to link together. Common people's symbolic actions, particularly pilgrimage and celebration, are a strong cry for life and global meaning. May our theologies be part of this hopeful movement.

Globalization and 'Postmodern' Culture Politics

Georges De Schrijver, S.J.

In November of 1996, I organized an International Symposium in Leuven (Flanders/Belgium) on the paradigm shift and paradigm crisis in Third World theologies of liberation. In my discussion paper,[1] I pointed out that globalization and also postmodern culture constitute the framework within which contemporary reflection from the underside of history has to take place, if we are to expect some renewal of liberation theologies. As far as globalization is concerned, it took the participants a couple of days to understand the urgency of exploring this domain; whereas the issue of postmodern culture got hardly any consideration at all. Now, some weeks ago a doctoral student of mine who lives in the U.S.A. sent me a book in which, to my surprise, the dismissed term figured in the main title: "*Liberation Theologies, Postmodernity, and the Americas*."[2] This reaffirmed in me a conviction to develop my theological reflections on globalization in the light of the ambivalent phenomenon of postmodernity. But before I start making this connection, I would like to dwell first on three aspects of globalization worth considering.

1. Globalization Unpacked

(i) At a first, experiential level the term globalization might cover what some call a growing sense of cosmopolitanism, as this is typical of the post-Cold-War period, and presumably already earlier, starting from the post-colonial and colonial periods. In the local

---
[1] See note 9.
[2] Ed. by David Batstone a.o., New York: Routledge, 1997

setting, cosmopolitanism comes to the fore in the mega-cities' capacity, worldwide, to bring about a melting pot of traditions, cultures, and ethnicities. Multiculturalism, mestizajes of every kind, as well as interracial, and interreligious contacts and intermingling seem to be inevitable in a world in which migration from countryside to the city, and from backward provinces to new metropolitan centers, wherever they may be located, have become the hall mark. In many West-European countries, Muslims are becoming the second largest denomination. Mosques are being built and Catholic and Protestant churches closed down. The former guest-workers have begun to organize themselves with the aim of having their identity recognized on the same footing as the long-standing cultural groups. Yet, what is startling for many Europeans took place already long ago in the United States, with their Japanese, Chinese, Vietnamese, Afro-American and Latin (Puertorican) immigrants; it is also not uncommon in the Two-Thirds World. Think only of cities like Sao Paulo, in Brazil, or Bombay, in India,[3] with their varied crowds of mainstream and subcultural (racial) groupings.

This local cosmopolitanism, however, only reflects on a microscopic scale what is happening at the macro-level where the world is becoming just one global village. Here one can witness a spread of facilities allowing people, especially the wealthier, to travel to distant localities for business, or to sell their specialized labor power to any taker. This flexibility is fortified by steady flows of instantaneous information and transactions that can now be materialized with the help of electronic means of communication. But to look at the material conditions that make cosmopolitanism possible is already to move over to its two grounding aspects, economic globalization, and the global information highway.

(ii) Economic globalization is the latest phase of the developments within neo-liberal economy, in which the basic principle of the free-market reaches its apogee. Typical of this phase is that the free-market is no longer checked or kept within limits by the governments of the modern nation-states. On the contrary, the World Bank and the International Monetary Fund (IMF) now dictate to

---

[3]. M. Featherstone, *Undoing Culture. Globalization, Postmodernism and Identity*, London: Sage Publications, 1995, p. 115.

what extent governments can engage in, or should refrain from, setting up socially protective measures, coercing them to comply with Structural Adjustment Programs (SAPs). Trans-national corporations have, thanks to their unhampered versatility, succeeded in putting pressure on the political bodies, using hereby their own strategies to reduce labor costs. What this flexible approach is all about is clearly shown, e.g. in the reshuffling of enterprises: "A sports car is financed in Japan, drawn up in Italy and constructed in Indiana (USA), in Mexico, and in France; it contains the most recent electronic components developed in New Jersey and constructed in Japan... Which of those products is a US one? Which one is not? How are we to decide? And is the answer really important?[4] Moreover, a new worldwide division of labor – in terms of spatial repartition – is coming off the ground: "American airlines' tickets originate from the Bermudas, Swissair's accounting is done in Bombay."[5] At sunset, Swissair sends the necessary data to Bombay, where they can be processed during the day. This, of course, leads to redundancies in Switzerland. But who should care?

(iii) This reshuffling of enterprises and the migration of subsidiary companies to countries with cheaper labor force is in the last resort made possible by the flow of instantaneous information these enterprises receive and pass on. The explosive means of communication, coupled with capital flows are, so to speak, the (secularized) sacramental symbol expressing and effectuating the world economy's defiance of all national borders. Indeed, sophisticated means of transportation, telephone connections, radio and TV broadcasting, even transmitted through satellites, as well as the information highway (faxes, E-mails, web-sites on the internet, etc.) have brought about a greater internationalization of contacts and exchange of expertise; they also facilitate lobbying, and the establishment of financial empires that exert control over the media, such as the Murdoch and CNN monopolies. Whoever holds sway over the media will be victorious in steering the direction of economic globalization, a total market which is primarily addressing consumers

---

[4] R. Reich, *l'Economie mondialisée*, Paris, Dunod, 1993, p. 103, quoted in F. Houtart, "The World-Encompassment of the Economy," in *Coeli Quarterly*, n. 68, winter 1993-1994, p. 8.
[5] *Ibidem*, p. 113.

and not geared to producers, as was the case in classical political economies (Marx).

2. Postmodern Culture and Globalization: A Janus-Faced Reality

Postmodernity, on the cultural level, boasts of having repelled the lure of mobilizing grand stories. Unifying centers have been replaced by webs of spinning signifiers which all refer to other spinning signifiers, without any rootedness in stable metaphysical verities. Aesthetic postmodernity is nomadic, characterized by transgression, and aware of the fact that the rules of the game have to be invented again and again; they are not given in advance once and forever in terms of a straightforward, undisturbed teleology. Playfulness, inventiveness, deviation, dispersal, and the magical lure of offering packages of novelty (difference, otherness, new attractive items brought unto the market) are the heralded qualities of the latest civilization.

When confronted with the phenomenon of spreading differentiations, all of them moving away from fixed centers, some authors tend to define postmodernity as the awareness, from within, of what the acceleration process of modernization is all about. Postmoderns, so to speak, are used to sitting comfortably in the high-speed train of modernity, and taking in the shifting panorama of the unstoppable innovations and changing perspectives. Postmodernity would then have to be seen as modernity having reached the stage where it became conscious "of its true nature – *modernity for itself.*"[6] Others, however, point to some distinctive features which make postmodernity differ from modernity, such as the cancellation of teleology, weakening of state interference, replacement of ethics by esthetics, celebration of the fleeting qualities of life (living on the surface of existence in terms of pure instantaneity), and weakening of historical memory.[7] Television, it seems, is the typical postmodern medium, for it succeeds in mixing up historical accounts of the past

---

[6] Z. Bauman, *Intimations of Postmodernity*, New York, London: Routledge, London, 1992, p. 187.

[7] Cf. D. Harvey, *The Condition of Postmodernity: An Inquiry into the Origin of Cultural Change*, Cambridge-Oxford: Blackwell, 1993 [1990], p. 59.

PART 3 : THE GLOBAL AND THE LOCAL 175

with advertisements of today, and this collage makes it difficult to differentiate entertainment from serious information.[8]

Therefore some venture to speak of postmodernity as the legitimating story of the neo-liberal free market gone global. As I wrote elsewhere: "The market's adaptable game of profit enhancement, with its free-floating codes and electronically steered mobility, is so to speak omnipresent, omnipotent, and infinite in inventiveness. Thanks to the electronic media of communication and to the dismantlement of state power, it meets no more borders that restrict the inroads of its empire. It creates at will jobs and unemployment, wealth and poverty, ordered life and crime, when and where it wishes. It acts, thus, as a dark providence whose decisions are not to be questioned."[9] Economic globalization in conjunction with the free-wheeling style of postmodernity, will, in short, lead to the globalization of a world of *apartheid*.[10] The 'total market' is, in its postmodern form, perhaps more than in the days of classical political economies, the deity or the chance/fatality which decides upon 'salvation' or 'damnation,' not just of individuals and social classes, but of entire nations and sub-continents.

However, this is only one side of the coin. Indeed, at the other extreme of the spectrum, some leftist authors, especially in the U.S.A, have in turn begun to use postmodern categories, but with different accents on them. They are convinced that the habit of looking at things from the underside of history will lead to a divergent selection of postmodern topics. They hereby refer to the fact that liberation theologies from the outset tended to 'dialectically move beyond modernity.[11] This move is clearly expressed in the 'irruption of the poor in history': those relegated to the fringes of existence, as non-

---

[8] See D.Harvey,*O.C.*, p. 61. Quoting in part from B. Taylor, *Modernism, Postmodernism, Realism: A Critical Perspective for Art*, Winchester: Winchester Schoolof Art Press,1987, pp.103-105.

[9] G. De Schrijver, *Paradigm Shift in Third World Theologies. From Socioeconomic to Cultural Analysis*, Leuven: Preprint, Bibliotheek van de Faculteit Godgeleerdheid, 1996, p. 51.

[10] M. MacClain Taylor, "Vodou Resistance/Vodou Hope. Forging a Postmodernism That Liberates," in D. Batstone,*op.cit.*, p. 170.

[11] F. Hinkelammert, "Taking Stock of Latin American Theology Today," in *Coeli Quarterly* , (1995-1996), p. 29.

entities, now lay claim to being part of the moral conscience in society. Their struggle for survival makes them the privileged 'other' whose voice cannot be stifled by any hegemonic center whatsoever. Liberationists, in other words, succeed in making theirs the strategies by which postmodern 'fragmentation' reacts against uniform standards of rationality, standards that were so much cherished in the hey-days of modernity. They thus join hands with postmodern critics of modernity, while maintaining a faultfinding distance from postmodernity's alliance with economic globalization.

The liberationists' selective readings of postmodern themes have in common that they all relate to breaking away from monolithic hegemonic centers. They insist on respect for the 'otherness of the other' (revival of indigenous cultures and religions, feminist movements, counter-cultures of the poor and marginalized) in order to develop a 'postmodernism of resistance'. The latter, it is said, "both collapses the distance between elite and popular culture; challenges the 'great narratives of western progress, and generates a new postcolonial narrative of historical space and destiny.[12] Emphasis is placed on particular locality, its historical destiny and its prospective chances, two items not held in great esteem by modernity's logocentrism – this particular locality being spelled out now as made up of 'people at the bottom'.

In this context references are made to Foucault, Derrida, and Bataille, in as far as these postmodern deconstructionists set out to 'delegitimize' hegemonic centers of knowledge and power, in view of opening up spaces where dissonant discourses undertaken by minority groups are given a chance to prosper. The more people realize that thinking is not free from place, time and interest, the more a 'decanonization' of conventional authorities will be put on the agenda.[13] At this juncture, the newest theoreticians of liberation theologies join in. They not only stress that Christian liberation movements should be given the right to interpret the scriptures from their particular place at the underside of history (hereby decanonizing

---

[12] Lois Ann Lorentzen, "Writing for Liberation. Prison Testimonials from El Salvador," in D. Batstone, *op.cit.*, p. 129.

[13] D. Batstone, E. Mandieta, L. Lorentzen, D. Hopkins, *Introduction*, in D. Batstone, *op. cit.*, p. 1.

PART 3 : THE GLOBAL AND THE LOCAL 177

conventional interpretations), but also point out that Liberation theologians did not go far enough in their attempts at doing contextual theology. However important the classical hermeneutic circle may be, it does not encourage people to engage in a radical decentering in terms of "multiculturalism," "polycentrism," and "ecumenism." In their study on *"Liberation Theology and the Quest for Syncretism in the Brazilian Context"*, A. Sathler and E. Nacimento assert that L. Boff, in his work *Church, Charism and Power*, still held on to a concept of syncretism in which the 'other' cultural and religious elements were seen as a possible enrichment of Christianity, provided they allowed themselves to be incorporated into Christianity. But, these authors go on, as long as incorporation into Christian patterns is simply being imposed, the 'different' voices are not taken seriously. Perhaps, what these voices want is to assimilate themselves selected Christian elements into their own cultural patterns. At any rate, the question of alterity becomes more crucial when liberation theology turns to employ also 'postmodern' cultural analysis. They conclude; "Liberation theology as a whole has neither taken the side of African Americans as the majority of the poor, the excluded, and discriminated, nor tried to see their movements of resistance and religion as equal partners in a dialogue of cultures and religions. Without a recognition and correction of this contradiction, liberation theology leaves untouched a whole tradition of conservative thought and action that systematically negates multiculturalism, polycentrism, ecumenism, and postcolonialism."[14]

The same refusal to be coopted into some dominant discourse can also be seen in some practical strategies that are recommended. As far as the means of communications are concerned, it is said, postmodern liberationist groups must not just wager on using the internet, since that monopoly is in the hands of economic magnates; they should also, and preferably, make use of alternative, informal communication networks, such as distribution of leaflets and newsletters, neighborhood visitation, group networking in disenfranchised communities, radio journalism, etc. When organizing gatherings in

---

[14] A. Sathler-E. Nacimento, "Black Masks on WhiteFaces. Liberation Theology and the Quest for Syncretism in the Brazilian Context," in D. Batstone, *op. cit.*,

halls of the academy, they should realize that this is, in fact, an improper place for the marginalized to meet; joined to these meetings they should also organize protest marches around action programs from below. And finally, they need to "enter into, or strike solidarity with, communities in which Vodou esthetics of practice and spirit are already being deployed with liberating effect"; whereby Vodou stands for a ethnicity inspired mystique of resistance, expressing itself in jazz, blues, gospel songs, reggae, rap, etc.[15]

How does all this relate to globalization? That the first panel of the diptych points to our usual idea of globalization is almost evident. Postmodern glitter and mobility, inventiveness and playful dispersal are, indeed, not only part and parcel of the migratory behavior of trans-national companies; they also serve as the latter's philosophical legitimization: The more 'decentering' in term of fresh free market initiatives occurs, the more an endless line of brand new items can be promoted and sold in an increasing number of close and distant places. This breaking away from fixed (immobile) centers of planning leads, paradoxically, to the emergence of a total and totalizing market whose specialized magnates exhibit strong signs of affinity among themselves. As far as this is concerned, versatile decentering only serves as a springboard for boosting a multi-layered, but world-wide expansion of the (diversified) market. Reduced to its essence one could say: the total market is primarily postmodern because it succeeded in establishing its empire beyond the control mechanisms of the modern nation-state. This emancipation makes the markets daring, inventive, and purely consumer-oriented, whereby ample use is made of the postmodern glitter of media-steered advertising.

Now, it is in reaction to this unbridled expansionism of post-modern economies that regional groups within the formerly authoritative nation-state begin to affirm their autochtonous character. Take, for example, the European case. While the United Europe in the making seeks to enhance its competitive position in the meandering global market, regional nationalisms that seemed no longer to exist within the one nation-state begin their resurgence, placing

---

p.117.
[15] M. MacClain Taylor, "Vodou Resistance/Vodou Hope. Forging a Postmodernism

an emphasis on local language, customs, and race. Think of the nationalistic movements in Scotland, Flanders, and Catalonia. In other words, the larger the perspective in terms of globalization becomes, the more there is felt a need for regional entities to go back to their (dormant or explosive) cultural roots. This is what the second panel of the diptych is all about. Uncertainties about the positive results of their insertion into a wider context make regional groups look back to ancient certainties, in the hope that the potential thereof will not be coopted in the hegemonic language of the global market, however much flexibility the latter may claim to have.

With respect to the Two-Thirds World, there is of course an additional element that must be given its due. Here, the postmodern suspicion of hegemonic narratives is in many cases born from the cruel experience of economic exploitation of the masses – and their exclusion from the 'good life'. For the destitute in the Two-Thirds World, economic globalization is understandably experienced as a new wave of neocolonialism, even more powerful than previous oppressive regimes. Hence the growing need for them to affirm their local, cultural, (sub-)cultural identities, an affirmation which includes involvement in networks of solidarity and engagement in the informal economy. Given their predicament of dire poverty, these people take the 'different' more seriously than postmoderns from the North, for whom 'difference' often boils down to just engaging in ever new experiments. They do so by sticking to their racial, cultural and religious 'otherness' in order to prevent their identities from being 'liquefied' in the ever new constellations of gliding signifiers. Their 'otherness' is for them something 'substantial' that cannot be done away with in the name of enthralling novelty. This consideration brings us to the question of the sacramentality of existence.

3. Sacramentality of Existence: Discernment of the Spirits

Leonardo Boff sees in the notion of transparency or translucency the most appropriate term to evoke what God's sacramental presence in the world means: "Divine reality (the lens through which all things are looked at) is, in its startling beyondness and nearness, not so much to be conceived of as a reality *above* the world which is also immanent *in* it; but rather and primarily as a reality which transpires *through* the very world... Transparency begins to shine 'in between transcendence and immanence'; as such it is formative of the whole world of symbols, signs, and sacraments. This 'in-between' is also the locus of 'sacramental thinking', which is essentially a thinking through symbols."[16] In sacramental thinking, in other words, one is able to see configurations and patterns in the world as translucent towards the hidden ground of existence. These configurations also involve human activities, which allows liberation theologians to acknowledge that 'every anticipation' of the construction of a more humane world is a 'sacrament' or 'visible sign' of God's grace and presence. Or as Boff puts it elsewhere: every great or small event that the people celebrate in their struggle towards a humane existence is a sacrament, a celebration in anticipation of God's complete salvation.[17]

From this background, I would like to develop some reflections on esthetics and celebration, including expressive forms of a mystique of resistance – a 'Vodou esthetics of practice and spirit', if you like. However, when embarking on these reflections, I realize perfectly that notions such as the beautiful, the symbolic, and the transparent may be full of ambivalence, whereas, on the other hand, aesthetics are welcomed in various, often disconnected aspects of culture today. The mystique of resistance has recourse to aesthetic categories (music, dance, painting), but so does postmodernity, in its globalized form. Here, too, the lure exerted by beautiful objects – commendable products of the market – comes to the fore. But does this mean that it therefore has something genuinely sacramental about it? A discernment of the spirits is thus in place, to see which beautiful forms and gestures may compete for sacramental status and which not. For not every symbolic expression is by its very nature revelatory of the divine. It might even be the case that things that have a natural capability for disclosure could seal themselves off.

That Liberates," in D. Batstone, *op.cit.*, p. 180-2.

[16] L. Boff, *Die Kirche als Sakrament im Horizont der Welterfahrung*, Paderborn, Bonifacius Verlag, 1972, pp. 123-125.

[17] L. Boff, *Sacraments of Life. Life of the Sacraments*, Washington D.C., The

In his book *Church, Charism, and Power*, e.g., L. Boff develops a sacramental vision of the church to which he immediately adds some possible pathologies. Unlike Protestants who are iconoclastic with respect to the transparency of the divine in human mediations, Catholics mostly define the church, its institutional forms included, as a particular set of mediating configurations which render God's grace visible in earthen vessels.[18] In Catholicism, he says, "there is great value placed on mediation. Faith is incarnated in the piety of the people. The Gospel is present in the promises made, the processions, the lighted candles, and the veneration of the saints , making (the church's) identity visible though these manifestations. They make the gospel historical. Thus there is the basic optimism of Catholicism. There is happiness, joy, and enjoyment in the presence of God's transcendence, and that of Jesus Christ, made present in this popular piety. The realities of this world are accepted as manifesting and mediating salvation.[19] This genuine translucency towards the divine, Boff goes on, is however obscured by the very institution that should testify to this 'shining forth'; indeed, to the extent that the hierarchical church places herself in the center – forgetting that she is only a mediation pointing to something else – her concern will be about maintaining her own power position, instead of fostering creative imagination. Self-maintenance in power makes the church vitiate her sacramental symbolism.

I appropriate Boff's basic scheme because it lends itself to application to various fields. Without denying the intimate link between the Catholic Church and sacramental visibility, I would first of all extend the phenomenon of translucency to the broader realm of sacramentality of existence. Events and celebrations outside the strict confines of ecclesial life can also be experienced as sacramental signs, as Boff himself has made clear when speaking of the sacrament of the cigarette butt (referring to his father's memory). Second, I would like to examine, in this context, to what extent the particular aesthetics of postmodernity (or high modernity) can or cannot become a bearer of sacramentality

---

Pastoral Press, 1987, p. 45.

[18] I leave out Boff's second characteristic of the church's catholicity, notably her ability to appropriate symbolic utterances taken from other cultures (the aspect that has met criticism from recent scholars; see above).

Because postmodernity has taken leave of grand stories, it is left with ever changing fragments, and the absence of ontological depth. It is no longer evident what translucency towards the divine should mean in a world where signs no longer refer to a primordial *referent*, but instead only refer to other signs, which in turn point to other signs or lines of interpretation. The interpreting community spins around in a hall of mirrors, in an endless labyrinth, engaged as it is in an 'erring' one should nonetheless learn to enjoy as an ineluctable fate. In an essay I devoted to this subject I called this the 'hollow sacramentality' of the postmodern condition.[20] In using this term, I attempt to structurally understand the situation; and to point to a paradox.

There has hardly been a period in history in which there was so much glamour and fascinating mobility. Rarely, if ever, has a culture been so visual, so exposed to sensory impressions elicited by electronic mass media – CD's, computer and television screens. And yet, all that is brought to the users' attention are floating surfaces with no substantial core, unless one should include the soft- and hardware employed to ground the spectacle. In the absence of a real 'ground' however, the notion of sacramentality undergoes a displacement. The media have become the visible and efficacious sign of the power construction of commercial monopolies, and in that sense designate the *latter's* 'sacramental' presence. The medium is the message. And the message is clear: 'consume what is being offered to your receptive capacities. Buy eternity and memorable enjoyment within your haphazard constellation of finitude.'

There is, however, a second approach to this 'hollow sacramentality' which consists in an option for the void, as a means to refrain from absolutizing the dance of images.[21] Here the 'gospel message' sounds: in the beginning was the void, and from the void a dance of changing impressions was born, with endless possibilities which in turn refer back to the abysmal void of the origin. Hence one has to deconstruct every attempt at attributing a straightforward finality to the ever-changing series of ciphers. Postmodernity

---

[19] L. Boff, *Church, Charism, and Power*, London: SCM Press, 1981, p. 86.
[20] G. De Schrijver, "Experiencing the Sacramental Character of Existence," in *Questions Liturgiques. Studies in Liturgy*, vol. 75, 1994/1-2, p. 20-21.

should remain a 'low-key thinking' – philosophically – and therefore place a ban on those who claim the ability to construct a solid edifice (or counter-edifice) on the shifting grounds inherent in a 'decentered' project still in search of the rules of the game. This approach develops a negative theology of its own kind: no clear formation should be regarded as final and conclusive. The next wave of the unpredictable future (with its own glamour) will wash away the glitter of today. This next wave, however, is not linked to an Absolute (or to a steering Providence); it is rather acting as a randomly deciding fate-deity. Yet, who would like to dance and sing before this Grand Destructor and Rebuilder? Sacramental celebration is again vitiated; it only thrives in the mode of frenzied dizziness (driving people into drugs and gambling). Or is this negative approach to be understood as paving the way, through cleansing, for an ultimately joyful celebration of existence?

I admit that the above reading sketches the logic of a system when thought through to the end. Whether everybody engaged in economic globalization is espousing this thought-through logic remains an open question. At any rate, two seemingly opposed obfuscations of a sacramentality of existence come to the fore: giving in to the lure of shining surfaces, and resignation before the threatening abyss of the void. This diagnosis permits a search for remedies. Indeed, what creates a sham heaven of glitter and/or the experience of a dark abyss in postmodernity is the premise of (western) individualism, in whatever form it may present itself: egoism, profit-making at any price, collective elitism. Only when this individualism is overcome by bonds of solidarity, especially with the weak sectors in our societies, can translucency towards the divine flourish again.

Genuine sacramentality of existence presupposes commitment to community structures, coupled with a world-wide search for the *bonum commune*. Only on this basis can one come in touch with something 'substantial' in the core of existence, with concerns that spur us on to commemorate small and decisive events in life with religious fervor. A Mystique of resistance is born from the discovery of substantial concerns regarding the community. "Solidarity," Gutiérrez writes, "implies a certain solidity, something consistent that one wants to do."²² It leads to looking at reality with new eyes, and to perceive and hallow in it signs anticipating renewal that can become a source of joy and praise – and "celebrative resistance."²³

4. Mystique of Resistance and Community-Building

The importance of community-building already came to the fore where it was explained how Two Thirds-World people make their own selection of so called postmodern themes, in stressing respect for the 'otherness' of the other, which means: respect for solid local values that give a deep sense of dignity to the members of the community. Without actually belonging to a community no one will be able to survive in the face of one or another threatening aspect of globalization. But here, too, one should discern between types of community-building.

It is well-known that almost everywhere in the world charismatic groups are mushrooming. Their success is partly due to the uncertainties people experience when seeing to what extent economic globalization is reshuffling their labor opportunities, for some for the better, for others for the worse. In both cases, the novelty of the situation causes anxiety. And how to exorcise these worries more easily than by luring people into the momentary exaltation offered to them in closed prayer meetings and healing sessions? A study examining this situation in South India shows that charismatic fundamentalism is on the increase in the urban settings: "The increasing pre-eminence of fundamentalist Christianity in urban south India (as elsewhere) can be read as a reassertion of religious certainty and exclusivity against the established churches' admissions of doubt, accommodation and ecumenism, ingredients of the social gospel which has been ascendant within the Protestant church and missions for the better part of a century.²⁴ Striking in this description is the elimination of the social gospel, of interreligious dia-

---

[21] Lyotard's reinterpretation of the 'sublime' (Kant) falls under this category.
[22] G. Gutiérrez, "Renewing the Option For the Poor," in D. Batstone, *op.cit.*, p. 71.
[23] M. McClain Taylor, *art. cit.*, p. 177.
[24] L. Caplan, "Certain Knowledge. The Encounter of Global Fundamentalism and Local Christianity in South India," in W. James (ed.), *The Pursuit of Certainty. Religious and Cultural Formulations*, London and New York: Routledge, 1995, p. 106.

logue, and of hermeneutics of the faith. On the other hand, a meeting between the global and the local is taking place, but only from a strictly religious perspective. The global is palpable in the fact that US preachers are invited, who during their performances announce the good news of healing, orchestrated with sound-recording and video clips, whereas their message is being received against the background of the local apprehension of malevolent spirits deemed to cause illness and make people lose their jobs. That these community gatherings have hardly any serious impact on social resistance is more than evident. Their 'mystique' lays elsewhere, in the religious certainties which do not allow of any doubt, and on which 'worldly affairs' are not given a chance to encroach.

However stable this return to certainties may be, it can not be taken as a model for the recovery of substantial values which lay at the roots of experiencing the sacramentality of existence. For this to occur, there must be small basic communities which commit themselves to questions of social justice in society, such as the eradication of bonded labor, unchecked child labor, and the rough treatment of lower classes and casts (races), not to mention the inferior position of women in traditional societies.[25]

Now, it is at this juncture that the question of utopias has been put on the agenda, in a self-critical sense. Increasingly since the collapse of the East-Bloc, leftist grand stories have been looked at with suspicion. A recent book in France has drawn up a balance sheet of the atrocities perpetrated during the Nazi-regime, and those of communist regimes, concluding that more people have died in communist concentration camps than elsewhere. Think of the Stalin period in Russia, or of the killing fields in Cambodia (Pol Pot).[26] In some liberationist circles, this is reason enough to lower the range of their utopias. Some fear that utopias (or grand narratives) may direct our attention to a place where we are not, thus creating a false consciousness in those who want to revolutionize politics from within the local and historical setting they find themselves in, and which

---

[25] I have treated the question of ecology elsewhere, See G. De Schrijver, "Paradigm Shift," *op.cit.*, 1996, pp. 43-44; 70
[26] S. Courtois a.o., *Le livre noir du communisme. Crimes, répression, terreur*, Paris, Laffont, 1997.

they are able to grasp.[27] Others caution, in the same line, against emancipatory programs conceived of in terms of an inflexible teleology: "Any emancipatory narrative adopted for political aims and goals must, of necessity, be a provisional narrative, a narrative open to questioning, and aiming at proximate goals. We cannot live or act without narrative, yet it may be possible to conceive of metanarratives as endlessly open, fluid, rather than static and reified.[28]

Considerations like these make sense, at least to a certain extent. However, they should not go so far as to let the pendulum swing in the opposite direction. It may be true, as Foucault and Lyotard point out, that the leftist grand stories have only produced an internalized replica of the grand stories of the right, in the sense that they have espoused the same belligerent character as the original model, not stopping short of bloodshed and barbaric extermination of opponents. Yet this state of affairs should not lead us to believe that the 'toothless strategy'[29] of First World postmoderns, is also imperative for the Two-Thirds World. As I have pointed out, one of the rationales behind the First World position is that of a resigned option for the void (*chora*) as the matrix out of which everything emerges. To confront this void may be a solution for those who find themselves at the 'upper side' of history, but must it also be the perspective of those living at the underside of it? Those people need a *telos* to hold on to. It is therefore consoling to see that at least one author writing in the volume from which I have often been quoting raises this question. He says: "If the locked out voices did not have a telos that promised that though evil might last through the night, joy comes in the morning (paraphrasing an old African-American teleological faith claim), then people without power, whether racial, gender, sexual, class, may as well go insane.[30]

---

[27] D. Batstone, "Charting (dis)Courses of Liberation," in D. Batstone, *op.cit.*, p. 162.
[28] L. A. Lorentzen, "Writing for Liberation. Prison Testimonials from El Salvador," in D. Batstone, *op.cit.*, p. 145.
[29] Batstone, E. Mandieta, L. Lorentzen, D. Hopkins, "Introduction," in D. Batstone, *op.cit.*, p. 10.
[30] D. Hopkins, "Postmodernity, Black Theology of Liberation, and the U.S.A. Michel Foucault and James Cone," in D. Batstone, *op.cit.*, p. 216.

The Global and the Local: An African View

Laurenti Magesa

Few now would dispute the fact that ours is an age of globalization. And even through people will differ on the details of what precisely globalization means, as well as concerning its effects on human thought and systems, its main outlines are fairly clear. They are no cause of much dispute. It is accepted that globalization is a complex process of interaction of economic, political and social forces throughout the world, producing a new way of looking at and understanding the world. It has its roots in the European Enlightenment period, but has acquired prominence as a system since the second half of the twentieth century.

One important characteristic of globalization is that it is double-edged. It effects close contact between peoples and societies on the one hand, while, on the other, it creates and accentuates sharp differences between them. Instrumental in this process of "compression" and differentiation are capitalist commerce and information technology. As far as Africa in general is concerned, what does this mean in practical terms?

The question can be reduced, without being reductionist, even for theology, to the issue of power. Globalization essentially involves the *power* of a superior -- though not necessarily better -- scientific and technological knowhow and/or access to the same. Those with this power, or with access to it, are therefore able to impose and spread their political will and cultural preference. The rest of the people and societies inevitably become recipients of this imposition. In other words, they become mainly consumers in every sense of the word, and whatever little they produce is subsumed in the superior knowhow.

It follows, then, that globalization is not only a question of power relationships between the economic North and South. It is also a question, in the same sense, between small Islands of power in a sea of powerlessness within the economic South as well as substantial Islands of powerlessness in a sea of scientific and technological knowhow within the economic North. The point is, however, that the theological questions the situation of globalization poses for both contexts are similar. They are ethical. Here I refer particularly to Africa, and want to suggest that for this continent the consequences of globalization have been no less profound than those effected by the slave trade and slavery in the more distant past and, in the recent past, by colonialism. It should not appear odd of me to make an intrinsic connection between socio-economic and political issues (i.e. the slave trade, slavery and colonialism) with theological concerns (i.e. ethics). Theological concerns arise out of social issues: Christianity is basically a response to questions of human relationships in the universe in which God is accepted as the supreme and final judge.

In this situation of globalization, it seems to me that the basic question to which Christian faith ought to apply itself involves the human cost of the global system. Given the wide variety of Christians' reception, understanding and experience of the one and the same Gospel, it is obvious that response to the same Gospel in the context of globalization will be just as varied. But it is still possible and necessary to point out the main orientations of any truly Christian response.

It is possible to distinguish at least two approaches to the challenge of globalization in theology: the theoretical and the practical. The theoretical approach, like all or most such approaches, is rather universalising and conservative. The practical approach is more particularizing and radical. Despite its current faltering steps under pressure from the global system itself, as well as from the centralizing trend in church institutions (itself an aspect of globalization), the particularising approach would seen to hold more promise for the Gospel to be, and be seen, as truly "good news" to and by those we might describe as the "victims" of globalization.

Theologians such as Robert J. Schreither represent the theoretical approach. Concluding his study on the interplay between global and local theologies, Schreiter (1997:133), for example, writes:

> Living in a globalized world, where time and space have been compressed, where those who have and those who have not are driven further apart, a truly intercultural way of doing theology between the global and the local is required of us. And a vision of a new catholicity can guide us to it.

Schreiter (ibid.: 128-32) describes the "new catholicity" as characterized by "wholeness, fullness, and exchange and communication." By wholeness he intends a theological appreciation that the various cultures of the world can receive the Gospel and communicate it through their own proper codes. Fullness means that the integrity (orthodoxy) of the faith must be preserved even as it is being transmitted and received across cultures and through the various cultural codes. Exchange and communication imply, for Schreiter, an intense and sincere inter- and cross-cultural dialogue. Such dialogue means to preserve both the integrity of the Gospel as well as that of the partner in dialogue as a human person. "To the extent that this catholicity can be realized," Schreiter proposes, "it may provide a paradigm for what a universal theology might look like today, able to encompass both sameness and difference, rooted in orthopraxies, providing *teloi* for globalized society."

There are two serious reservations to such an approach. The first is that it seems to accept the global system too much as an invincible given, with little possibility of adjustment or reversal. Secondly, it does not take into sufficient consideration the theoretical and practical inequalities endemic in the global system which often render the wholeness, fullness and respectful exchange and communication proposed by the new catholicity unworkable in human relations.

There are those, of course, who dispute the possibility of resisting the global system in any way, and they would describe any such attempt as both foolish and futile. But that kind of position is extremely dangerous. Unchecked or unmodified, globalization is sure to spell disaster of great proportions on its victims. In the interests of reducing the human cost of globalization, which, as I previously indicated, is the Christian task, the global movement must be managed so that it can be channelled in less destructive ways economically, politically, culturally and religiously.

Contextual theologies, which constitute the more practical approaches, try to do just this. They are not content with considering the outward "rewards" of the global system, but they are also concerned about its destructive, anti-Gospel spirituality. Their intent is to enable regions such as Africa, and their social equivalents in the power game of the global system, to maintain their identity so that dialogue can be as nearly as possible an equal exchange and communication.

The practical approach is exemplified by theologians like J.N.J. Kritzinger from South Africa, Michael Amaladoss from India, Jean-Marc Ela from Cameroon, and Uttich Duchrow from Germany. Amaladoss (1996:77), for example, describes the Christian mission today to be "a call to be counter-cultural." The christian community as a counter-cultural community, he asserts, must not only suggest a different vision of life in the world than that promoted now by the global system. This is theoretical. More than this, the Christian community must be actively involved in advancing its alternative vision in truth and love. Amaladoss proposes what he (ibid.: 68) calls "a two-pronged strategy."

> On the one hand we have to show in practice that people can meet their needs through alternative technologies and alternative economic and commercial practices. On the other hand the people must progressively gain participative control of the systems that govern their lives and, in this manner, humanize and socialize them. This strategy has to be pioneered by small groups of people who link themselves into networks, nationally and internationally, to put the pressure on the powers that be and to bring about progressive change.

Ethical considerations must therefore yield somewhat, or, even better put, mature themselves into, pastoral considerations. The central issue is really not, as it might first appear, sheer resistance against globalization (antiglobalism) in any of its manifestations. The central pastoral issue, as Amaladoss makes perfectly clear in the above-quoted passage, is the ability of people -- here the victims" of globalization -- to "gain participative control of the systems that govern their lives and, in this manner, humanize and socialize them." In other words, it is a question of sharing of power in the very basic sense of being able to determine the orientation of one's life. Here eschatological issues are involved.

One is the Reign of God and his justice. It should be clear that in denying participative control of systems that govern their lives to people, as the global system mainly does, it perpetrates injustice. But injustice is incompatible with God's present and final order. It creates chaos. And arguably, beneath the veneer of order and tranquility that globalization presents itself to be, there is a storm of dissatisfaction and frustration. This is evident in the many forms of violence that are now spread all over the world. But such violence is a manifestation of the spiritual and moral chaos that is the spirituality that the global system perhaps unknowingly promotes.

Another eschatological issue has to do with the element of moral choice, which globalization tends to deprive people of. It has been said that God cannot save us without us, so that the ability to choose to accept or reject God's gift of salvation is a necessary aspect of the Christian story. The diversity that globalization appears to offer is not genuine. On the contrary, it promotes a homogenization which few find it possible to resist, and those who try may be crushed under the wheels of the global system. Where there is no choice, can one really speak of free will?

While, therefore, global theologies of the theoretical kind are part and parcel of the global system and do influence the local church, local theologies of the practical kind will help better to reorient the Church towards it original mandate even in the current world context. I do not think that we need a hybrid theology of universal application. What we do need today is a local theology, or local theologies, which never tires of reminding Christians of their call to wholistically promote and protect the integrity of human life in all its forms.

REFERENCES

AMALADOSS, M. (1996) "Mission in a Post-Modern World; A call to be Counter-Cultural," *Mission Studies*, XIII: 1-2.

SCHEREITER, R.J., (1997) *The New Catholicity: Theology Between the Global and the Local* (Maryknoll, N.Y.: Orbis Books)

PART 4 :

Emerging Alternatives to Globalization

Emerging Alternatives to Globalization and Transformative Action

Horst Sing

1. Poverty and the fight against poverty in the process of globalization

Following the collapse of the "real existing socialism" - most visibly documented by the breakdown of the Berlin Wall in 1989 - the waves of globalization enforced tendencies and developments in the global society which had been looming up already: while the "Gross Global Product" and the GNP of many states are steadily increasing and the rich become even richer, the absolute number of human beings living in poverty is also continuously growing. The variety of options for organizing one's own life and life style is enlarged nearly every hour for those who can afford - I like to mention the developments in the fields of virtual reality, communication, mass media and genetic engineering, while new causes and sections of poverty and suppression emerge, for instance, the sequels of AIDS, new methods of state terrorism such as ethnic cleansing, the instrumentalization of ethnic or religious differences in order to gain political or economic power.

This somehow simplified description of the social status quo of our global society cannot seriously be doubted and is continuously documented in great detail covering many aspects by surveys and statistics even of, for instance, the "World Development Report", published by the World bank or the "Human Development Report", published by the UNDP-Programme.

By reviewing these reports and documentations and their precursors until the beginning of the perception of poverty and exclusion in a global perspective - which might be dated back to the Magna Charta of the UN in 1948 or Truman's "Point-Four-Programme" in January 1949 - one will nearly everywhere and always find the following topic: the poor and the rich are linked together by a global system of communicating tubes that does not sufficiently reduce poverty, but often leads to exclusion and to extremely unequal conditions of life. Therefore it is important to analyse the water flow in this system of communicating tubes in order to divert currents producing inequality or to create new currents which might help to overcome unequal conditions.

This example is quite impressive. The problem, however, is that all of us are part of this picture, swimming in the stream of the communicating tubes. By trying to analyse and observe the water flow, we will realize that - at best - only parts of the tubes are made of glass and transparent; therefore the water stream can only be observed in part. The globalization processes of the last few years have shown that the speed of these developments, their simultaneity and their linkage to nearly uncontrollable global players have destroyed the hope and the expectations rising from the concept of hegemony to what was designed quite often by the best intentions and was thought to create better living conditions for the poor in "developing countries" by implementing self-reliance strategies starting from the economically and politically most powerful global centers and contributing, by a kind of trickle-down effect, to overcome poverty in cooperation with the national elites of the South. In many cases, however, the contrary was the result: already in the early 50's modernization and growth strategies in many countries of the South led to the destruction of poor but in fact functioning societies, for instance in the tribal areas.

This ambivalent outcome - to use an euphemistic term - of the global development intentions and processes has been recognised since the 1950's on various levels of human sciences and by some change agents (especially NGOs) as well, but its recognition could not prevent that today 1,3 billion people live in poverty, most of them in the South. Social awareness and self-reliance groups as well as bigger social movements of the poor themselves and of activists identifying themselves with them have taken place on local, regional, national and international levels since the 1950's in showing the ambiguous structure and impact of modernization and globalization and in implementing strategies for prevention and eradication of the negative effects of development.

Reviewing the development of these movements from their beginnings, one cannot help but be highly impressed by their achievements taking into account the status quo of the 1950's, 60's and 70's: living conditions of the poor and social realities have been brought to light, the interpretation of poverty as a God-given or totally self-caused fate has been identified as a myth. Hunger, epidemics and illiteracy have been diminished, the self-consciousness, self-esteem and self-reliance of many poor people as well as their organizations and movements have increased.

This balance, however, has to be seen within the context of the global development process: if one accepts the idea that the poor-oriented NGOs are the organizations most closely linked to the poor, the result of a UNDP report (1993) indicating that only 250 million people are reached by them, of which only a part belong to the weakest groups which should be reached by them according to their intentions and philosophy will be disappointing and eye-opening. This disappointment and disillusionment is even bigger when one realises that the new poverty problems are not simply caused by new emerging "external" challenges like AIDS, but quite often by those which are meant according to their function and to their ethics to diminish or prevent poverty, inequality and oppression, i.e. by the political classes or so-called elites.

Therefore, it can be doubted that our concept of communicating tubes implying that we could control the development of the global society by relatively simple methods and strategies is sufficient. But where should we begin to try to understand why the fight against poverty reminds us of the race between the hare and the hedgehog or the fight of Heracles against the snake of Hydra?

2. Normative conflicts in the global society: the paradox of the modern welfare state

Besides the comparison with the communication tubes to describe the relationship between the North and the South the perception of the big difference between what should be, what should not be, and the status quo is another topic in the discussion about global society.

Human rights as they were implemented in particular since the Declaration of Independence of the United States and during the French Revolution in Europe resulted in a continuous differentiation into social rights and with the Magna Charta of the United Nations and its amendments to an universality on a high social and ethical standard which is in principle accepted by all modern states. Irrespective of whether they call themselves explicitly "Sozialer Rechtsstaat" in their constitution as, for example, the Federal Republic of Germany, to all of them belongs as an integral part the obligation not only to protect each citizen from discrimination because of his origin, race, language, native country, religion, philosophy of life, but also to save him from situations or assist him in overcoming them which have to be considered from the viewpoint of the respective society as being beneath human dignity.

At the same time - and that is the other side of the coin - all modern democratic states have in common that by their constitution every citizen is permitted "pursuit of happiness", whatever he understands by it. As a result, a right of inequality is embodied in every modern state that under certain circumstances leads to such a differentiation that the fundamental values of the constitution understood as a consensus of the whole society are often shortened by social reality and at times are even reduced to the absurd[1].

Increasing individualization reinforces in that case the tendency towards discriminating against values promoting solidarity and acting in solidarity.

Therefore the identity of modern societies will consist, above all, in "the incapacity of identification" (Luhmann). Moreover, this tendency is strengthened by the fact that in the present phase of development the successful inclusion of individuals in society is

---

[1] See for instance Niklas Luhmann, *Politische Theorie im Wohlfahrtsstaat*, München 1981; idem., "Die gesellschaftliche Differenzierung und das Individuum," in: idem., *Soziologische Aufklärung 6. Die Soziologie und der Mensch*, Opladen, 1995, pp. 125-141; Uwe Schimank, *Theorien gesellschaftlicher Differenzierung*, Opladen, 1996.

mainly dependent on technologies. The more they succeed, the fewer jobs they need, but, on the other hand, attract more and more capital and at the same time yield more and more profit.

The processes taking their course in this connection are generally oriented according to the guidelines of universal ethics, but, unfortunately, only in a rhetorical way. As a matter of fact, they orient themselves according to special ethics or codes so as to be fit for competition in the best possible way. As these partial rationalities do not dispose of any braking device they will become almost unstoppable if they enlarge in attractive fields of self-realization and consumption the variety of options of those that profit by inequality. If they are able to do so in every respect as much as possible - particularly in the course of waves of globalization of the past decade - successful global players - e.g. in energy, nuclear, computer and gene technologies as well as in selling capital and work - have succeeded in building up gigantic productive capacities of technological and, last but not least, of legitimizing rationality. This has, among other things, led not only to economization and colonisation of environment and traditional forms of organization on the job market, but also to the phenomenon that these partial rationalities have managed more and more to "socialize" the negative side effects of their activities and at the same time to take the profits of the latter into private ownership. Share - holder - value has become more important than the causation principle.

However, the increase of inequality and the differentiation of poverty, oppression, marginalization and exclusion shows that globalization - in particular that of the markets - provides no absolute positive date for the dissolution of the ambiguity in the development of global societies.

This ambiguity is based on an indissoluble paradox but whose consequences can and must be arranged in a tolerable way. An indispensable requirement is that these paradoxes of modern societies are recognized without illusions and that effective conclusions are drawn for the fight against poverty.

If in the end the development of a global society is veiled, this does not mean that it may be left to an inhuman and uncivilized evolution of the market that is irrational on the whole, despite the fact that it has at its disposal huge institutions and enterprises producing "rationalities". Even globalization does not improve the situation to its best level.

Actually the risk of its descending to irrationality is rather increased than reduced.

Therefore alternatives to movements towards globalization are not only justified for accidential reasons, but they are equally necessary for principal considerations. The question, however, remains what they can achieve.

3. Emerging alternatives: Functions and perspectives

From the assumption that the development of the global society at its base shows a paradoxical structure that in principle is indissoluble, it follows that it is the same with alternative movements. It is true that a great deal of evidence supports the assumption that the global players in spite of or just because of their specific functions, their partial rationalities and successes are joined to a kind of system whose supreme maxim is not to succumb to competition. But this connection is so complex that it does not offer any gap for a global alternative, at least not in the near future. Marxist socialism also failed because the world and knowledge about this world were too complex for it. It is not even possible to protest against complexity as a whole effectively, i.e. to produce a global opposition.

Proceeding on the assumption that there are different starting points for alternatives to the negative effects of globalization, one could ask from which starting point are they developed, what perspectives could they have and what about other perspectives of other systems. Pursuing this development of alternatives to destructive globalization processes, perhaps the most genuine starting point - the mobilization of the self-reliance of the poor - is best suited for analysing the possibilities and the limits of such alternatives. This starting point seems to be a very characteristic example of self-reliance because it issues from the concerned people themselves, that is to say from those whose dignity and existence are thoroughly affected by the negative effects of the development, not in an abstract or statistical way but in a concrete way both individually and as a community.

As early as the 60's the point of view of the persons concerned were, however, already combined with the rationality of scientific construction in the field not only of applied research but also of basic research. They developed the method of "participatory research", which not only opened up interdisciplinary horizons on all levels but above all a self-awareness of the people concerned of their own point of view. Thus a new a way of rationality was developed with whose help one can see some things that others don't, that things are very important.

Another particularly important result in the context of this starting point is that the voices of the victims of history have found, at least in some fields of the global rational discourse, a capacity of truth and of self-articulation that had hitherto been withheld from them. Besides sheer protests, and appeals to morality it is now possible also to argue with rationality, that is to say with a medium that the parties responsible for the negative side effects have considered as their monopoly up to now.

The second realm in which the starting point of self-reliance led to serious and indispensable alternatives is the mobilization of the poor themselves and of the potential that can be released in the social context with the help of activists.

When coping with social problems, these movements of self-reliance are of vital importance where next to nothing or only a totally insufficient social infrastructure had been set up by the state.

It is the dominance of "vested interests" of locally, regionally, nationally and internationally influential groups that prevents the building up of a social infrastructure which could contribute to overcome poverty. In this context the setting up of social net-works are aimed at immunizing the poor against the strategy of *divide et impera* of the representatives of these "vested interests" and at creating a climate of solidarity and confidence in order to overcome fear, insecurity and attempts at blackmailing.[2]

---

[2] See Hans-Bernd Schäfer (Hrsg.), *Armut in Entwicklungsländern*, Berlin 1994, passim.

In this connection also strategies were developed to include the technical sector as well as the technological one. One should not overlook the development of well-adjusted technologies that have decisively influenced the origin of comprehensive concepts of a "sustainable development" in ecology.

The third realm in which the starting point of self-reliance has begun to take effect and, in view of globalization, gains even more importance is the process of developing political objectives. Movements of self-reliance have become everywhere social movements, NGOs, associations and even integral parts of political parties, not only on a local and regional but also on national and international levels. NGOs contribute, for example, on a worldwide scale to prepare political decisions.

The "international regimes"[3] in the fields of ecology and of the fight against poverty do not yet possess the political weight of similar organizations with military and economic aims. But they are developing more and more into platforms of international discourse aimed at forming people's opinions and political objectives. And they are becoming "pressure groups" which the policy-makers cannot neglect easily.

We cannot expect that in the near future a global institution will establish or build up an international order, which offers an all-embracing global plan to put an end to inhuman poverty and misery and to the waste and destruction of non-renewable resources or at least to mitigate the effects. Because of all this and the prevalent social inequality in the present phase of globalization one will give precedence to the development of alternative movements and plans. If it is clearly recognized by the present global players, that, from the standpoint of their partial rationalities and special ethics they endanger themselves and others owing to their narrow-minded and stubborn way of thinking and acting, then these alternatives are a great asset. Extreme social inequality is not only inhuman but also too expensive in the long run and illegitimate in a democracy.

---

[3] See Harald Müller, *Die Chance der Kooperation. Regime in den internationalen Beziehungen.* Darmstadt, 1993; Klaus Dieter Wolf, *Internationale Regime zur Verteilung globaler Ressourcen*, Baden-Baden, 1991.

This is true of all serious negative side effects of globalization. For instance, all over the world, in the long run, money is not provided by the bank, but has to be earned honestly, i.e. by everybody's work and for everybody's benefit. It seems to me that coupling (that does not mean to harmonize!) the rationality of alternative movements with global players is the critical moment when attempting to civilize globalization because it is there that initially diametrically opposed points of view and interests appear to collide. Leaving out of consideration the insight that the development of the global community at the level of the norms and control is based on an indissoluble paradox, one will have to take a disillusioned but nevertheless determined approach to civilize the world society in those areas where it is possible. These are considerable. One will have to make use of them resolutely.

However, this does not work without certain previous achievements as I would like to show in relation to the social doctrine and commitment of the Catholic Church.

4. The Catholic Church as a starting point for alternative movements

It is obvious that the Catholic Church has great importance in this global society. I mention only two reasons:

1. Since the beginning of industrialisation Christianity has, more than any other religion, dealt with the social question. In this context it is particularly the Catholic Church that has developed a social doctrine that is not only to be understood in a theological sense but also corresponds to non - theological - philosophical understanding.

2. On account of its intellectual as well as material potential the Catholic Church is one of the most important pressure groups in a democratic state even in the so-called post-Christian-Societies of the North as well as in those countries in the South where it is a minority.

Perhaps one of the striking characteristics of the Catholic Church is, after all, a very high degree of "corporate identity" shown by its believers.

This is not so true of the social doctrine and of the response to it within the Church. To put it in an nutshell, one might say that there are two different approaches whose advocates are opposed to each other, at times even very controversially.

The first one was developed by the Church in answer to the challenges of the first industrial revolution since the first papal encyclical "Rerum novarum" dealing with social issues. This approach was evident in a lot of official statements by the Church as a whole as well as on a regional level. With the emergence of a global society, economic and other issues of this global society were taken into consideration.

Though the statements of the regional churches of the Third World focus on the extremely difficult conditions of life of the poor, declarations of the official Church at higher levels hold the view more or less overtly that the poverty without human dignity of a large part of humanity could be sufficiently relieved by some more responsibility in politics and the other relevant groups of society as well as by cooperation of "men of good will".

Apart from a few rare exceptions, as for instance the document of Medellín, they are rather guides for others than results of realistic self-reflection and change. There is great belief on the whole that with a traditional theology connected with the universal ethics of the human rights and the right political theory, guiding principles to make the world more human have finally been found.

The second approach starts where such confidence is no longer or has never been prevalent. In Latin America in the 50's Christians engaged in social affairs (in the context of a "preferential, but not exclusive option for the poor") happened to discover that Catholic social doctrine could not save a Catholic continent from degrading poverty. And, what is even worse, the social doctrine was evidently not sufficient to find means of improvement as long as the general set-up and the social structures did not allow that. This would mean, however, putting the cart before the horse. It is a well-known fact that in this context the "Theology of Liberation" was worked out by partly integrating socialist or Marxist views. If we leave theological premises of the supporters of either approach aside, and ask ourselves what the contributions of the Catholic Church are in the context poverty in the present phase of globalization, I would make the following suggestions:

1. If there is no generally accepted formula to understand reality, every attempt to propose a new absolute formula is doomed to fail. The classical social doctrine of the Church is no longer adequate.

2. Theories and strategies of development which hope that the negative side effects of globalization will be dealt with by politics in an appropriate period of time are refuted by the actions of global players and partial rationalities. They run the risk of sacrificing the poor and the excluded even in the future if they accept the immunization of politics and the political classes - and the classical social doctrine as well - against criticism.

3. If the Church wants to provide a voice to those who are not able to speak, it must not give up its prophetic talk, i.e. it must condemn misery and injustice wherever and under whatever name they may appear.

4. In a global society in which 1,3 billion people live under the poverty line in conditions unfit for human beings and where politics and partial rationalities are evidently not capable of overcoming this "irrationality", the Church will have to cope with these challenges in the form of new arguments and new strategies. Taking the paradox of modern states as a starting point, this can only mean that even a social doctrine of the Catholic Church cannot resolve this paradox. It can only help to make the resulting consequences bearable.

That means having to give up some of the self-confidence (which leads often to arrogance against the "option for the poor") of the classical social doctrine and, at the same time, to encourage and enable people to take their destiny in hand. "Advocacy" alone is not sufficient, "empowerment" is indispensable.

Because the development of western concepts of rationality shows us, that this rationality cannot be the sole rationality[4] of the global society, the "preferential option for the poor" will have new functions and new scopes. We should see this opportunity in the process of globalization. The Church should act more globally, not in a global uniformity, but by globalizing local, regional, national and international networks.

In this area, the Church is a very under-developed "global player". We should change this in order to promote the alternatives which Christians indeed have against the negative effects of globalization.

---

[4] See Richard Münch, "The Dynamics of Societal Communication," in: Paul Colomy (Ed.), *The Dynamics of Social Systems*, London, 1992, pp. 56-71.

Alternatives to Globalization: Philippine-Asia-Pacific Experience

Mary John Mananzan

Introduction

One of the most debilitating effects of Globalization is the attitude that there is no other alternative and all we have to do is to capitulate to what is already there and to make the most out of it. Any alternative to Globalization has to break through this attitude. We should first of all be capable of saying NO to the values of globalized economy. It calls for the *Grosse Verweigerung* which Marcuse challenged society already in the '60's. It calls for what Brueggermann calls "prophetic imagination", which C. Rene Padilla understands as "the imagination that provides the courage to conceive new possibilities for the future on the basis of our confidence in the God of life." (C, Rene Padilla, 1996)

This paper will focus on how women are saying "NO" to Globalization and will describe some of the ways they have concretized their "prophetic imagination" in searching for alternatives to globalization. I will select four areas in which I am personally involved, namely:

1. Women's advocacy in women's organizations
2. Consumer protection
3. Alternative agriculture
4. Academic Advocacy

Women's Organization and Globalization

Women's organizations in Asia have awakened to the tremendously negative effects of globalization on the poor of the world. An example of such an organization is GABRIELA, a federation of about 200 women's organizations in the Philippines with about 50,000 members founded in 1984. We can see from the strategies, campaigns and activities of the organization its committed struggle against the policies, projects of globalization in the country.

1. Organizing: GABRIELA puts a tremendous efforts in the organizing of grassroots women , namely peasants, workers, and urban poor dwellers because it believes that only by organizing the women can they have the power to oppose the forces that oppress them. This effort also includes the training of grassroots leaders. It is noteworthy that in public demonstrations, sectorial leaders are among the main speakers to denounce the effects of globalization on their particular sectors.

2. Mobilizations and Campaigns. – It is in this area that women's organizations give loud and concrete expression to their protest against different aspects of globalization. In April, 1994, The Ramons government hosted the Miss Universe Contest in Manila to kick-off the development of tourism under the Medium Term Plan of the Philippine Government. GABRIELA launched a series of education and information activities among the grassroots women and organized a demonstration on the opening day of the Ms. Universe event. In October of the same year, it called for a national day of protest against the signing of the GATT. In its annual celebration International Women's Day, GABRIELA mobilizes thousands of women to march to Malacanang Palace and the themes of these marches are against price hikes (1994) , the plight of Migrant Filipinas (1995) and the Denunciation of the Oppressive Labor Policies (1996) all of which have to do with the effects of globalization.

Women are well known for their creativity and sometimes dramatic ingenuity in their protest actions. We all know of the laudable gesture of the Indian women of the Chipko movement when they embraced the trees of the Himalayas to save them from being cut down by logging companies. In the Philippines, the protest action of the indigenous women of the Cordillera against the Chico River Dam has become legendary. When the protesting women were confronted by the military, at a signal from their leader, they took off their blouses, which startled the men and caused them to run away. A peasant movement in the Philippines, the AMIHAN launched a land occupation campaign where its women simply tilled an unoccupied land and planted and harvested food for their families.

3. Education: GABRIELA has an education desk that gives systematic education on current national issues to its members and to the public. Some modules are on globalization, Structural Adjustment Programmes, GATT, foreign debt, price hikes, labor policies, APEC (Asia Pacific Economic Council) etc. AMIHAN has launched international conferences for Asian peasant women on the Structural Adjustment Program. During the APEC summit held in the Philippines in November, 1996, GABRIELA sponsored a workshop on Globalization and Women attended by women from 7 countries.

4. Alternative Projects: Ulrich Duchrow in his article "God or Mammon: Economies in Conflict" (1996) advocates micro-alternatives. He writes:

Every person, household, neighborhood, group of friends, congregation, church, mission and charity organization, etc. has a certain freedom, a niche, to introduce life-serving financial and economic micro-alternatives. To make it quite clear from the beginning: small-scale alternatives are not the whole solution but a start, the humus, signs of the new vision. Yet as such they are highly important to break the taboo of the idolized system paralyzing the people by saying that there is no alternative. (Duchrow, 1996)

In this regard women organizations have pioneering projects. A woman's organization SAMAKANA , belonging to GABRIELA, has set up alternative day care centers and primary health care centers in urban poor communities. Small credit projects have been set up giving small loans to vendors. Small trading projects (buy and sell) run by women's unions have been established. An urban poor community in Iloilo has set up a successful business of banana cues which they are exporting to Switzerland. Because of the high cost of medicine, women have resorted to alternative healing . There has been a return to the traditional herbal medicines. Many herbal gardens have sprung up in the country and groups of women are engaged in selling herbal medicines, biodegradable soap, and some are engaged in acupuncture, acupressure, reflexology, crystal-healing and pranic-healing.

The Peasant Women's Organization, AMIHAN, undertook a land occupation project in Mindoro where they planted on land that had not been in use for 20 years. They were able to sustain these for several years until the landlord and the military put a stop the project. This is attempted in many other parts of the Philippines with greater or lesser success.

Another alternative women's project is the alternative marketing initiated by the Okitama Women's Network in Japan with organic banana growers in Negros, Philippines. The project is assessed thus:

> These Japanese consumers are consciously paying for both healthy bananas and healthier community in Negros. Alternative marketing CAN work with consciousness raising efforts toward both producers and consumers. It provides an opportunity to grow, eat and create together. Alternative markets like this create people to people trade which can replace the present trade system which is having detrimental effects upon communities-both farmers and consumers. This is just one idea working to change the system beginning at the grassroots level. This example is a small effort, but if everybody in the world starts this way—small—we can build many networks of alternative marketing which WITH and FOR people and their communities. (From a Report in a Rural Women's Workshop sponsored by ISIS, Manila, in Rome in 1996)

Women in Consumer Protection

Consumers are most vulnerable to globalization propaganda. For example, to promote import liberalization, consumers are told: You should promote import liberalization, because this will ensure your having many products to choose from and because of the competition you will get things more cheaply. Consumers who are shortsighted fall for this seductive promise. However consumers who are socially aware argue that on a short –term basis, this is true but in the long run import liberalization will kill local industry and will make people depend on foreign goods for their basic necessities. This will not insure sustainable consumption. This is very crucial especially in the area of food security. And although all are consumers, women as consumers are the more affected because in our present family set-up women not only buy for themselves but for the whole household. This is the reason why women take active part in consumer protection.

In the Philippines, women constitute the majority of the members of the Citizens' Alliance for Consumer Protection, which is one of the organizations of civil society that monitors the effects of globalization on the Filipino people. It has made consistent educational efforts to enlighten the citizens about such topics as food security and food availability, the rice crisis, energy crisis, water crisis but most importantly it has disabused the minds of the people about the seductive promises of import liberalization regarding choice and cheaper prices of products. It has launched campaigns against oil price hikes, smoking, junk foods, banned drugs, baby food advertising. It has mobilized other consumer groups in the country around these issues.. Together with other NGO's in the Philippines it has joined nationwide general strikes that have succeeded in winning a rollback of oil price or of a restraining order from the Supreme Court against oil price hikes.

An example of a successful action by women consumers was regarding their electric bills. One of the conditions of the Structural Adjustment Fund is the removal of government subsidies for basic services such as electricity. Already suffering from the rise of their electric bills, women consumers noticed that this was aggravated by anomalies in their electric billing. So about a hundred women resolved to monitor their electric bills for a year and pinpointed unexplained raise in their bill . They prepared a well-documented presentation of their case using an overhead projector and they made an appointment with the President of the Manila Electric Company (Meralco). They won their case.

The Pacific Island Women's Consumer Education Resource Book likewise documents an alternative action to solve the growing dependence of the islanders on imported food, which was regarded as "the single, most dramatic consumer problem identified in the Pacific Islands." (p.17). The project is called the Supsup Garden and is described in the following:

> A creative solution to the complex problem of dependence on imported food is the Supsup Garden. Supsup is Pidgin English for Soup. The recipe is simple: boil up any vegetables available with what fish or meat you have on hand and you have a nutritious and tasty meal. The key is to cultivate your own garden. (p.16)

Several Supsup gardens have been established in Honiara, Solomon Islands. These gardens use mixed cropping, recycling of waste, composting and use of natural methods of pest control. No pesticides or chemical fertilizers are used. In the center of each garden a kitchen is constructed where the soup is cooked. Many groups visit the gardens to learn how to start their own. The writers of the Resource Book evaluate the supsup garden project thus:

> The supsup garden provides a simple, effective and practical solution to the problems of poor nutrition and dependence on imported foods. In place of canned fish, rice and salted beef people are encouraged to eat more fruit and vegetables. People can be taught to establish small gardens in difficult environments such as on coral atolls, where "gardens in a bucket" using old tins or tyre casings are grown.

The supsup garden is an important means of ensuring that nobody starves in Paradise. (p.17)

Sustainable Agriculture

One of the more successful alternative projects engaged in by women is the cultivation of small, sustainable bio-diverse farms. At present, globalization has reduced land area for food cultivation by turning them into golf courses, real estate, or commercial complexes. And those that are cultivated are used for monoculture cash crops using chemical fertilizers and pesticides. Farmers who till this land never rise from their poverty and indebted existence. A visit to one of the alternative, bio-diverse farms gives hope to the possibility of families becoming self-sustaining.

The farm we visited is a two and a half hectare land in a barrio in the province of Pangasinan in Northern Luzon. It is cultivated by a family and is named Geo-farm. Five years ago this land was a rice field, flat with hardly any trees. Now it is full of trees and planted with varied plants. Its objectives listed in its brochure include:

1. Natural Food Production- The farm applies bio-dynamic concept and organic approach featuring home gardening, agro-forestry, agro-ecology and permanent culture.

2. Alternative/Renewable Energy-The farm runs with alternative power from biogas, solar and wind energy.

3. Total waste management- Human, animal and plant waste are transformed into biogas that runs the kitchen's refrigerator and some lights.

4. No pollution- In the farm there is no air pollution, no water pollution no soil pollution, no social, cultural or technological pollution.

5. Promotion of Health and Well-being- Through the use of herbal plants, and organic food, clean air and good relations, people living in the farm live in a healthy manner and in harmony with nature.

6. Combat malnutrition- The farm has a spirulina culture, which is an algae that has complete food nutrients in proper proportion and can be the answer to malnourishment and undernourished population.

7. Technology transfer- The farm provides seminars in which it shares the vision and the practice and skills of sustainable bio-diverse farming.

Since its beginnings in 1992, the farm has been visited by hundreds of groups and thousands of people both from the Philippines and abroad and all who take the seminars are converted to healthy, nutritious food and some have even started their own bio-diverse farms. They have seen for themselves that the family has developed from food security to poverty alleviation and to 80%

sustainability. It provides a possibility as a "termite strategy" to gradually undermine the false claims of globalization with regard to the provision of basic necessities.

The School as Agent of Social Transformation

When people today speak of Civil Society as a force to confront globalization, they don't usually include schools and yet schools when properly oriented can be one of the most effective agents of change. I give as an example, St. Scholastica's College, a school for women run by an all-women administration in Manila. It has 6,500 students and three departments: Grade School, High School and College. German Benedictine nuns founded it in 1906. It soon became an elite school that educated the daughters of prominent Filipino Families. In 1975, confronted with poverty, injustice and oppression under Martial Law, the school launched a re-orientation of its vision towards Education for Justice. It revised its curriculum, its methodology, and its policies according to this vision. In 1985, it added the gender perspective to its vision not only mainstreaming Women's Studies in its curriculum but it likewise established an Institute of Women's Studies that gives alternative courses for women and publishes women's books. Its social orientation has also adopted an ecological approach establishing an Institutional Project Team for Environmental Concerns (IPTEC) to ensure the continued awareness and practice of environmental conservation by the academic community.

This year, in the annual orientation talk of the College President, she announced the special focus of study of the whole academic community, namely : Globalization and its impact on the Filipino people. This topic is incorporated in the syllabi of the faculty, is the topic of convocations, symposia and fora, and is incorporated in the co-and extra curricular activities of the different departments.

An example of an institutional activity is the Health Food Campaign, which has been launched. A Health Food Committee has initiated a series of lectures for all sectors : teachers, staff, maintenance, students, parents and canteen concessionaires. By the end of the campaign, healthy food preparation will be expected of the canteen concessionaires and all junk foods and soft drinks will be removed from the school canteen.

The Institute of Women's Studies has acquired a one hectare lot which is being developed into a bio-diverse farm and which will be the home of the Women and Ecology Wholeness Center. It will feature, besides sustainable and organic farming, holistic healing and eco-feminist spirituality. It will also provide organically raised vegetables to the Geo-Garden café, which the College is opening. This will be the official practice house of the Hotel and Restaurant Department of the College. It is a unique kind of café, which will offer only healthy foods and alternative entertainment such as chamber music, indigenous music and alternative cinema. In its own little way this is an alternative to the globalized Coke and Macdonald culture.

A significant involvement of the students of the college is in the struggle of Hacienda Looc, an 8,650.78 hectares of beautiful land in Nasugbu Batangas, home of 10,000 farmers. The gist of the problem is :

Ten thousand peasant families are about to be displaced from their land, their rights as land reform beneficiaries forfeited as Fil-Estates Harbortown transforms their nature-endowed coastal villages into an exclusive playground for the rich. When completed, Harbortown will include 4 golf courses a 5-star hotel, beach resorts, a marina for yacht anchorage and neighborhoods of luxurious homes.

Tension has begun to grip this once placid farming and fishing community, Fil-Estate's security guards have already killed two members of the local peasant organization. Of late, military troops came in the area in the guise of conducting training but which is believed by the local population as another attempt by Fil-Estate to sow terror and fear among them .(From an unpublished Situationer on Hacienda Looc)

The involvement of the students of St. Scholastica's College began when four students majoring in Social Development Through Community Organizing made their required practicum in Hacienda Looc. They made a study of the situation. They lived with the farmers for a year and in the many meetings they had with the farmers, these resolved to fight the Fil-Estate. They staged pickets and rallies both in front of the Department of Agrarian reform and Fil-Estate offices in Manila. They called for a press conference and the Philippine Daily Inquirer assigned a special reporter to cover the whole process. When the Fil-Estate started bulldozing the place, human barricades were set up. When Fil-Estate cut down a tree, the women of the community went to the place and celebrated a ritual of atonement. Two of the students who have graduated continue to work in the area as volunteers of the Work-a-Year Program of the school. Due to the vigilance of the people, the Fil-Estate has not been able to continue with their "development" project in the place as of this writing.

Conclusion

Globalization continues to seduce governments of developing countries to be integrated into its fold. Meanwhile the greater majority of the people of many countries both, developed and developing, are suffering from its ill-effects. This should provide a more solid basis of international solidarity, since First World people are no longer just commiserating with the miseries of the Third World people but somehow experience the same negative effects of globalization even if not to the same degree. There is no blueprint for an alternative to globalization. The different efforts, different forms of resistance, and initiatives at alternative systems such as the ones described in this paper must be encouraged and shared and somehow coordinated. Out of these radial energies a tangential energy could somehow bring a quantum leap to something qualitatively new and bring about a fundamental societal transformation.

But for this to happen there must be a political will of the people to resist. So I would like to conclude with the Filipino Women's Manifesto declared by GABRIELA on October 28, 1985:

Our Nation is in crisis

WE, the women, know because we live the crisis everyday.

This crisis has exacerbated the specific forms of oppression that we have to contend with as women.

We are the housewives who can barely make ends meet because of the dwindling value of the peso and spiraling prices.

We are the consumers, victims of monopolies, price fixing, hoarding, and false advertising.

We are the mothers who grieve over the future of children we can neither clothe nor educate.

We are the mothers who desperately watch our children waste away because of hunger and disease.

We are the peasant women who do not have access to basic social services, who do not have a voice in the decisions that our lives, and who bear the double burden of unpaid labor at home and in the fields.

We are the urban poor who live in extreme poverty, yet must defend our shanties and meager possessions against harassment and demolition.

We are the street demonstrators whose legitimate protests are met with water canons and truncheons, tear gas and bullets.

WE, WHO MAKE UP THE BULK OF THE SILENT MAJORITY, WILL NO LONGER BE SILENT. WE, WHO HAVE BEEN CALLED THE WEAKER SEX, WILL NO LONGER BE COWED. WE WHO HAVE BEEN RELEGATED TO THE HOME WILL NO LONGER BE CONFINED.

IN UNITY WE WILL RAISE OUR COLLECTIVE VOICES, WE WILL BUILD OUR POLITICAL STRENGTH.

Sources:

Behind Our Smiles: Pacific Island Women's Consumer Education Resource Book, New Zealand: South Pacific Consumer Protection Program, 1994.

Mission Studies, Vol. XIII-1 & 2, 1996.

An Assessment of Impact: GABRIELA's Three Year Plan (1994-1996)

Citizens' Alliance For Consumer Protection Progress Report (1995-1996).

Unpublished Manuscript: *Hacienda Looc*

Conclusion
Towards Global Community

Michael Amaladoss, S.J.

When globalization is seen from the point of view of its victims the tendency may be to see it as an unmixed evil. Such evil and sinful aspects have been evoked many times in various ways in the preceding papers. In opposition to it we tend to stress the local reality and community and an eventual networking among them. One might even look favourably at post modern pluralism, provided it does not become anarchic. I would like to suggest however that the plan of God for humanity and the world has global dimensions. God's salvific will is universal, not merely in space and time, but also in its human and cosmic depth. The goal of history is the reconciliation of all things so that God will be all in all. (1 Cor 15:28) A clearer understanding of God's global vision will throw a counter-cultural light on the evils of the human attempts at globalization as we experience it today.

The Vision of the Kingdom as Global Community

The mystery of creation is God wishing to share God's life with us. God's life is a gift of God's unconditional love. This life is experienced as freedom from every bondage, as fellowship in the community of God's people and as justice expressed in equality and sharing. Jesus in his life experiences this unconditional love of God and seeks to share it with the people. He proclaims the Kingdom: God's nearness to and concern for God's people. He frees people from the structures of unfreedom, both personal (Mammon) and structural (Satan), as manifested in the various illnesses of which the people were victims. He struggles for justice in solidarity with the publicans and sinners, the prostitutes and the marginalized in society. He protests against the prevailing economic, political and religious leadership who oppress the people in various ways. He exhorts people to love and to share their goods and to assert their freedom from empty ritualism and legalism. He gives them a new commandment of love which must show itself in mutual service, in sharing and in self-giving even unto death. He shows that it is in loving the other that one loves God: when God is experienced as parent, all people become brothers and sisters. His solidarity with the poor leads his to conflict with the rich and the powerful, with the political, theological and religious establishments of his time. He does not hesitate to lay down his life as the ultimate witness to his Good News. God raises him. The risen Christ and the Spirit animate a new movement of people, who seek to be symbols and servants of the Kingdom.

In the power of the Spirit, the disciples of Jesus create new communities of sharing and fellowship in prayer and mutual service. They realize that this Good News is for all peoples and fan out into the then known world. Particularly Paul and John, contemplating the mystery of Jesus' life, see in it the mystery of God's plan for the whole universe. Paul envisions a new cosmic community, in which God seeks to gather all things (Eph 1:10), reconcile all things (Col 1:20), reunite all things so that God will be all in all (1 Cor 15:28). There will be equality and community between the Jew and the Greek, men and women, masters and slaves. (Gal 3:28) The diversity of the gifts of the Spirit will find a common purpose in the service of the community. (1 Cor 12:4-11) Even the cosmos will be integrated in the freedom and glory of the children of God. (Rom 8:21) John sees the Word of God enlightening every one (Jn 1:9) and becoming flesh to share with us his fullness (Jn 1:16), so that all will be in Jesus as he is in the Father (Jn 17:21-23). John also sees God making all things new, so that there will be a new heaven and a new earth, where there will be no more tears and suffering. (Rev 21:1-5) Such a vision is an echo of the expectation of the prophets. (Is 60-62)

The vision of the coming Kingdom then is not the saving of individual souls in a spiritual and other worldly heaven but the reconciliation and reintegration of the whole universe in a community in which God dwells as the goal and fulfillment of history.

Inequality and discrimination of every kind will disappear. Love and life, justice and sharing will characterize this community. Even material creation will be part of this communion. This is a vision, full of hope. It does not exclude conflict with personal (Mammon) (cf. Rom 7:14-25) and structural (Satan) (cf. Rev 17-20) evil powers. But in the risen Jesus we have the "first fruits of the Spirit" (Rom 8:23), who makes us children of the Father (*Abba*), who assures us of victory and who makes us free and creative.

Opportunities and Challenges of the Present Moment

Looking at the world today we can see many factors that make us dream of the possibility of a new global community. In the last 150 years science and technology have grown tremendously. Science, by helping us to discover the causes of natural process, has made possible increased production and control. Technology has perfected the instruments necessary for this. Today we can produce enough food to feed every one. We are also able to detect and control diseases and disasters through appropriate remedies. We can, if we wish, meet the basic needs of people in terms of nourishment, health, housing and communications. Facilities for rapid communications has made the global sharing of goods, through trade or exchange, feasible. Interaction between peoples and cultures through travel and encounter has become frequent. The media has promoted both the extent and the rapidity of the exchange of information and knowledge through such means as the television, fax machines and the internet. Not only news of disasters, but also aid travels fast. With the disappearance of the cold war there is a new awareness among peoples of belonging to a global community. Economically, the world is becoming one big market place. Capital as well as goods traverse borders easily. A network of exchange can be built up in which each country contributes its best to the benefit of all. With the disappearance of political colonialism sovereign states are able to manage their own affairs and collaborate with others in freedom and mutual respect. It seems as if we have all the elements necessary for building up a new global society.

But one look at the daily news paper is sufficient to warn us that this promise is not being fulfilled. On the contrary, behind a superficial global mirage created by the presence of consumer goods like jeans and Coca cola every where there is a growing fragmentation among peoples, ethnic and religious conflict, a growing gap between the rich and the poor both internationally and in each country whether rich or poor. In a brief diagnosis one can say that in a world deeply divided between the rich/powerful and the poor, the forces of globalization are exploited by the rich/powerful to increase their riches and power at the expense of the poor. This is an indication that today injustice and globalization are closely linked and that we cannot promote justice anywhere except in the context of promoting a global community. Injustice, while local, may be imposed by a global situation. Our actions to promote justice at local levels will have to reach out necessarily to global levels.

Let us look a little more closely at the many factors that contribute to the deteriorating global situation.

Market and Money

The globalization that people speak of today is primarily that of the market. The market is the new idol. It is supposed to be left autonomous to regulate itself. The principle according to which such self-regulation happens is the maximization of profits. Production and exchange (trade) are driven by the profit motive. Capitalism or the accumulation and control of resources is seen as the best way to promote production and exchange. Since profit is the only consideration the producers of primary goods either in agriculture or in mining are paid very little by the traders who market these goods with astronomical profit margins. Monopolies can create artificial scarcities that push up the prices. Industrial producers establish their production units where cheap and controlled labour is available. The labourers often get only a subsistence wage. Or children and women are exploited for low wages in the labour market. This leads to rising unemployment in countries where labour is more costly. Looking for efficiency production processes are increasingly mechanized. They are not labour intensive. So more and more lower level workers lose their jobs. Today it is the information and service industries that animate the market. Even these units are shifted to poorer countries with lower wages, so that even the middle classes in the more affluent countries face increasing unemployment. Such globalization of the economy is being managed by the multinationals in collaboration with the richer classes in every country, rich or poor. So the gap between the rich and the poor in every country is growing.

Behind this international economy of industry and trade are the money markets. In the past money generated profit through being invested in industry. Today money makes more money through financial speculation. Vast amounts of capital are moved from country to country to profit by differences in tax laws. A whole country can be ruined through such flights of capital which has nothing to do with industry or production. International debts can be multiplied by the creditor country simply raising its interest rates to meet its own internal financial needs.

Politics and Power

The market is supposed to be free. This is the ideology. But in practice the political power has become the servant of the economic power. The richer countries, the G-7 for example, concert together and dictate financial policies to the rest of the world. They control the international financial institutions like the International Monetary Fund, the World Bank and the World Trade Organization and, through them, impose financial structural adjustments on poorer countries. These are forced to cut subsidies to various social projects in favour of increasing savings and investment. This not only further increases the gap between the rich and the poor, but also leads to the deterioration of the general quality of life, since the necessary infrastructures for common life are also neglected. This is economic colonialism. In the past the richer governments used to support politically 'stable' governments in poorer countries, usually run by dictators, to provide them a captive and controlled labour market. Today the structural adjustment programmes imposed by international financial institutions can achieve the same effect in an indirect manner. The alternative for the poor countries is total marginalization in the international market place. The social unrest that such policies will inevitably give rise to are put down by armed might, within and across national boundaries. This necessitates a flourishing arms industry, which not only fills the coffers of the arms producers and merchants, but also wastes precious resources of the poorer countries who buy them - resources, which could have been used for development. The State is thus forced to become the agent of the market economy. Its aim is to create the ideal climate that will attract investment. Even the creation of infrastructures like schools, roads and communications systems are geared to the market. The concern for the common good or for the needs of the poor majority does not enter into their calculations. At the time of the elections promises will be made to the poor and then soon forgotten. Such a situation in which the government, that is the politicians and the bureaucracy, has the power to distribute scarce resources also gives rise to corruption. Politically, the smaller and poorer countries seem to have very little power to decide their own policies. A rich and powerful elite in them is functioning in more or less willing collaboration with the rich and the powerful elsewhere to the detriment of the poor everywhere.

A Narrow Vision

Underlying these economic and political choices is a world vision and a system of values. Science is based on the principles of rationality and immanence. It tries to understand through the use of reason the material world in itself without having recourse to external causes. It refuses to see miracles every where. But people go further and deny anything that is not material and that cannot be understood by reason. Technology develops the technical means that uses the discoveries of science for the control of nature and production of goods. It can be used for increased food production and control of diseases. It can also be used for the production of arms or for the unlimited exploitation of the earth. Industry uses technology for mass production of goods. But rather than serve the needs of the poor, artificial needs are created through advertisement and consumerism and the markets are promoted. The media can be used for rapid communication of information and of mutual encounter. But controlled by market forces they are used rather to misinform people, to promote consumerism though advertisements and to provide people with alienating entertainment. One can even say that the media is made use of to propagate the consumer culture of the market as a sort of universal culture.

The human person is valued as a producer, and perhaps even more as a consumer. In a society governed by the market, what is important is how much a person can earn and how much he can spend. A person is valued for what s/he has rather than for what s/he is. In a competitive society, it is each one for oneself. There is no sense of community. No one things of the other or of the common good. Individualism is rampant. The individual as a consumer also becomes egoist. There is no urge to share; one tends rather to hoard and to put something aside for moments of scarcity in the future or in old age. One talks often about rights of all kinds. But they are all centred on individuals. There is no corresponding discourse about duties and obligations to the others and to the community. Sometimes it looks as if every relationship is reduced to a contractual one. Only claims, not gifts, seem meaningful. If one identifies with one's class or ethnic group, it is more in defence of one's own interests. Such an egoistic identification is itself a differentiation from other groups who are seen either as enemies or as competitors.

Nature is there to be exploited. It is treated as an object. There is no sense of it being God's gift to the whole of humanity, to present as well as to future generations. One looks only at one's own immediate consumeristic, not real, needs. In a competitive atmosphere, one does not bother either about the unjust appropriation of what is more than one's due. It is said that 20% of the people consume 80% of nature's resources today and that nature's resources are fast being depleted and polluted.

It has been remarked that people's attitude to nature is often on a par with their attitude to women. Women continue to be exploited in every way. They are not treated as equals. Their dignity is often violated in various ways. They are made into objects of pleasure. They are used to attract attention in advertisements. Their work is poorly paid. Especially among the poor, they often carry the whole load of the family and bring up the children. Poverty often has a feminine face.

The Transcendent has no real role in the human community. One speaks about secularization, which does not care to deny God, but is quite indifferent to God. People are so busy in making money and in pursuing pleasure that they have no time for God. In any case, the realities and structures of this world - economic, politics, science, industry, etc. - are seen as autonomous from any religious control. They are ruled by the law of the market. If there is still a feeling for religion, it is seen as useful for satisfying private needs for peace and meaning - a refuge in times of personal tension and turmoil. Religion and values have no place in the public sphere, where rationality, efficiency and profitability are the main moving forces.

Peoples' Movements Questioning Globalization

This movement towards a global world based on the market is not going unchallenged in recent times. Various types of peoples' movements have emerged all across the globe. We can explore, for example the ecological, feminist and different subaltern movements.

Ecological movements protest against various types of activity destroying nature. Some think that modern technology and industry is over-exploiting the non-renewable energy resources of the universe jeopardizing the future. Others object to the pollution of present atmospheric and water resources and the destruction of forests and bio-diversity that are detrimental to the quality of life here and now. Peasants and indigenous people protest against such exploitation of nature because they affect their life itself by attacking the sources of their food, water, and fuel. Their dwellings and their sacred spaces are destroyed when forests are cut down either for trading in wood or for substituting them with cash crops. Forests may also be submerged when dams are built for the development of people elsewhere. The ecologists point to the need of the humans for living in harmony with nature, to alternate, renewable sources of energy like the sun and to sustainable patterns of development that do not destroy nature.

Feminist movements question the domination and the exploitation of the women socially, culturally, politically and economically. They protest against the innumerable atrocities committed against them all over the world from female infanticide to dowry deaths. They demand both equality, especially in terms of opportunities, at every level and respect for their identity and originality. They point to the religious legitimation of male-dominant structures and ask for reform and liberation.

CONCLUSION

Subaltern Movements

Oppressed groups everywhere like the Dalits in India, the Afro-Americans, the indigenous peoples and ethnic and religious minorities are reasserting their identity as a source of a culture, alternate to the locally dominant one. They clamour for equality, respect and justice. Besides these groups, the poor everywhere feel excluded from the material affluence that they see all around them. They demand a say in decisions that affect them. Their protest may sometimes take violent forms, which are often a sign of desperation.

There may be a lot of ambiguities in these movements, especially in the subaltern ones. Their protest against injustice is authentic enough. But they may have interiorized the worldview and values of the modern West. Their action may represent a collective form of selfishness, in which their very solidarity in the name of class, caste, ethnicity, religion or language may exclude others who may be similarly poor or even poorer, but who do not belong to their group. They may be easily be led to a certain religious or ethnic fundamentalism and may even find in it an escape. The homogenizing effort of modernity itself may be at the origin of these movements as means of defending one's identity and of protesting against one's exclusion.

We can also note many positive elements in these movements. The oppressed have woken up. They are no longer passively submitting to their oppression. A certain experience of democracy, however inadequate and imperfect, may be one of the causes of their self-assertion. A few people from these groups who may have had the privilege of education and development are not running away from the group to look after their private well-being, but are willing to conscientize and lead their people. The mass media, while it could flood them with alienating entertainment or false propaganda, are also offering them images and information about the wider world, its progress and its opportunities. This opens them to perceive new possibilities for themselves. Images of a revolution, even partially successful, elsewhere, can inspire hope and commitment at home. Some movements have used the media to conscientize and organize their group. Others have known to profit by the media to inform the wide world of their plight and purpose and receive international solidarity and support. We note here the positive impact of a certain globalization, perhaps unintended.

Empowering the People

What can we do in this situation? I would like to suggest here a three pronged approach. We can empower the people by being in solidarity with them. We can be symbolic counter-cultural communities that present an alternative to contemporary global culture. We can be prophets to the dominant forces, either in the First World or the local elite who collaborate with them for their own narrow benefit, linking together in a network with peoples' movements everywhere.

We have to acknowledge in the first place the conflict that is going on in the world between the rich and the poor. It may not be open; it may not be always violent. But it is there, even if it is only visible in the powerless rage or dispirited fatalism of the poor. In this situation we are called to make an option to be in solidarity with the poor. We must not dilute this option with finding different meanings for the term 'poor'. Poor are the economically poor. Poverty may be cumulative; but economic poverty remains always the foundation. They make take different forms today as migrants, refugees, the unemployed, the excluded, etc. They are oppressed by the economically, politically and socially powerful.

To be in solidarity with the poor does not mean that we take their place. Only the people can liberate themselves. They have to become aware of their situation; they have to get organized; they have launch a movement; they have to claim and fight for their rights; they have to make use of the existing democratic facilities to assert themselves and to make their voices heard.

Though economics and the market are the motors of the globalization of injustice, in today's world order they are still subject to political power, exercised either by individual States or by groups of States. The people can bring pressure on the State only through the political process. For this many groups, with common or converging interests, will have to act together, using not only peoples' power, but also moral authority and media power. Today many democracies are not really participative. Often the governments are not even elected by a majority of the people. Once elected, the representatives are not responsive to the people. The need then is to move towards democracy from the grass roots where people will be able to participate at every level.

Working in solidarity with the poor, we will get involved in conflicts. Conflicts would bring suffering, even martyrdom as recent history has shown. Our quest should be, not peace and order at any price, but peace with justice. We can help the people to network with other groups nationally and internationally, especially when multi-nationals or international institutions are involved. Even exploitative institutions are careful about their image. So they are vulnerable to certain types of publicity. In a struggle like this the poor will never make it alone. They will need the support of sympathetic groups in the middle class, intellectuals and journalists.

Witnessing to a Counter-Culture

I have pointed out above that the problem about globalization is not the resources of science and technology but the world-view and value system that use them for their own purposes. I have also suggested that the poor too may have interiorized some of these values. These are constantly made present and instilled into public awareness by the media. It is a challenging task to present a counter-cultural vision which proposes an alternate world-view and system of values. This can be done effectively, not by talking about them, but by living them. We could the nuclei of counter-cultural communities that give active witness to these values. These values are those of the Kingdom that Jesus proclaimed and started to realize on this earth. I shall spell out these alternate values as a set of affirmations.

Affirming Life

We have to affirm *life* in all its forms. The life that needs to be affirmed is not life after death, but life before death. This would include the protection of nature, the defence of the unborn, especially the female infant, the support of children and women. Any human society will have to assure the basic necessities of life to all its people. Today's these necessities would be not only food, health and a place to live, but also others like the right to basic education and to employment.

To affirm human life is to affirm a life worthy of the humans, who are not machines, but spirits-in-bodies. They are entitled to freedom and to creative self-expression in its various forms and to appropriate spaces and opportunities for such creativity. To live humanly means also a life that is not dominated by the urge to consume. A human knows to transcend the body, even when rooted in it. The body becomes the expression of the spirit and not its master. One humanizes oneself through a certain self-discipline. One learns to measure one's pleasures. In a world in which the body and even the human person are turned into objects and commodities to be exploited and to be experimented upon we have to witness to a spiritual humanism.

To affirm the spirit in the human is also to affirm the divine presence in the human, the transcendent which is immanent. The humans and the world itself then become symbols and sacraments of God. We experience the presence and power of the risen Christ and the creative gifts of the Spirit. One would then reject the materialism and secularism of modernity and seek to humanize science and technology so that they become instruments in human hands to promote life rather than turn the humans themselves into machines. Ultimately it is a sense of freedom, measure and control over the self and over the world, which is not seen as imposed from the outside, but which emerges as the normal self expression of the human. One will no longer be the victim of structures of any kind, but will be able to dominate them even in the midst of suffering. Becoming human in this manner is a life-long project. It is the process of self-realization. The Christian tradition seems to have lost this art through the formalism of its spirituality. On the contrary, the oriental traditions of Hinduism and Buddhism have kept alive such methods of self-development and attract western disciples. It is a programme of personal discipline, which through breathing, posture and meditation, combined with an appropriate life-style, improves the quality of life.

Affirming Community

Secondly, we have to affirm *community*. The human is born in a family and is humanized by a culture. From the beginning we are humans-in-a-community. This is our natural way of life. To be individualistic is to artificially isolate oneself. In life we experience ourselves as interdependent at every stage. It is in the love of the other that we discover ourselves and experience the presence of God among us. The experience of community is lived at various levels from the family, to the group, to the nation and to the world. The new commandment of Jesus to love one another as he has loved us makes us reach out to every one so that we all feel one as the body of Christ.

To affirm community is to respect and accept the others with all their differences of caste or creed, sex or ethnicity, culture or social status. We cease to be egoists. We are ready to share, to give ourselves even unto death. We set the common good over our own personal convenience or preference, because we recognize that our own well-being depends on the well-being of every one. In the world of today it may be difficult to convince the affluent that their own peace and well-being depends on the well-being of all. And yet the various measures they take to protect themselves from others and the fear that dogs them wherever they go is an indirect acknowledgement of this truth, which however they refuse to recognize.

To affirm community is to affirm peace. Real peace in the community will come only with justice. Otherwise violence in its various forms will continue to plague us. Inequality in whatever form can be maintained only through violence, whether open or hidden.

Pluralism and Public Space

To affirm community is to affirm pluralism of all kinds because of the variety of God's gifts and the creativity of human freedom. This is experienced as the pluralism of cultures. Such pluralism is accepted as richness. Community as a communion of free human beings is not a given, but has constantly to be built up. Dialogue then becomes a way of life.

Today religious pluralism poses a particular type of challenge. But it is possible for believers of different faiths to collaborate for the defence and promotion of common human and spiritual values while finding justification for such action each in his or her own religion. Hinduism and Buddhism have produced liberation theologians much before Christianity. Gandhi in India and Buddhadasa in Thailand are examples. Given the past and present hostility and even open conflict between religious groups this is not easy. But communion in a multi-religious community is not possible without collaboration in common ethical and social projects. Common praxis is more important than a common ideology spelt out in rational categories with the pretension of being global. Today most communities in the world are multi-religious, whether or not they acknowledge themselves as such.

To build up community in this manner we have to cultivate a public space, different from the State, in which ongoing conversation, dialogue and even controversy is possible so that consensual relationships can be built up in a human manner. It is in the public space that public opinion is created which is basic and necessary for any common political action. Educational institutions, the media, cultural and associative groups and religions would contribute to the animation of such a public space.

The Global and the Local

Justice issues are primarily local issues. But they are often linked to global structures. The global players have allies in the local economic and political elite. Action for justice therefore has to be both local and global. One may have to tackle local issues in the global context; one may also have to tackle global issues both locally and globally. The phenomena of economic migrants and political refugees seem to be offshoots of globalization and demand international attention. Global action is possible only through networking. The media today make such networking easy and possible. Some international institutions like the United Nations and some of its agencies may facilitate such networking, though their official status may render them powerless. At this level, public-spirited lawyers, journalists and social activists serve as catalysts. Coalitions for action may be longstanding or temporary. But one will have to be discerning in choosing one's collaborators, because of possible vested interests, though a strategic, temporary alliance may tolerate even these.

There will always be a tension between the global and the local. The global will tend to impose homogeneity in the name of unity. The local will defend its specific identity. For us the focus is the Kingdom. But the Kingdom is a vision, a set of values, not concrete structures. The Kingdom will find local expression, given to it by the local people with their culture and history. Today even the local may be specified not in geographical, but in cultural or ethnic terms. Ongoing dialogue between the different concretizations of the Kingdom will lead to mutual respect, understanding, enrichment and communion. One could think of a convergence of communities. It is not easy to visualize because the principle of unity is not found somewhere in itself, but always contextualized somewhere. Therefore it is always unity-in-difference.

A Role for the Church?

Where does the Church stand in relation to the phenomena globalization and the various counter-cultural and subaltern movements. As the symbol and servant of the Kingdom in the world, the Church is called to be a catholic (universal) communion of local Churches and communities. But unfortunately, the Church is very far from living this ideal. One could even say that it seems to be doing everything to subvert it. Uniformity of thought and structures are imposed everywhere in the name of unity, even though one speaks constantly of cultural pluralism. Its sacralized hierarchical structures keep the people of God away from real and effective participation. Even the communities of Religious suffer from the same drawbacks. Many of their educational and other institutions in the Third World seem to be active promoters of the wrong kind of globalization. Fortunately, the Church too has its subaltern groups that keep alive in word and deed the vision and ideals of the Kingdom as a global community. These groups are called to network with other similar groups elsewhere who share their vision and goals, promoting in this manner God's own mission in the world.

Conclusion

In recent years, the political divide between the East and the West has been succeeded by the economic divide between the North and the South. In trying to perpetuate its hegemony, the North is imposing the economy of the market supported by political and even military power and is seeking to homogenize culture in its own western image. In contesting the inevitability of this division on behalf of the poor and in the name of the liberator God, the Gospel does not have ready-made economic and political blue-prints. But it offers a new system of values that does not reject the positive benefits of science and technology but submits them to human control and purpose. It builds up new prophetic communities that seek to symbolize and promote these values. It opts for the poor and the marginalized, empowering them and calling the rich and the powerful to conversion. It celebrates cultural and religious pluralism as the embodiment of God's gifts and human creative freedom and seeks to promote communion and harmony.

We are sent into the world as symbols and servants of this new global community of freedom, justice and harmony. We are invited to read the signs of the times and to discern not only God's activity in the world gathering every thing, in heaven and on the earth, but also the new peoples' movements that are working for a new world order. We are inspired by the Spirit to prophetic action. It is for us to spell out what are the concrete ways in which we can help people build the new global community which is God's dream for God's people. This demands from us an openness to relate and to network, to dialogue and to collaborate. While rooted in the economic and political reality of life, we may need to concentrate on the personal, cultural and religious dimensions of the peoples' movements. Our animating vision will always remain the Kingdom that Jesus preached, which is God's gift to all peoples and which will bring the whole universe together into a new global community of the peoples of God.

Reports of Group Discussions

Group I

Group I discussed "globalization" in the sense of "integration of the economies of the whole world including the 3rd world in the liberal capitalist economy dominated by Group 7."

A large number of farmers are displaced through mega projects (e.g. mega dams) and through new lifestyle (e.g. farm houses, golf courses). They lose their lands and live in slums. Indigenous people and the urban poor are excluded from society. The labourers have lost the security of their work. The economic exclusion of the poor is at the same time depolitization. In the process of victimization there is always collaboration between foreign and internal agents of economics as well as politics. Globalization is deeply antidemocratic, against the real participation of the people in controlling the system.

The evil strategy of globalization is to keep people in the dark. The consequences of consumption are not merely superficial; they have their own power to strengthen the internalization of the system by the victims. Therefore to counter the globalization process one must became aware of its negative consequences.

The growing unemployment in all countries has shown that globalization has negative consequences for all countries and all people.

The group's discussion moved from the ambiguity of globalization to the ambiguity of the Churches. They can become instruments of the globalization process. They can also become centres of a counter culture, a culture of resistance. They can become centres of creativity to bring out alternatives.

Alternatives

1. **Advocacy and empowerment.** This means organizing people, training grassroots leaders and forming pressure groups to effectively influence decision making processes in society (government, business etc.) for the benefit of the people

2. Cooperating with sisters and brothers of other faiths as well as people of good will in all movements. By doing so the churches are more credible and not suspected of proselytising.

3. Appreciating the wisdom of the marginalized people, their cultural symbols that maintain and promote human dignity, as well as supporting their sense of sharing and mutual responsibility.

4. Building pressure groups at micro and macro levels, both in the 1st and in the 3rd worlds, from the perspective of social justice in economic and political structures

5. To force ethical investment by the states, private and institutional investors (e.g. Churches) to finance and develops enterprises and companies which respect ecological, social and cultural goals.

6. To manage our schools and educational institutions as agents of conscientization and social transformation.

7. To educate the consumers to know and protect their rights, to inculcate simplicity of life-style and to work for sustainable consumption and self-reliance.

8. To encourage small and sustainable biodiverse farming, to ensure food security, to lessen the need of imported food.

9. To recognize the great potential of women's organization for advocacy and to encourage their alternative initiatives countering negative aspects of globalization.

10. To appeal to the common humanity of everyone (the rich and the poor, the powerless and the powerful) and to the reality of our universal sisterhood/brotherhood. Everyone who claims to be human has a responsibility to see to it that global economics and politics are so restructured as to ensure that every child the

world over is properly fed clothed, sheltered, educated, protected from every exploitation and abuse, as well as honored and offered a human future. Short of this there can be no civilized life. Short of it all talk about democracy, freedom, human rights etc. is hollow and hypocritical. Short of this we are betraying our humanity and retreating to the jungle and the deep sea where the big prey on the small.

Group II

Contemporary sociological theories of globalization of the world-system have by now taken several forms, with varying ideas as to what the most important elements of globality are. These include the capitalist world economy, the global political system of sovereign states, communication technologies and global/local culture. Without ignoring other elements, this conference and the members of our group place economy at the centre, without ignoring political power and cultural forces. The Speakers tend to see very basic tensions as characteristic of the global system, tensions which most often pit the larger systemic or structural elements such as economy, technology, and polity against a varied and in some way embattled "non-systemic" domain. In Habermasian terms, globalization features a typically modern struggle between system and life-world, in which the former in various ways is in the habit of "colonizing" the latter. Accordingly, culture, identity, and the self are the various battlegrounds on which this rudimentary conflict takes place.

1. Without for the moment trying to defend or criticize this prevailing view of an inherently problematic and conflictual globality, I note that in our group religion usually entered the discussion as a cultural non-systematic force. Religious institutions, actors, and ideas are sources of identity, cultural assertion, anti-systemti-elements, and the like. They were also, though not so often, put forward as "coloniser," as a structural component of globality, in short as system. We did not however reflect on the evidence of what might be called the shaping of a global religious system along with other differentiated social systems in global society in which we and the victims of history increasingly live today.

2. Globalization and localization are themes of such universal moment and importance that it is clear that they represent a new frontier of experience as well as awareness for the church and the theologians everywhere. We see, that the efforts of constructing local theologies as alternatives to universalizing and universalised systemic patterns of christianity will have to be continued. Furthermore, the theologians will have to become "globalization managers" within our cultures.

The issues of inculturation, deculturation, acculturation, and interreligious dialogue will be with us.

Throughout these days the group was aware of the "beast" side of globalization: `the bulldozer', `steamroller', `whirlpool', `the trap' -- a perspective which is seen with the eyes of the poor and of the marginalized of a globalizing world. Fighting globalization from within, in the mode of guerilla activity, was largely seen as the required response to it.

3. The role of the church in the situation of increasing globalization was seen to be threefold: The church facilitated globalization, so that we need to recall christianity's historical contribution to economic and cultural globalization. As a global player christianity can be analysed in terms of its own systemic global formation. Religion has anti-systemic potential to support either anti-globalizing forces or to promote new global theological flows (Schreiter), which may renegotiate globalization.

4. As we look at the connection between globalization and culture three paradigms are seen:

   1. There is a widespread understanding that growing global (economic) interdependence may tend towards increasing cultural standardization and uniformisation, in the global sweep of consumerism. A shorthand version of this momentum is 'McDonaldization'.

   2. A second understanding is that various forms of difference have come to the foreground, for instance in relation to identity politics, gender, minority rights, indigenous peoples, and ethnic and religious movements. There seems to be

cultural revivals as a response to globalization. We are presently experiencing a 'clash of civilizations'.

3. A third position focuses on cultural change, saying that what is taking place is a process of trans local cultural mixing or hybridization.

— Along these lines we discussed experiences of change of values under modernization and globalization. In different areas of the world, different cultural modes of globalization are highlighted. We tried to look how globalization creates and transforms cultures, how it creates a consumeristic mind set and culture, how the resonance to globalised culture products can be seen in poor countries.

— As culture is always a rather dynamic than a static entity it can be detected, controlled, accepted, rejected.

In this regard three aspects, mainly in the form of questions, were put forward.

— Who are the elite people controlling the economy and forming a globalized culture?

— How can the promotion of cultural identity be part of power formation? How does it disadvantageously lead to cultural self-exclusion?

— We felt that cultural rootedness best allows for acceptance and critical openness to globalizing cultural moments.

5. Though the section on theology and globalization had several inputs we mainly got stuck with Felix Wilfred's distinction of motivations versus content in the new theological endeavour. We understand that a theology is required which gives space mainly to the context. Against centralised and reformist proposals an anthropologically based ecclesiology is required, which is suggestive for a motivational hermeneutics, which opens up history and reflection beyond settled foundations and beyond theological and historical determinations. How we theologise is more important than the content. We learned that e.g. Tamil theology seeks to identity Jesus in the Dalits' own context; that

content is less important than the effort to provide motivational hermeneutics. Contrasting terms as context vs. dogma, theological determinism vs. global opening up beyond settled foundations pointed to the need to hear more about the obvious eipstemological presuppositions behind what was termed as preference for motivation over content in theologising.

Three further questions for discussion.

(i) One would be: To what extent such a theological way would really be new compared to all the efforts of let's say former proposals of constructing local theology from a cultural starting point or the effort of pastoral theology taking into account the data of social sciences and cultural sharing.

(ii) The second in a self-reflective way points us to the question of how far we were representing "the victims of history."

(iii) A third set of questions came to the foreground when the question of normativity was raised (in regard to the motivation - content issue). How do we understand the tension between normativity vs. openness and dialogue?

6. With regard to alternative strategies, we hold that further *involvement* is needed (empowering; mobilizing marginalised people; counter-cultural formations); *participatory research* will support this; ways to *beat the system on its own ground* have to be discovered. The GRAMIN Bank in rural Bengal is an example. Anti-big-dam activities are another example of how victims learn to use the tools of globalization in order to strike back and become, though unwanted, participants in the power struggle to fight globalization's bad consequences. Indeed cultural resistance can be a means to renegotiate from below what globalization is all about. For the moment, we need to continue to *unmask the direct link between wealth and the poor, support local movements*, build up *networks on all levels*, train *new appropriate leadership*, learn to *participate in the big power process* and how it is *controlled*. Finally, *communication* worldwide is the big issue. Communication has changed through globalization and the people of the shadow side of the global systems will have to make strong efforts to learn to participate

and communicate with the different global power players - we can give voice to the voiceless. So that the marginalised and the victims can become participants in constructing a just interconnectedness in the world.

Group III

The various points discussed are reported under three Titles.

I. Understanding of Globalization

The concept of globalization has an inherent ambivalence from the perspective of the victims of history

On the one hand Globalization is understood as a cultural process in which human fellowship and solidarity is promoted through international networking and collaboration leading to a global community.

On the other hand, Globalization is interpreted as a new form of hegemony of developed countries over under-developed countries. In this sense, Globalization has three aspects:

1. Economic domination: It is a new, intricate exploitative and capitalistic economic domination of the developed countries through international financial institutions like the IMF, World Bank, W.T.O., GATT

2. Cultural aggression: It is a cultural aggression of imposing a mono-culture of consumerism and market economy on the third world through modern media which is controlled by the mutinationals of the developed countries.

3. Political imperialism: It is political neo-colonialism in the sense that through cultural aggression and economic domination, the first world is deciding the political visions and destinies of the third world for their own advantage.

II Concern of Globalization

1. Ignorant of the implicit dangers of globalization, the poor people of developing countries consider the availability of consumer goods like, T.V., autos and computers in the local market as

signs of development and progress; they are blindly fascinated by the consumer gadgets; they never think that these goods are beyond their purchasing power. Consequently it creates an illusionary concept of development.

2. The mono-culture which is propagated by the values of consumerism and market economy, silently and subtly displaces the root-paradigms and belief systems of the indigenous people of the third world and make them rootless and alienated from their cultural heritages and archetypes; it creates a cultural and ethical void in their life values and vision.

3. Contrary to general thinking, globalization does not lead to human solidarity or fellowship but to fragmentation of human community owing to the utter faceless profit oriented competition and rivalry in the dynamics of market economy.

4. The consumerist values promoted by the Global market economy lead the present generation to individualism and egoism. Consequently the sense of social responsibility and social justice is forgotten in the religiosity of the present generation; religious experience is more and more privatized; religion is sought after for personal consolation. It leads to a strange synthesis of self-centredness and God-experience in religiousness of the consumerist generation.

5. The Prophetic mission of the church in this context could be achieved through:

   1. Rereading the Bible in terms of local, cultural paradigms giving more importance to '*form*' than to '*content*' so that the message of Christ could be translated directly in local idioms and root-paradigms.

   2. The message of the Gospel is to be presented more in terms of a servant 'community of creation' rather than in traditional anthropocentric rationalities and hermeneutics.

III Responses

At the outset we should admit that a sense of helplessness and powerlessness prevails over us when we know that we are totally controlled by the invisible forces of opaque power structures of globalization through the systems to which we indispensably belong. Nevertheless there exist valid alternatives to counter the onslaught of Globalization on our culture, history and religion.

1. First of all there should be a prudent realism that evils of globalization is to be envisaged in a long term perspective. Overnight results should not be entertained.

2. The invincible evil forces of globalization could be fought against, to start with by small initiatives prompted by faith commitment through local social action groups.

3. These action groups should not be formed by unrealistic grandiose Utopian dreams but on an experimental basis and with concrete projects and targets.

4. As a second stage, attempts are to be made toward strengthening the action groups at local levels through conscientizing and educating the people.

5. Then, at the next stage a networking of action groups is to be realized, first at a local level, followed by sectorial, territorial, national, regional and lastly global levels.

   Such net-working of action groups empower the people in their fight against globalization at a global level.

6. This webbing is envisaged as a social contract or covenant which creates a prophetic and counter cultural social texture supplying continuous and consistent support and inspiration to the victims of society.

7. This web of action groups will naturally lead to political action without which no real lasting change takes place. This spilling over to political action does not aim at party or power politics but transformative politics through pressure groups and political actions of counter-cultural movements.

8. It is a long process in long term perspectives. In this it is a prophetic and counter cultural pilgrimage of civic actions which should be seen as social, cultural and religious attempts through

human communities in the vision of a kingdom of justice, peace and joy.

9. Some suggestions

1. A concerted campaign against the Debt dynamics of the Banking system in view of the Jubilee year 2000
2. Educational institutions and Seminaries.
3. Inter-religious fellowship and dialogues.
4. Church associations and action groups.
5. Vigorous theological reflection and articulation taking into account the concerns of Globalization
6. Collective and vigorous support and promotion of the cause of women and the gender questions.

Globalization from the Perspective of the Victims of History

FINAL STATEMENT

An international Consultation on *Globalization from the perspective of the Victims of history* was jointly organized by Vidyajyoti, College of Theology, Delhi, India and the Institute of Missiology, Aachen, Germany at the Indian Social Institute, Delhi, on January 18 - 22, 1998. 30 participants from the five continents - men and women, theologians, social scientists and activists - shared their experiences of the effects of globalization on people, particularly the poor, and explored concrete action-plans which they can get involved in and promote at local and international levels. Through a series of exposure programmes to local alternative action groups, conferences, group discussions and plenary sessions a consensus emerged. The following points present the highlights of that consensus.

Some Aspects of Globalization

— Globalization is the domination of a uni-polar economic system, facilitating the free movement of capital and trade. In an unequal situation it works in favour of the rich. Capital itself is used more for profitable speculation than for useful production. It is a one-way accumulation of wealth: from the poor to the rich. It does not affect the people in the north and in the south in the same way. Off-shore banks facilitate laundering of money.

— It relativizes and threatens national economies and deprives people of a say in what happens to them. People are no longer respected as persons, but become cheap labour. The women are particularly vulnerable. There is not only rising unemployment; the poor are excluded, when they are not needed even as cheap labour.

— International debt and structural adjustment programmes trap people into economic, political and social dependence.

— A consumer culture, creating artificial needs, is promoted by the media.

— An easy availability of goods may give a false impression of development. Agriculture is diverted from necessary food production to cash crops.

— Industrial development and 'scientific' agriculture lead to the pollution and destruction of the earth.

— Globalization is destructive of the family and its structures and relationships.

— Rising individualism goes hand in hand with lack of social responsibility and solidarity. Where true brotherhood and sisterhood disappear God is no longer the provident parent. A practical atheistic and materialistic attitude sets up Mammon as an idol in the place of God. People are subordinated to material forces. Violence and corruption become rampant everywhere and at all levels. In a consumer and technological culture the people become expendable.

Possible Responses

— Cultivating a fundamental ability to say "NO" to the forces of globalization and to suggest alternatives.

Economics: Joining movements for the abolition of international debt at various levels.

— Opposing in a reasoned manner structural adjustment programmes. Promoting research and analysis that will help in supporting such movements.

— Encouraging investment guided by moral principles. Economic control, through taxation, of financial speculation. Campaigns against money-laundering. Forcing the change of the actual interest system. Continuing the search for a new international economic and juridical order.

—Making sure that the remission of debt is not tied to conditions harmful to the people.

— Supporting consumer protection programmes.

— Promote and support environmental protection programmes.

— Give shape to alternative agricultural projects that respect bio-diversity and meet the real needs of the local people - Encouraging people-oriented development projects. - Promotion of microprojects.

— Promote alternative patterns of employment: less working hours, creative use of leisure also for the workers, abolition of child labour.

Politics: Empowering the people through organization to assert and defend their rights - formation of local action and pressure groups. Make people aware of their duty of responsible participation in civic life.

— Confronting the local economic and political elite who cooperate with globalizing forces.

— Advocacy through legal means and through transformative, not power, politics.

— Net-working locally, nationally and globally with alternative movements and with all people of good will - net-work particularly with committed people in the First world where pressure needs to be exerted, by providing information, etc.

— Continuing efforts to reform international organizations like the UNO, WTO, etc to make them more democratic, transparent, accountable and open to periodic independent evaluation.

Social: Promote a sense of solidarity (against individualism) - cultivate quality of relationship among people, respecting the other.

— Initiate programmes particularly in favour of the poor and the weak: farmers, workers, women, youth, tribals, migrant, the displaced and the oppressed in general.

— Promote women's rights and their participation in the world and in the Church.

Cultural: Conscientize the people of the true characteristics and effects of globalization, not only through popular means but also through institutional means like schools, seminaries, the media, etc.

— Help people appreciate the quality of life rather than multiply needs or indulge in greed.

— Facilitate the rediscovery and return to the wisdom of the indigenous peoples and subaltern traditions. Unearth their liberative potential.

Religious: Help people to focus on God in the other rather than on the merely human (anthropocentrism), the self (egoism) and matter - all religions advocate selflessness, sharing and simplicity of life.

— Cultivate a sense of social responsibility. Explore the socio-economic implications of sacraments like the Eucharist. Oppose movements that seek to privatize religiosity.

— Enable people to be agents: building up the local Church at all levels - promoting autonomy and relevance in reinterpreting tradition - people are more important than buildings. Invite people to celebrate life.

— A new sense of mission: the Kingdom proclaimed by Jesus as directed against Satan and Mammon (personal and social structures of injustice) rather than against other religions and cultures.

— Promote and network the prophetic movements in every religion (including Christianity)

— The Church needs to be self-critical so as to avoid encouraging and legitimating factors of globalization and to support alternative movements. The Church itself must avoid giving the image of being a globalizing agent in its own internal life and structures.

— An eschatological vision of the Kingdom as a global community of freedom, solidarity and justice, which we are called to commit ourselves to.

— A vision of the Church as a symbol and servant of the Kingdom, as a communion of local Churches, called to dialogue with other believers and all people of good will.

Authors

Amaladoss, Michael teaches theology at Vidyajyoti College of Theology, Delhi, India.

De Schrijver, Georges is Professor of theology at the Catholic University of Leuven, Belgium.

Diouf, Léon is Professor of theology at the Catholic Institute of West Africa, Abidjan, Ivory Coast.

Fernandes, Walter is the head of the Programme for Tribal Studies at the Indian Social Institute, Delhi, India.

Gorostiaga, Xabier teaches at the University of Central America, Managua, Nicaragua.

Henriot, Peter is Director of the Jesuit Centre for Theological Reflection, Lusaka, Zambia.

Hoffmann, Johannes is Professor at the Faculty of Catholic Theology at the University of Frankfurt, Germany.

Irarrazavel, Diego is Director of the Institute for Aymaran Studies at Puno, Peru.

Magesa, Laurenti is Pastor of Bukama Parish at Tarime, Tanzania.

Mananzan, Mary John is at St. Scholastica's College and Director of *Gabriela*, a women's Organization, at Manila, Philippines.

Paunga, Mikaele N. is from Tonga, completing Doctoral studies in Rome.

Sing, Horst is the Dean for Social Questions at the Catholic University of Eichstätt, Germany.

Wijsen, Frans teaches in the Department of Mission Studies at the Catholic University of Nijmegen, Netherlands.